GERRY HASSAN is a writer, commentator and policy analyst. His books include *The Modern SNP: From Protest to Power, The Dreaming City: Glasgow 2020 and the Power of Mass Imagination* and *Scotland 2020: Hopeful Stories for a Northern Nation*. More details of his activities are to be found at: www.gerry hassa .com.

ROSI ILETT is Deputy Director, Glasgow Centre for Population Health and Honc ary Senior Lecturer at University of Glasgow. She recently co-edited *Trans- form g Sexual Health in Scotland: Cultural, Organisational and Partnership Appr aches*.

Pra for *Radical Scotland*

[*Th ook*] brings together twenty-six writers and thinkers in a wide ranging set ssays, conversations and interviews, to develop a new culture of civic en ment, cutting across politics, community, arts, education and society as a u e.
C/ AN GALLAGHER, Open Democracy

A p erful, incisive, and groundbreaking set of accounts of, and challenges to, entrenched power of the British political class.
P! SSOR MICHAEL GARDINER, Warwick University

Viewp ts is an occasional series exp' relevance.

Luath Press is an independently owned : any based in Scotland, and is not aligned to any

D1514380

Radical Scotland

Arguments for Self-Determination

Edited by GERRY HASSAN and ROSIE ILETT

Luath Press Limited

EDINBURGH

www.luath.co.uk

First published 2011

ISBN: 978-1-906817-94-7

The paper used in this book is recyclable. It is made from low chlorine pulps
produced in a low energy, low emissions manner from renewable forests.

Printed and bound by
Bell & Bain Ltd., Glasgow

Typeset in 11pt Sabon by
3btype.com

© Gerry Hassan and Rosie Ilett and the contributors

Contents

Acknowledgements

The motivation, thinking and idea for this book was born of numerous conversations, public talks and articles. These involved friends, people in public life in Scotland, the UK and further afield, and a number of the contributors in the book.

Many thanks go to all of the contributors who gave enthusiastically of their time, effort and writing to put pen to paper and shape and articulate their thoughts. In particular, we would like to thanks the authors who took part in the conversation pieces which are contained within this book; these were designed as a deliberate attempt to change the kind of public conversation we have about policy and ideas in Scotland, and draw upon a wider range of opinion than what sometimes passes for the policy community.

We would like to specifically thank a number of people who gave encouragement, support and time to this project and its ideas: Sandy Campbell, John Carnochan, Sara Dybris McQuaid, Phil Denning, James Egan, Liz Gardiner, Geoff Huggins, George Kerevan, Mary Miller, Pete Seaman and Eleanor Yule. We would also like to thank all those who aided and supported the project but would prefer not to be named.

Our appreciation goes to Rebecca Lenagh-Snow for her professional translation of the Anthony Barnett-Will Hutton conversation; to Ricky Fleming and Laura Hudson Mackay for photos and to Laura for inspiration for the cover; to Samuel Sparrow, *A Dundee Wave of Change* and the Hot Chocolate Trust for the front cover illustration; and to Jennifer Scott and Gavin MacDougall at Luath Press for their professionalism and support of this project and who were a pleasure to work with from the conception of this book to its publication.

Finally, we would like to dedicate this book to someone who has inspired us and countless others – Alison Bigrigg, founder Director of the Sandyford Initiative – a pioneering sexual health service in the West of Scotland who we are proud to know and call a friend and who is an example to all of us.

Gerry Hassan and Rosie Ilett
February 2011

After Devolution: The Search for Radical Scotland

GERRY HASSAN AND ROSIE ILETT

The Stories of Modern Scotland

WHAT HAS BEEN THE dominant story and set of expectations about contemporary Scotland? Has it been the establishment of the Scottish Parliament and process of devolution? Particularly in its early years, the latter brought with it public expectations and a narrative about a 'new politics', transformation and far-reaching change which was always going to be difficult if not impossible to deliver and sustain.

What of the other stories of modern Scotland? What of the story of the changing dynamics of Scotland's economy, society and culture in the last few decades? The rise of new companies, winners and entrepreneurs some claim has given Scotland a sense of place and worth. Or what of narratives on the scale of inequality, exclusion and lack of power and voice which exists across large parts of society? Even across the decade of the boom a sizeable section of the Scottish population were excluded from the wealth and prosperity generated. How does that fit with Scotland's sense of itself as a compassionate society?

Then there is the account of Scotland post-crash, with our leading banks disgraced, masters of the universe knocked off their pedestals, economic assumptions questioned, and yet at the same time there is a discernable feeling in our political elites – in Scotland and the UK – of restoration and returning to the pre-crash world order pre-crash. Scotland's story of change these last 30 years has been less centre stage than expected. The extent of transformation – economically, socially and culturally – can be measured in changing employment and the nature of society, but just as important has been a shift in people's attitudes across a range of areas from the economy and jobs to aspirations, housing, inheritance and inter-generational issues, which have resulted in a more individualised society. This has produced more diversity, choice and opportunity, but also insecurity, fragmentation and dislocation.

Many of the changes which have happened to Scotland in recent times have not been explicitly Scottish, and have been part of a global journey with a palpable feeling of 'being done to us'. They have made us feel less unique and more like everywhere else. In consequence, there has been ambivalence about whether to celebrate or commiserate what has happened. This can be encapsulated in the Scottish reaction and attitudes to Thatcherism still to this day, and the question of whether her government and legacy did anything positive or was a complete and utter unqualified disaster. The prevailing Scots opinion would still be the latter.

The account of modern Scotland has less emphasised this complex story of change and has instead focused on politics and political change. This has put to the fore the devolution narrative: the idea of the Scottish Parliament as both a new start and the continuation of an old story: 'the reconvening of the Scottish Parliament' in Winnie Ewing's famous phrase.

This should not be surprising as there were always two opposing accounts of the Scottish Parliament. The first was the *instrumental* perspective: a Parliament was a means to an end not an end in itself; the objective was good governance, rationalism and the power of expert opinion. The second was the *intrinsic* account which emphasises the Parliament as an end in itself; as being an expression of nationhood and national voice (Hassan, 2003).

These two accounts are related to Lindsay Paterson's 'two stories of modern Scotland': a devolution and nationalist story (Paterson, 2009). Devolution Scotland is seen in the long story of institutional, professional society. This is the Scotland which ran society from 1707 onward, and gave birth to the corporate state in the 1930s – improving health and education, alleviating poverty and overseeing mass slum clearance. Paterson describes this order as 'networks of committees and agencies, staffed by disinterested professionals, drawing upon the distilled wisdom of civil society' (2009, 114).

The nationalist story is summarised thus, 'Allegiance to both Scotland and Britain is hypocrisy and dependence. Professional self-confidence, echoing Thatcher, self-interest' (2009, 115). The most influential thinker in this account is Tom Nairn, but Paterson identifies three other strands: the anarchic left, the cultural left and a Tory anti-welfare strand.

The Scottish Parliament has become, according to Paterson, a triumph for the first story; a vehicle for professional Scotland and for a self-validating public conversation between the elites of our society. The SNP's caution and its failure to challenge 'Labour's dense network of supporters in the professional classes' is described as the SNP adopting a gradualist strategy, and marginalising 'the MacDiarmid-Nairn critique' (2009, 117). This latter perspective is put up to be shot down: an unrealistic, troublesome, utopian outlook which was not equipped for the pressures of grown-up politics with its necessary compromises and difficult choices.

Paterson ends by acknowledging that Devolution Scotland – the world of 'ancient networks', experts and professionals – has taken us back to the 1950s:

> The Scottish Parliament, faithful to the rational democratic story of how it came about, has indeed given us no more (but also no less) than the 1950s Scottish governing system made more democratically transparent. (2009, 118)

The Demise of Radical Scotland

There are many assumptions that need examining in this account. One is the Scottish predilection to identify with professional vested interests and elites, and to dismiss the challenging of professional self-interests by Thatcherism and radical critiques of right and left. Another is to pose the idea of 'civil society' in a non-theoretical, uncritical way. Civil society is often seen as synonymous with the institutional Scotland which gave expression to the Scottish Constitutional Convention and Parliament; the parameters and dynamics of civil society, who are insiders and outsiders are seldom examined, and instead civil society becomes a term which seems to mean the new class of devolution. In some of the literature, the terms 'civil society' and 'civic society' are used interchangeably – with the latter never defined, nor the differences between the two, and whether the latter is a subset of the former or vice-versa; related to this the concept of 'civic Scotland' is often invoked without ever being adequately described (Paterson, 2002).

A third factor is the lack of influence of the new left in Scotland. This is important because it is one of the reasons which made Thatcherism so contentious. The experience of Thatcherism was the only political tradition which seriously attempted to challenge the professional elite order which governed Scotland.

There was no serious new left perspective in the 1960s or has been since devolution. Two brief dawns can be identified of new left influence: the Upper Clyde Shipbuilders work-in of 1971–72 led by Jimmy Airlie and Jimmy Reid, and the pro-home rule journal 'Radical Scotland' which was published between 1983–91, drawing together an array of rising left voices such as Lindsay Paterson, David McCrone and George Kerevan. The first was quickly incorporated into the then dominant left Labour account of Scotland, while the second became part of the new establishment of devolved Scotland. In both cases potentially radical, challenging perspectives were closed down. The exception to this is the writing and influence of Tom Nairn, while a whole generation of post-new left voices have emerged – from Pat Kane to Alastair McIntosh.

This absence of a radical Scotland has had implications for Scotland post-devolution. One characteristic has been that for all the rhetoric of transformation, Scotland post-devolution has been shaped by continuity compared to pre-devolution: the same professional groups and interests have worked the system, accessed the corridors of power, and broadly produced the same overall policy outcomes. Scottish policy-making is dominated by the same bodies and groups, post-devolution as pre-devolution. A study of Scottish Government consultations between 1999–2007 showed that of 13,746 acts of evidence given by 3,083 distinct contributors – 38.2 per cent came from government and public sector agencies (Halpin et al, 2010). The top respondent to Scottish Government consultations was the Scottish Government itself with 337 responses; followed by COSLA in second place with 196; the Scottish Trades Union Congress, a non-state body, finished joint seventh with Highlands and Islands Enterprise and the Association of Chief Police Officers with 74, and Scottish Enterprise in tenth with 68.

An interesting case study is the Scottish business lobby – with the Federation of Small Businesses in 15th place with 53 responses and CBI Scotland in 27th with 40. These corporate bodies claim to be the representative voice of Scottish business. However, what is seldom asked is who are they representing and giving voice to? CBI Scotland one might suppose speaks for a broad swathe of Scottish businesses given its prominent voice and public role in campaigns such as supporting the Calman Commission proposals and opposing fiscal autonomy. Yet CBI Scotland for all their lobbying and visibility represent a miniscule part of Scottish businesses. One study of the CBI Business Directory estimates that they have only 90 members out of 296,780 business enterprises in Scotland; taking away the various universities and public bodies who are CBI members one is left with 62 members out of 148,760 Scottish companies (0.04 per cent) (Cashley, 2011).

So, despite access to Scottish Government consultations through websites and direct mailings, those who respond to help shape national policy and legislation are drawn from a narrow strand. However, since devolution, and even more so since the SNP minority government took power with limited legislative scope, there is an argument that the amount of national policy generation on everything from, at the time of writing, the protected geographical status of the Stornoway Black Pudding to the monitoring of Dounreay and from the protection of dead people against defamation to the treatment of prisoners in Scottish prisons, has caused policy fatigue that can advance minority interests and, although it provides activity for civil servants and parliamentarians, fails to inspire widespread engagement (see the following table for a sample as of January 2011).

There is a direct correlation between this closed world of consultation, exchange and representation, and the narrow world of institutional Scotland found in government, public bodies and quangos. This after all is the modern expression of the system of committees, commissions and bodies which has historically administered Scotland through its patchwork nature in the 19th century, corporate state in the 1930s, and post-war Labour order.

How has this world of patronage and preferment changed under devolution? The answer is it has not in substance; the only real change being the expansion of the public agency preferment state. This produced a network world which sustained and supported a very narrow, select part of Scotland: the professional male, middle aged or retired, professional, with few women, ethnic minorities or ordinary people (Roy, 2010). A survey of 81 non-departmental public bodies showed that of the 81 part-time chairs only 11 (13.5 per cent) were women, while 10 bodies (12.3

**SAMPLE OF SCOTTISH GOVERNMENT CONSULTATIONS
JANUARY 2011 : source Scottish Government website
http://www.scotland.gov.uk/Consultations/Current**

Consultation Document	Main Themes (Summarised)
Consultation on the Milk and Milk Products (Pupils in Educational Establishments) (Scotland) (Amendment) Regulations 2011	To amend the Milk and Milk Products (Pupils in Educational Establishments) (Scotland) Regulations 2001 to account for new Commission and Council Regulations.
Defamation of the Deceased	To review the extent to which law and regulatory regimes protect against defamatory statements against deceased persons, and consider options for enhancing.
Right to Adapt Common Parts in Scotland	Consultation on the use of regulation making powers under s37, Equality Act 2010 to ensure that disabled people have a right to adapt common parts of premises in Scotland.
Extension of Permitted Development Rights and Permitted Changes of Use to Finfish and Shellfish Developments	Consultation on proposals to allow fish farm operators to make minor changes to farms without needing local authority planning permission.
Building A Hydro Nation – A Consultation	Proposals for Scottish Water to develop its commercial activities.
Amendments to the Pollution Prevention and Control (Scotland) Regulations 2000	To introduce provisions to enable the Scottish Environment Protection Agency to take more risk-based and proportionate approach to regulation across a range of lower risk activities, consistent with the need to protect health and the environment.

Consultation Document	Main Themes (Summarised)
Stornoway Black Pudding – Protected Geographical Indication Application	Consultation on application for Stornoway Black Pudding to gain Protected Geographical Indication (PGI) status.
Consultation document on amendments to the Public Contracts (Scotland) Regulations and the Utilities Contracts (Scotland) Regulations 2006	Consultation on amendments to the Scottish Procurement Regulations including outcomes of judgment of European Court of Justice and new offences relating to serious organised crime introduced by Criminal Justice and Licensing (Scotland) Act 2010.
Dounreay Waste Substitution	Proposals are to allow two forms of waste substitution.
Wheelchair and Seating Clinical Standards for the NHS in Scotland	Consultation on clinical standards for wheelchair and seating services provided by the NHS in Scotland.
Implementing Scotland's Zero Waste Plan: regulatory measures to require separate collection of waste materials, and restrict disposal in landfill and input to energy from waste facilities.	Consulting on proposed regulatory changes including establishing a rolling programme of material based landfill bans and property based landfill ban over approximately three to seven years and extracting as much recyclable metal and plastic from mixed waste as reasonably practicable.
Consultation on Independent Monitoring of Prisons	Consultation on views on the system for monitoring quality and safety of prisons and treatment of prisoners in Scotland.
A draft National Strategy for public space CCTV in Scotland	The consultation is to seek feedback on a draft national strategy for public space CCTV in Scotland.

per cent) had not one single woman on their governing bodies (Roy, 2009). What it includes is a fair number of serial quangocrats and an entitlement culture whereby people build up part-time appointments into full time remuneration (Coutts, 2010).

At the apex of this is a 'Scottish establishment' or clubland which consists of a tiny group of decision makers who went to the same schools, go to the same social clubs, and often play the same golf courses. Magnus Linklater, editor of the Scottish edition of *The Times* once wrote, 'It would ... be very hard to talk about a Scottish establishment', ironically doing so in the foreword of a book entitled *Anatomy of Scotland* (Linklater, 1992, xiv).

Such an attitude touches on a prevalent opinion in Scotland – which may seen seem inexplicable given our story of ourselves as an egalitarian culture: our disinterest in who has power and voice. Scots seem to prefer the sentimentalised and romanticised story of themselves as 'radicals' – whether it is standing up to the English at an ancient battle or the struggles and myths of 'Red Clydeside'. Therefore, a nation which prides itself on its 'democratic intellect' and inclusiveness has been hidebound to deference, authority and elites, while seeming to have a complete lack of curiosity about this (Wightman, 2010).

Idea Scotland

Given this narrow public conversation and the closed nature of much of Scots public life, where do ideas, creativity and policy innovation come from? This is one of the perplexing issues in devolved Scotland – a political system with a government, parliament and network of public bodies. The lack of dynamism and resources in many of the bodies, and generally in 'civil society', would come as a surprise to many outsiders. Business bodies, public agencies and the voluntary sector often draw up policy documents and responses without consultation with their own members, and on occasion without much expertise or research. A survey of member based organisations responding to Scottish Government consultations found that 44.4 per cent said that they submitted responses after consulting their entire membership while 25.9 per cent engaged in minimal to no consultation (Baxter et al, 2010).

Such a discussion can often lead to commentators believing the problem is the lack of think tanks in Scotland, with only one conventional think tank currently in existence: Reform Scotland. However, this is a very superficial analysis; it ignores the gathering critique of the think tank industry in London – an Anglo-American model of doing politics based on the outsourcing of policy and the importance of access and money (Hassan, 2008).

Instead, the Scottish ideas question is about resources, capacity and capability. The Scottish public sphere whether it be the media, academia or policy community does not have a huge amount of resources to spend on policy or research, but nor has it, along with the civil service shifted substantially from some of the attitudes of pre-devolution. What this means is that pre-devolution there was a propensity of this small world to act together, emphasise unity and act as 'a Scottish lobby' trying to lever money or influence out of Whitehall: an approach singularly ill-suited to the demands of making vibrant and real a new political dispensation.

There is a wider cultural issue of who we as a political community give permission to be players, and who the gatekeepers are in this. Scotland has a slender tradition and space for political entrepreneurs: people who make things happen, who ruffle feathers and bring about change. There are a few examples of such people, but without naming them, there is a more prevailing culture of believing political change comes from conventional politics while any political change or initiative requires permission from authority. This is one of the many paradoxes from this supposedly radical nation.

Scotland as a Centre-Left Nation

Scotland is a centre-left nation, even to some still a 'socialist country', to more a politics shaped by 'a social democratic consensus' or a 'progressive politics', often seen enviously by those on the centre-left south of the border.

This is one of the defining communal stories of Scotland post-1979. We are firmly on the left, much more so than England; we never voted for the Tories, never liked or wanted Thatcherism and yet had it imposed on us. It is a popular refrain and one many of us are familiar with and find comforting. Scotland is the land that resisted the charms of Thatcherism and remains anti-Tory to this day; the only part of Britain immune to 'the Cameron bounce' in the 2010 general election.

There are two problems with this. First, there is the anti-Thatcherite myth of progressive Scotland. Thatcherism has provided one of the most important mobilising stories of progressive Scotland – one which led to the establishment of the Parliament. At the same time, while all Scotland's mainstream political parties have painted themselves – Tories included – with anti-Thatcherite colours, each of them has been changed by, embraced and adopted parts of Thatcherism.

Alex Salmond famously got into trouble for commenting about Thatcherism that 'We didn't mind the economic side so much. But we didn't like the social side at all' (Torrance, 2009, 257). This inadvertently blurted out a long disguised truth about Scottish politics: the use of anti-Thatcherite rhetoric to hide the substance and extent of our political classes embrace of Thatcherite ideas.

Second, and even more problematic: who is Scotland exactly social democratic for? A social democratic nation would have a cohesive society and dynamic economy, low levels of poverty and inequality, and a powerful sense of national mission connecting of all of these. Scotland does not have any of these, and clearly lacks – despite a decade of devolution – an over-arching sense of national mission and purpose.

Critical in this is the disfigured nature of much of the Scottish economy and society, with huge swathes of population written off, permanently excluded from the labour market, on welfare benefits such as what used to be called incapacity benefit, and condemned to a life where huge health and social inequalities shape and limit their lives. This is 'a forgotten Scotland' where some professional groups are more than happy to ignore or, even worse at points, patronise people living in poverty with glib talk of 'welfare dependency' to 'the underclass' and 'Shettleston man'. This can end up invoking psychological, individualised solutions, shorn of wider social and structural issues. It may be the case that, in discussing poverty and social exclusion, some of Scotland's vested interests have, after decades of efforts and money, basically lost patience with such groups. This does not auger well for Scotland's 'social democratic consensus'.

The scale of our inequalities, poverty and dislocation should shame all of us and jolt anyone who buys into the nice, cosy story of social democratic Scotland. We have the worst male life expectancy of all Western Europe; the highest concentration of poverty and disadvantage in the UK; large parts of our biggest cities have over half of all households workless; and even across the decade of the Blair-Brown boom huge parts of Glasgow and the West of Scotland were excluded from work. And we know thanks to extensive work on 'the Glasgow effect' that all of this is not just about material poverty or social stratification, but other factors such as culture, lifestyle, individual motivation, as well as the gendered nature of how men and women experience and react to this differently (Hanlon et al, 2006).

Scotland's social democratic story works for the political and professional elites who run it. There are many in these groups who are animated by a genuine sense of care and compassion for disadvantaged people in the population, but in too many places, and judging by the reality of Scotland, there are many people and bodies content to do too little or to care about the state of the nation. This is social democracy for institutional interests, and it is not an edifying or sustainable picture. It is one which is leading to increasing disquiet about our politics, widespread cynicism and falling levels of political participation. Part of this is the global story of Scotland embarking on devolution and its Parliament in a profoundly anti-political (or anti-party political) age. The process of the hollowing out and disillusion with formal party politics is a process which can be seen the world over. Therefore, we have to acknowledge the ambiguity, loss and confusion which this produces: a public culture which once prided itself on its power of mission, purpose and morality, and which feels increasingly unsure how to articulate such sentiment in the present day.

The Limits of Self-Government

It is not surprising that one of the untold aspects of post-devolution Scotland has been the exhaustion of the mainstream. Professional and interest group Scotland expends a lot of time and energy maintaining its position and influence, facilitated by in many instances, relatively easy access to the devolved government machine. But what though are the ideals and values of mainstream Scotland which allow it to exercise this hold? There is a sense that we are all centre-left and anti-Tory – but as we have shown this is increasingly questionable. This has become 'the official story' of the nation and our public sphere.

One of the ways the Scottish experience is framed by some – in a kind of counter-story – is to present a critique of the Scottish state which has some truth, but which spills over into caricature, presenting it as too large, too powerful and too anti-private sector. The solution is a familiar one: free market policies, massive public spending reductions and deregulation (Miers, 2010).

Another account found in institutional circles and part of the language of the new establishment is to emphasise that the public sector and bodies need to embrace a culture of constant innovation, measurement and improvement: themes taken up in a recent NESTA report (Bunt et al, 2010). What an analysis like this does is appropriate warm words such as 'radical' and 'localist' for the orthodoxies of the age. It lacks any understanding or reference to the real, varied experiences of the lives of Scottish people; no voices of individuals are acknowledged and instead everything is reduced to the mantra of an accountancy-style logic, measuring output and productivity – as if in a far-off foreign country that we do not need to visit to understand. This is a template kind of politics and mindset which you can just purchase off the shelf.

It is not an accident that such institutional accounts, informed by technocratic, managerial determinism and utopianism, don't have a space for real people and their voices. People don't live their lives in neat, tidy policy boxes which correlate to smart, successful government initiatives. The rise of this type of perspective can be seen across the Western world and is directly linked to the promotion of a certain kind of 'official voice' and the denial of alternative voices, which aids the language, philosophy and policy prospectus of the new conservatism (Couldry, 2010).

The Scottish mainstream has produced no defining arguments or publications in the first decade of devolution. It isn't an accident that the original, interesting Scottish non-fiction books published have nearly exclusively fallen into two areas, history and alternative Scotland. In the former, there has been a renaissance of Scottish history, with Christopher Whatley (2006), Tom Devine (1999; 2005), Michael Fry (2001), Michael Lynch (2001), Richard Finlay (2004) and Catriona MacDonald (2009) publishing path-breaking books. These have looked at important parts of our history in new ways: the nature of the union of 1707, Scotland's leading role in Empire, and the nature of the private life of Scots men and women in the 20th century.

In the world of alternative Scotland, a parallel nation has found form:

a Scotland that is magical, surreal and filled with mystery, humour and mischievousness. Two books stand out: Bill Duncan's hilarious and serious *The Wee Book of Calvinism* (2004), wonderfully described as 'a self-help book' which plays with caricatures of Calvinism. And as impressive is Momus's *The Book of Scotlands* (2009), bringing together over 150 parallel universe Scotlands, from past, present and future, some plausible, some fantastical.

What these two developments tell us is that the Scottish exploration of ideas, our curiosity and sense of discovery has not left us. It has just abandoned the mainstream of our society, and the mainstream of much of our society, politics and policy community.

This takes us to the search for a new political mission and project for Scotland. Some will believe that project is independence. Others will believe it can only be found by stopping our supposed obsession with constitutional change and staying in the union. And yet both beg the question: what kind of Scotland do we want to live in? Surely that is the substantive issue which should inform our public conversation and would even make sense of our constitutional debate.

Scotland's experience in this last decade has been one of self-government. This has involved the narrow political project of focusing on establishing a Parliament with its resulting political class and this becoming the fulcrum of our political debate. What it has also done is constrain our very idea and imagination of what political change is.

All of Scotland's political parties collude in this, but there is a case for arguing that the most potentially radical of the parties, namely the SNP, does this the most. When the SNP is making its case for independence it nearly always does so by emphasising that Scotland will become 'a normal nation', that the Parliament will become 'a full Parliament' with 'full powers' and 'increased powers'. The dominant narrative of independence to the SNP has been about the Parliament and politicians, not wider societal transformation which would give meaning and substance to independence.

The SNP, in part, do this to make independence appear unthreatening and something Scotland can evolve into; they also make it appear boring and uninspiring, and something which – by being so focused on the Parliament and politicians – excludes most people. In this the SNP are only articulating this widespread Scottish sentiment of politics and change being narrowly focused on institutions and elites. Independence has to be about a wider, more radical and ambitious vision of change in order to have relevance.

From Self-Government to Self-Determination

For Scotland to shift from the narrow notion of self-government it has to embrace the idea of self-determination – at the level of the individual, community and society. There is now an increasing body of evidence on self-determination theory which emphasises the importance of autonomy, competence and relatedness at the level of the individual and wider society to assist both in prospering (Deci and Ryan 1995; 2002). Pivotal to both self-government and self-determination is the idea of 'the self' and the notion of authority and agency and with it the potential of challenging the marketised, consumer-orientated concept of 'the self' (Mitchell, 1996; Przeworski, 2010).

Self-determination has the potential to offer a way of connecting politics, power and psychology, and in so doing to articulate a set of ideas which develop a less institutional concept of change, and one which both challenges the stasis of Scottish civil society and its professional elites. Through this it also has the prospect of making real and relevant the ideal of self-government.

This would entail a different approach drawing from self-determination theory across the parameters of public life, economic, social, cultural, developing. If we were to assess modern Scotland in terms of autonomy, competence and relatedness how would we fare? In autonomy and our universal desire to be the agents of our own lives and have an integrated sense of self; in competence, to being effective in the immediate environment as an individual; and in relatedlessness, the fundamental want to interact, be connected and think of others. How would Scotland rate in terms of economic and social inequality, dislocation, educational achievement and health outcomes? It would not rate very well on all of these indicators and more, and that tells us something rather serious about the state of contemporary Scotland.

A politics of self-determination has to have four crucial dimensions of policy and ideas. First, there is *economic self-determination*. How do we deal with the massive concentrations of power which contemporary capitalism throws up in corporations and the market? How do we re-imagine economic democracy and corporate governance? And how do we develop a different idea of the state which is not equally oppressive and suffocating?

Second is *social self-determination*. In what ways can we bridge the chasms of inequality which have reached record levels? How can we breakdown the separate development which has seen whole communities trapped for 30 years on 'welfare dependency', often literally sitting cheek-to-jowl to the new global winners? And how do we combine an approach which acknowledges the power of structural factors, while recognising the importance of individual issues as well?

Third is *cultural self-determination*. How can we nurture a public culture which is not totally at the mercy of commercial and corporate interests and acknowledges the role of public goods? How can we aid dissent, imagination and diversity in a way which a self-regulating market or all-powerful state cannot?

Fourth and perhaps the most important as it binds together all of the above is the area of *futures self-determination*. The notion of self-determination is fundamentally about the concept of the future: identifying the future, democratising the future, and then taking the hesitant steps to imagine and create that future: the notion of futures literacy and aiding people to believe that they have the capacity to bring that future into being. Futures self-determination has within it a sense of the future, the impermanence of human existence, 'the long now' and environmental sensibility. This is a direct challenge to 'the official future' of globalisation that presents itself as an elemental force of nature which we have no opportunity to debate, change or depart from. This explicitly says 'don't bother worrying or thinking about the future as it has already been decided'. This is a deeply harmful message and one which has to be contested; the future cannot be pre-determined and closed, and must always be debated, discussed, remade and reimagined.

Such a shift involves a fundamental political and cultural change. It requires breaking with the economic and social orthodoxies which define British politics and most of the West. People will say that this is not possible, and not possible in Scotland: that this is a cautious, conservative land. However, we are now living in an age of the end of devolution: the decade of ever increasing public spending, avoiding hard choices, and incremental caution. We now know the best devolution can offer us in the most benign environment imaginable and one not very energising. Lindsay Paterson wrote that Devolution Scotland offered a 'Back to the Future' promise of a return to a 1950s world:

> So self-government has not challenged the power of civil society or the authority of professionals. What we have not had is a revolution, whether of social structure (which was never likely), or of the power of organised interests, or of the authority of the professional technocracy – including academics – in public debate. (Paterson, 2009, 118)

What Paterson's analysis misses is the multi-fold pressure on professional Scotland. First, there is the public spending constraints of the next few years. Second, the challenge of corporate power and increasing concentrations of economic power across every aspect of life. This will express itself in ways which Scotland's professional interests will find uncomfortable and challenging (along with the rest of us). English education and health reform will have massive consequences and spill-over north of the border, and which parts of elite Scotland may even collude with. It is also important to note that along with the impact of public sector reform, and the need to develop alternatives to the marketising and outsourcing approach, Scotland will face the prospect of significant public spending cuts having a disproportionate effect on both public service workers and members of the public.

Finally, there are the popular expectations of people, on living standards, public services and society. Some of these may be challenged in the future, economic growth assumptions being one area, but people are more questioning, challenging and demanding, and less deferential, tribalist and blinkered. The Scots professional classes days of benign despotism and their vision of 'planned freedom', a phrase used in the modernist utopia of 1950s Scotland is facing more and more challenge.

This book brings together a group of radical, informed and passionate voices on the subject of change in Scotland. In a book such as this not every contributor will agree on every single point, but there is a broad agreement on challenging the limits we have set ourselves, and making the case for self-government and self-determination. And unusually for a book on Scotland we have undertaken a wide set of conversations, one set exploring Scottish policy and ideas and the other placing the Scottish debate in a wider global context. This later series includes an examination of the problems of global capitalism and the British state, an exploration of the crisis of progress and modernity, and the nature and future of the United Kingdom.

The context of the Scottish debate does not as it is presented in many perspectives sit in splendid isolation from developments outside Scotland: the nature of the UK, the state of the European Union, global capitalism and the future of the world economy. Related to this is the flux and flow of politics and political ideas: the retreat and exhaustion of most of the Western left, the crisis of social democracy, and the challenge of market fundamentalism and neo-liberalism. In particular, the character of the British state and the commitment of the British political classes to a unitary state interpretation of the UK – when the UK is a union state – or as has been recently argued a 'state of unions' (Mitchell, 2009). The tradition of unitary state politics are deeply entrenched in British politics, in Labour and the left, and on the right and Thatcherism, and shows no sign of weakening.

Then there is the issue of England, which seems to have turned its back for the time on a territorial rebalancing of itself through regional decentralisation. This would not have addressed 'the essential asymmetry of the UK' (Keating, 2009, 178) and in particular the over-concentration of wealth, power and status in London and the South East which distorts and disfigures the British economy and politics. Yet it could have offered the prospect of beginning to develop a differentiated territorial politics in England which began to explore such issues.

The failure of such an English counter-story has several consequences. First, the British political classes belief that the British constitution remains fundamentally unaltered and untouched by constitutional change and devolution has to be recognised. They remain committed to the unitary state story of Britain, and seem to have no interest in rethinking and radically altering the state of Britain.

Second, the continuation of this approach is likely to lead and encourage eventually massive change in the form of the more avert assertion of a unitary state England which will lead inexorably to a new set of relationships across the UK with this having major implications for Scotland. There has long been an assumption north of the border that the future of the UK would be decided by the Scottish dimension, but it is more than likely that a decisive shift could emerge from England. And then there is the European dimension, from the Tory Eurosceptic outlook of trying to hold the dam back and entrench parliamentary sovereignty to the current standstill of the Europe of the Regions.

Scotland will be influenced by all of this and more as will its public conversation, but while recognising the wider context we sit in we at the same time need to move to being more active agents of our own destiny. Scotland is entering a new era of Scottish politics, society, and as a nation. It is going to be characterised by uncertainty, difficulty and tough choices, as well as the opportunity to be more daring and imaginative. The era of devolution as we have known it is over and it is time to embrace a shift from self-government politically to self-determination as a society and nation.

References

Baxter, G., Marcella, R. and Illingworth, L. (2010), 'Organisational Information Behaviour in the Public Consultation Process in Scotland', *Information Research*, Vol. 15 No. 4, http://informationr.net/ir/15-4/paper442.html

Bunt, L., Harris, M. and Puttick, R. (2010), *Radical Scotland: Confronting the challenges facing Scotland's public services*, London: NESTA.

Cashley, C. (2011), 'CBI Scotland: Who Does It Speak For?', January 5th, http://calumcashley.blogspot.com/2011/01/cbi-scotland-who-does-it-speak-for.html

Couldry, N. (2010), *Why Voice Matters: Culture and Politics after Neo-Liberalism*, London: Sage.

Coutts, G. (2010), 'A quango king hits back', *Scottish Review*, October (n.d.), http://www.scottishreview.net/Coutts36.shtml

Deci, E. L. and Ryan, R. M. (1995), 'Human autonomy: The basis for true self-esteem', in Kemis, M. (ed.), *Efficacy, Agency, and Self-Esteem*, New York: Plenum, 31–49.

Deci, E. L. and Ryan, R. (eds), (2002), *Handbook of Self-Determination Research*, Rochester, NY: University of Rochester Press.

Devine, T. M. (1999), *The Scottish Nation 1700–2000*, Harmondsworth: Allen Lane.

Devine, T. M. (2005), *Scotland's Empire 1600–1815*, Harmondsworth: Allen Lane.

Duncan, B. (2004), *The Wee Book of Calvin: Air-Kissing in the North-East*, London: Penguin Books.

Finlay, R. (2004), *Modern Scotland 1914–2000*, London: Profile Books.

Fry, M. (2001), *The Scottish Empire*, East Linton: Tuckwell Press.

Halpin, D., MacLeod, I. and McLaverty, P. (2010), 'Committee Hearings of the Scottish Parliament: Who Gives Evidence? And Does it Contribute to 'Policy Learning'?, Paper presented to the Political Studies Association Conference, http://www.psa.ac.uk/Proceedings.aspx?JournalID=5& ParentID=3

Hanlon, P., Walsh, D. and Whyte, B. (2006), *Let Glasgow Flourish: A Comprehensive Report on Health and its Determinants in Glasgow and the West of Scotland*, Glasgow: Glasgow Centre for Population Health.

Hassan, G, (2003), 'Talking about Devolution: A Decade of Constitutional Wish-Fulfillment', *Renewal: The Journal of Labour Politics*, Vol. 11 No. 1, 46–53.

Hassan, G. (2008), 'The Limits of the 'Think Tank' Revolution', *Open Democracy*, 8 September, http://www.opendemocracy.net/article/yes/the-limits-of-the-think-tank-revolution

Hassan, G. (2010), 'Scottish political classes in a smug comfort zone', *The Guardian Comment is Free*, 4 May, http://www.guardian.co.uk/commentisfree/2010/may/04/scottish-political-classes-smug

Keating, M. (2009), *The Independence of Scotland: Self-Government and the Shifting Politics of Union*, Oxford: Oxford University Press.

Linklater, M. (1992), 'Foreword', in Linklater, M. and Denniston, D. (eds), *Anatomy of Scotland: How Scotland Works*, Edinburgh: Chambers, xviii–xv.

Lynch, M. (ed.) (2001), *The Oxford Companion to Scottish History*, Oxford: Oxford University Press.

MacDonald, C. M. M. (2009), *Whaur Extremes Meet: Scotland's Twentieth Century*, Edinburgh: Birlinn.

Mitchell, J. (1996), *Strategies for Self-Government: The Campaigns for a Scottish Parliament*, Edinburgh: Polygon.

Mitchell, J. (2009), *Devolution in the UK*, Manchester: Manchester University Press.

Miers, T. (2010), *The Devolution Distraction: How Scotland's constitutional obsession leads to bad government*, London: Policy Exchange.

Momus (2009), *Solution 11–167: The Book of Scotlands*, Berlin: Sternberg Press.

Paterson, L. (2002), Civic Democracy', in Hassan, G. and Warhurst, C. (eds), *Anatomy of the New Scotland: Power, Influence and Change*, Edinburgh: Mainstream, 56–64.

Paterson, L. (2009), 'Civil Society and the Parliament', in Jeffrey, C. and Mitchell, J. (eds), *The Scottish Parliament 1999–2009: The First Decade*, Edinburgh: Luath Press in association with the Hansard Society, 113–18.

Przeworski, A. (2010), *Democracy and the Limits of Self-Government*, Cambridge: Cambridge University Press.

Roy, K. (2009), 'The all-male clubs paid for by us', *Scottish Review*, 14 October, http://www.scottishreview.net/KRoy153.html

Roy, K. (2010), 'Why do Garry, Willy and Mike, the kings of the quangos, have to do it all? Treading the Boards: Part One', *Scottish Review*, 19 October, http://www.scottishreview.net/KRoy34.shtml

Torrance, D. (2009), *'We in Scotland': Thatcherism in a Cold Climate*, Edinburgh: Birlinn.

Whatley, C. A. (2006), *The Scots and the Union*, Edinburgh: Edinburgh University Press.

Wightman, A. (2010), *The Poor Had No Lawyers: Who Owns Scotland (And How They Got It)*, Edinburgh: Birlinn.

Devolution without Self-Government

JAMES MITCHELL

Introduction

DEVOLUTION HAS PROVED successful in a number of ways: it created a representative institution; its membership looks much the same as Parliaments in any number of liberal democracies, though it sounds distinctly Scottish; and it can reasonably be argued that Holyrood is the sound of Scotland. However, its success as a representative institution has not been mirrored as an institution for developing public policies to meet the challenges facing modern Scotland. In this latter respect, it resembles the old system of government in which Scottish institutions proved effective means of articulating Scottish interests within the system of government, which essentially means asking for more money. The Scottish Parliament has been less successful as a form of self-government in which these authoritative voices are able to deliberate and weigh up the costs of benefits of policies and programmes (Mitchell, 1996, 9–34). This chapter outlines the reasons why devolution has taken the form it has and identifies key issues and areas that will need to be explored if meaningful self-government is to be calculated.

Why devolution?

If the existence of the Scottish Parliament can be summed up in a single word it would be *Thatcherism*. While evidence suggests the existence of majority support for a Scottish Parliament for many long years before 1979, what provided the impetus for its establishment was the belief that Scotland needed protection from alien policies. There was far less unity when it came to what the electorate was voting for in the 1997 referendum. In origins, devolution was a defensive institution, best summed up in the words of David Melding, Welsh Tory Assembly Member, who described Scottish devolution 'as a prophylactic against Conservative rule' in Scotland (Melding, 2009, 2). It is a moot point whether Scotland today would have its own Parliament without Mrs Thatcher but what is beyond doubt is that she was devolution's best recruiting sergeant. The perception that Scottish representative opinion was marginalised in the Westminster system meant that the focus of the campaign was on ensuring change in our representative institutions. In the rhetoric of the time, Scotland suffered a 'democratic deficit'. The rhetoric exaggerated the problem. The problem was a growing lack of legitimacy as Scots called the system of government into question.

This does not mean that there were no positive reasons for devolution. A myriad of progressive causes, most notably the women's movement, fed into the campaign. It simply meant that the emphasis amongst campaigners for devolution was to ensure that the Scottish Parliament would be a truly new representative institution, reflecting Scottish opinion to a greater degree than the Westminster system permitted, in order to ensure that Scotland did not suffer the imposition of policies it did not vote for again. Consequently, considerable effort went into debating the electoral system and the representation of women. Effort too went into how the Parliament should operate. It was as if the creative energies of its supporters concentrated on questions of representation. All would be well so long as the new institution embodying Scottish interests was representative.

Implicit in the negative motive was the positive assumption that devolution would allow for *Scottish solutions to Scottish problems*. What this meant was never clear. What were the Scottish problems that were to be solved? When it came to discussing the powers available to the Scottish Parliament, its founders had less to offer. Powers tended to be understood as lists of responsibilities and modeled directly on the Scottish Office. This was understandable. First, the Scottish Office was the focus of criticism, headed by a Cabinet Minister appointed by the Prime Minister regardless of Scottish opinion, an inevitable feature of a system in which government was accountable to Parliament as a whole rather than Scottish MPs. The Scottish Office was perceived to have failed, indeed to have corrupted its primary task. What had begun as a late 19th century institution to take account of Scottish distinctiveness and allow for diversity within the UK, by the end of the 20th century had come to be perceived as a manifestation of the imposition of policy on Scotland.

Secondly, it was far easier to draw up a scheme of devolution that was based on an existing model, albeit one that had evolved piecemeal with little obvious rationale and quite unrelated to the demands of anything approaching self-government. Scottish Office responsibilities had evolved over a century and more as the state's reach into the economy and society had increased. The job of devolution's architects would have been made far more complex had they started from scratch. It simply made sense to use the Scottish Office as the base in determining the responsibilities of the Scottish Parliament. If it was to be an endpoint then it would fail to address the fundamental weaknesses of the pre-devolution system of government.

It is worth recalling the Scottish Office's impact on Scottish politics. While it was the institutional manifestation of Scottish distinctiveness and lay at the heart of much that distinguished Scottish politics, it also meant that at the heart of Scottish politics was a deeply debilitating politics of grievance and a culture of oppositionalism. The Scottish Office was the focus of Scottish grievances within Scotland and the conduit through which these were articulated in Whitehall and the cabinet. It was extremely successful in making the case for Scotland, which usually meant making the case for more resources. Scottish distinctiveness was all too often measured in how much more Scotland received. In terms of public spending across a range of subjects, Scotland did relatively well. Industries that were under threat in Scotland could always rely on the Scottish Office to come to their aid. Whereas equivalent threats to industries in England relied on strong support from local politicians and might also have a 'sponsoring' Ministry, few could rely on an unfailing 'national interest' argument as those in Scotland. Scottish Secretaries were expected to make the 'case for Scotland' and most did so effectively. Hard choices could not always be evaded but what made Scottish politics distinct was its protective institutional layer – Scottish politics was essentially the politics of grievances and special cases. The breakdown in the system came when the Scottish Office was no longer able to protect, when the prophylactic institutional layer failed.

The most significant importation from the Westminster system was the financing of devolution. There had been much talk of tax-*raising* powers, latterly changed to tax-*varying* powers, and a separate question in the referendum on the subject. In the event the tax powers were largely symbolic and the funding mechanism was simply continuity of that for the Scottish Office. The Barnett formula, named after the Chief Secretary to the Treasury in the late 1970s, though Joel Barnett himself was not involved in its creation, became far more controversial even though its provisions remained largely as before. The real *power* of the Parliament would be measured, not in terms of a list of responsibilities inherited from the Scottish Office, but in its autonomy to pursue policies distinct from those either pursued in the past by the Scottish Office or from those pursued by Whitehall departments. That had been a power already held by the Scottish office. The key difference was that a Scottish representative institution would make these decisions.

The difficulties in creating an alternative form of devolution should not be underestimated. Nor should its success be understated. The Parliament can be measured a resounding success in terms of the logic behind its creation. Legitimacy was restored to the system of government.

Devolution in practice

Two features of the context in which the new devolved institutions came into being proved auspicious. First, the Conservatives were out of power at Westminster. Devolution would have been highly improbable so long as the Conservatives continued to govern at Westminster, although it is possible that pressure would have built up, forcing a Conservative Government under a new generation of leaders to implement a scheme of devolution. This is not as fanciful as might be imagined. Constitutional change, including major extensions of the franchise, have been introduced by Conservative Governments recognising that change was coming, fearing that the form it might take would be less attractive than that which a Tory Government might implement. *Thatcherism* involved a constitutional purism that prevented the party considering devolution other than in negative terms, as an attack on the foundation of the constitution, and prevented it contributing to debates on the form devolution should take. The defeat of the Conservatives meant devolution became possible but also removed for the moment its immediate need. In broad terms at least, there was 'congruence' between the governing party at Westminster and that elected in the first elections to the Scottish Parliament in 1999.

The second auspicious feature was barely remarked upon at the time but was at least as important. Labour inherited a buoyant economy producing tax receipts that allowed for increased public spending, limited in the early years by Labour's promise to stick with Tory spending plans and borrowed heavily. Nothing oils the wheels of government more than money. Devolution finances benefited due to the operation of the Barnett formula. Increases in spending by Whitehall department meant increases for the Scottish Government. Over time massive sums of money were spent on a range of services by Whitehall and consequently also the Scottish Executive. Additional money became the answer to problems rather than consideration of whether money was what was really required or whether it was spent wisely.

Increased public expenditure ensured that devolution had an easy birth. It meant that devolution had the appearance of greater autonomy than it in fact had. Policies were introduced that seemed and indeed were affordable at least while the money was available. There was an expectation that devolution would allow for Scottish solutions to Scottish problems; for policy divergence. Devolution's flagship policies in these early years were possible because of this largesse, money that had little to do with devolution *per se* but everything to do with the state of public finances which would have been available whether or not devolution existed.

Devolution made possible policies which would not otherwise have been pursued as these would have created significant policy divergence north and south of the border. It was inconceivable that there would have been divergence on care for the elderly or tuition fees without devolution. That was testified by the opposition to these policies by the Labour Government in London which found itself powerless to prevent the Scottish Parliament pursuing these Scottish solutions. This is where the aforementioned changes in representation made a difference. Coalition with the Liberal Democrats meant that Scotland did not follow England in introducing tuition fees and Donald Dewar and the coalition had initially rejected to proposals of the Royal Commission (Sutherland) on long term care, a policy reversed by Dewar successor Henry McLeish against his own party's inclination.

The key point about these flagship policies was that they were only possible in the moment and ran contrary to the institutional design of devolution. The relationship between Whitehall spending decisions and what was available under devolution under the terms of the Barnett formula meant that these expensive innovations which were possible would prove unsustainable over the long-term. It was easy to opt for expensive Scottish solutions in the early years when money was awash in the system. It would prove much more difficult to balance the books when money became tighter *and* the Parliament had no significant alternative source of revenue. The financial regime governing devolution meant that any Scottish solution relied on one of three conditions: it had to involve little or no additional cost; it had to be a one-off without involving any long-term financial commitments; or it relied on continuing 'good times' and generous Barnett consequentials. The only alternative was that London would be willing to provide Scotland with more money beyond that available under the Barnett formula, especially during difficult times. The last was never a serious likelihood. Devolution did not create the Barnett formula but it did place it on the agenda as never before. Views differed as to whether it worked to the advantage or disadvantage of each part of the UK but on one thing there was agreement: Barnett was understood as a mechanism that tied the devolved administrations to Whitehall and prevented meaningful financial autonomy. But while Barnett was pushed up the agenda, pressure for reform was limited as all parts of the UK gained more resources. There was less concern whether one part gained disproportionately more or less than another so long as all were gaining.

Therefore, the absence of financial autonomy was masked in this first phase of devolution due to increasing public expenditure alongside a reasonable degree of ideological congruence. There was some resentment surrounding the allocation of financial resources but this was muted in the context of expanding budgets. Devolution appeared to permit not only Scottish solutions to Scottish problems but relatively generous solutions.

The end of the devolution honeymoon

The end of the devolution honeymoon came with two changes in context. The combination of 'party incongruence' and economic and fiscal difficulties created a wholly different context. It exposed the extent to which devolution's early establishment had depended on substantial sums of money. It had become apparent that it was less Scottish solutions to

Scottish problems than public expenditure solutions to Scottish problems that had allowed devolution to bed down. Moreover, it became painfully clear that policies created in the good years involved recurrent expenditure. The commitments made were not one-off payments but would have to be paid over many years and, in the case of care for the elderly, would increase given demographic trends.

There was the added problem that these commitments could not be reversed without substantial political cost. Public policies create interests at least as much as interests create policies. Scottish policy on tuition fees, distinct from that south of the border, and Scottish policy on long term care created interests that could easily be mobilised in their defence. It would be difficult to reverse policies that had established privileged interests through generous policies. The policies themselves were defensible, attractive and grounded in public support but had emerged at a particular period in time when money was available. The problem that would have to be confronted was what to do when the financial regime created fewer resources.

The fundamental weakness of devolved government was that it created a system of government that addressed the lack of legitimacy but failed to address the enduring and debilitating grievance culture that had been inherited from pre-devolution. Cuts in expenditure across the state as a whole would be seen as attacks on distinctive Scottish policies. Much debate has focused once more on whether Scotland was treated unfairly by London. Each side of the argument started from the same premise: Scotland looked to London for the money. It might be devolution but this was not self-government. During its first phase, devolution had given the appearance of greater autonomy than would prove really existed as it moved into its second phase. Tied to funding decisions made in Whitehall, devolved institutions have proved and will continue to prove incapable of living up to devolution's limited ambition of acting as a prophylactic against London rule. The Calman report and proposals from the Coalition in London will make no substantive difference.

Self-Government

Over the next few years as the devolved Parliament proves incapable of preventing cuts biting deep, there will be a full-scale return to the politics of grievance. There will be substantial differences with the past. The existence of the Parliament provides Scotland with an authoritative voice and a policy inheritance. Devolution will become, as was inherent in its design, a factory of grievances rather than a form of independent decision-making. From an English perspective, and indeed from the perspective of territorial justice, it is anomalous that Scotland has services unavailable to other parts of the UK while not having to pay for them. There is a difference between arguing that Scotland should have special assistance on account of need, but Scotland is a relatively wealthy part of the UK and is in less need of special services and assistance than many parts of England. The instability of the system will become apparent. It has frequently been noted that supporters of devolved government disagreed on the end point but the far more significant contradiction lies in the fact that the same supporters of devolution see it both as a form of self-government, permitting divergent public policies, and a lever for demanding more from London.

The corollary of improved costly services must be that those who wish them should have to pay for them. This requires fiscal powers that are unavailable and not yet under consideration. The Parliament's existing tax powers evaded difficult questions and proved more significant symbolically than as a public policy tool. Calman was established in response to the election of an SNP Government rather than in response to the weaknesses of the devolved system. Its logic was driven less by the need to create an improved system of government but to maintain unity across the three parties opposed to the SNP. The starting point for any review of devolution needs to be a more thoroughgoing understanding of the public policy purpose of the Scottish Parliament and Government.

We need to return to first principles when considering its fiscal powers rather than consider these in party political gamesmanship. Broadly, taxation and fiscal policies serve three purposes: raising revenue to pay for goods and services; redistribution of wealth; and as a lever to encourage or discourage behaviour. The debate within Calman focused on only the first of these and even its proposals in this respect have been found wanting.

Each of these three purposes is relevant for meaningful self-government. Having the power to raise sufficient revenue is vital to pay for services. As we have seen, devolved government was not short of money in its first phase but is now as it moves into the second phase of devolution.

The simple fact is that the level of services cannot be maintained with the funding available to Holyrood. Moreover, the choice of maintaining the level of services by increasing taxes is unavailable to the Parliament. It is possible that the policy programme would have been different had it required a decision to increase taxes. It is this choice that needs to be available to ensure that decision-making neither lacks fiscal responsibility nor blocks costed and considered options. The problem with the Calman-Coalition proposals is that the choice of improved services remains unavailable.

The second purpose of fiscal policy is to allow government to redistribute wealth. This is not the same as providing money for services such as education and health. Over the long-term, such services may have redistributive consequences. For example, investment in education allows for redistribution over a generation as children gain an education that allows them access to better paid employment than their parents' generation. But the most effective and immediate means of redistributing wealth is through the tax and benefit system. Scotland's record in redistribution of wealth reflected changes in the UK as a whole as the main levers were held at UK level. Stein Ringen's work is amongst the best overview of the record coinciding with the period of devolution. Ringen's conclusion is that Britain was a 'society of entrenched inequality' in 1997 and after ten years it had 'become a yet more unequal one' (Ringen, 2009, 60). This was not for the lack of trying, nor the lack of resources poured into services designed to help the least well off but because when it came to income distribution, Government in London 'paid careful attention to the broad middle class – which of course represents the bulk of the electorate – but failed those at the bottom of the distribution and gave too much to those at the top' (ibid, 18). The key phrase here is that in parenthesis. The 'contented middle classes' needed to be appeased. Labour's instincts may have inclined it towards more redistribution but electoral imperatives prevented it doing so across Britain. The issue is whether that would have been the case in Scotland. There is some evidence that there are only slight differences in attitude on matters of redistribution north and south of the border but this evidence tells only part of the story. Political leadership plays its part in the shaping of public opinion and the dominance of left of centre parties pursuing a more redistributive agenda in Scotland has never really been put to the test. More important is what happens when

Scottish opinion is no longer in step with opinion elsewhere in Britain. This is where the real impact of the second phase will be felt: party political incongruence combined with severe fiscal constraints.

The third function of taxation is also important. There is no institutional incentive to encourage economic growth. Economic growth brings dividends to government in the shape of increased tax receipts and savings on public services required for those left behind. Devolution is a system in which only the savings from public services from economic growth benefit the Scottish Government while any tax receipts accrue to Westminster. But beyond this, taxation allows government to alter behaviour by creating incentives and disincentives. This is unavailable to the Scottish Government. The absence of such powers embed the imbalanced nature of devolution encouraging the politics of grievance.

The great problem with devolution is that it was created in reaction to a perception that the old system lacked legitimacy but failed to give sufficient consideration to what powers were required to create self-government. If devolution is to be more than a means of wringing money out of London and more than a factor of grievances as we move into a period of financial austerity and become a meaningful form of self-government then greater attention needs to be paid to the three functions of taxation.

Beyond Devolution

But devolution alone cannot deliver meaningful self-government. Just as devolved institutions need to do more than look to London for resources to become meaningful self-government, so too must local communities and citizens do more than look to devolution for solutions and assistance. Our system of government experienced a gradual erosion of local autonomy over a number of generations. The UK, and Scotland within it, is highly centralised. The pervasive command and control attitude that marked the culture of pre-devolution days remains largely in place. Scotland needs the reinvention of local autonomy, with financial autonomy central to this and less dependence on central grants.

Meaningful self-government cannot be achieved simply by focusing on institutions operating at the Scottish level. For many citizens these are as remote as any in London. Large sections of the public have become passive by-standers. In an age when novel forms of deliberation, involving citizens in different corners of the world have been shown to be as responsible and intelligent as any elected representatives, there are grounds for embracing more participative forms of democracy. The challenge ought to be how to harness technology in pursuit of meaningful self-government and breaking down the barriers between the governed and government.

Self-government in this sense is not nationalism. But neither is it unionism. It is on an altogether different plane involving a redistribution of power. Indeed, redistributions of power and wealth go hand in hand. Efforts in one will fail without the other. Redistribution of wealth is essential to facilitate citizen participation, yet even more challenging is acknowledging that no single body at whatever level can achieve meaningful self-government on its own.

Conclusion

Peter Hennessy, the historian and now member of the House of Lords, has argued over the years that there are three great institutions that had succeeded in wringing substantial resources out of the Treasury: the military, doctors and the Scottish Office. Devolution has proved to be a continuation of the old Scottish Office system in important respects. But its success should not be ignored. It was an important step but only a step in the direction. It is best to view self-government less as an end point than a direction of travel. Devolution marked a change of direction but one which has not been accompanied by enough further steps. It has become a cliché to describe devolution as a process, not an event. Sadly, if clichés are self-evident truths, this one has yet to live up to the billing.

References

Melding, D. (2009), *Will Britain Survive Beyond 2020?*, Cardiff: Institute of Welsh Affairs.

Mitchell, J. (1996), *Strategies for Self-Government: The Campaigns for a Scottish Parliament*, Edinburgh: Polygon.

Ringen, S. (2009), *The Economic Consequences of Mr Brown*, Oxford: The Bardwell Press.

The Political Economy of Self-Determination

MICHAEL KEATING

Self-Determination and Independence

SELF-DETERMINATION IN A minimal sense is about deciding about one's own constitutional future. This is never, and can never, be a matter of unilateral decision, since nations and states exist in a world of other self-determining communities with which they need to reach accommodation. For most of the 20th century, self-determination was associated closely with the demand for independent statehood. This followed the collapse of European empires at the end of the World War I and then decolonisation in Africa and Asia after the World War II. In a longer perspective, however, self-determination has been about negotiation and accommodation, especially for small nations which are unable to get their way by main force. European nationalities movements in the 19th century typically sought autonomy within larger imperial structures. This is true of the nationalities of the Habsburg Empire, of Scotland and of Ireland; even Sinn Féin was founded in the early 20th century to seek a dual monarchy for the United Kingdom.

While self-determination was associated with separation, its attractiveness in Scotland declined. The experience of the inter-war period demonstrated the perils of an independence not backed by massive force and the wisdom of those pre-war nationalist leaders who had warned that absolute independence for nations located between Germany and Russia was an illusion – a lesson the Catalans had learned a couple of centuries earlier. Following the World War II, the future seemed to belong to large states which could provide extensive markets and mobilise resources for social security. Only large states, it was argued on the left, could effect serious social redistribution or guarantee against risk. These arguments dominated such debate as there was on the Scottish question between the 1930s and the 1960s. Independence was just not 'viable'.

There were, however, counter-examples, which received increasing attention from the 1980s. Some of the smaller European democracies were learning to operate rather effectively in world markets, not seeking to control trade but adapting to it. The Scandinavian countries, in particular, demonstrated both economic growth and impressive levels of solidarity and social provision. Indeed, far from needing a large state to develop welfare, it seemed that the small states could do it better. To accusations of selfishness, being rich countries running their own welfare regimes, they could point to their generous record in development aid.

Globalisation and European integration have made these arguments all the more relevant (Keating and McGarry, 2001). Worldwide liberalisation of trade and the European single market have weakened the argument that large states are necessary to ensure market access and exploit comparative advantage to ensure an optimal division of labour. Supranational security regimes have undermined arguments about national defence, although the United Kingdom continues to conduct a somewhat fantastical debate about defence as though it were still a world power. Social solidarity may be weakening and no longer based on the old concept of social class but there may be opportunities to foster it at other levels and in new forms of community. The wider process of rescaling across Europe and the world means that we need to rethink the territorial basis for public action.

If we see independence and self-determination as purely legal categories, based on formal sovereignty, then they constitute an all-or-nothing choice. However, such categories are misleading since there is a whole range of possibilities between no self-government at all and unfettered sovereignty. More broadly, we must see self-determination as more than a legal category but rather a way of achieving social and economic goals. Some formally sovereign states have almost no capacity to elaborate their own social and economic project, while other non-sovereign entities have quite a lot. It is for this reason that we must examine the political economy of independence as an important aspect of the argument. Once again, the choice is not between subordination on the one hand and absolute freedom from constraint on the other, but rather of where on a spectrum a nation is located.

The Arc of Prosperity

The experience of small European democracies has had a strong influence on thinking about independence in Scotland and the SNP has paraded a series of successful examples to demonstrate the viability of its case. Until the collapse of the Irish and Icelandic economies, these were bundled together with the Nordic countries as the 'arc of prosperity', later lampooned by Labour as the 'arc of insolvency'. Both labels are so misleading as to provide no help whatever in the debate about self-government. The North Atlantic periphery, and Europe more widely, provide a range of very different models of small nations adapting to global markets. There is a neo-liberal model, associated with some of the central and east European states (an extreme example is Estonia) and in some respects Ireland. This involves competing on low taxes, light regulation, flexible wages and labour markets, and inward investment. The corollary is an under-developed welfare state. There is a section of opinion in Scotland that has recently been pushing this idea; for example, through Reform Scotland and some sections of the media. Michael Russell, shortly before becoming a minister in the SNP government, argued the case in a book (MacLeod and Russell, 2006). But as the Thatcher Government found, and the current UK Government is finding out, however, it is not as easy as it might seem to roll back an existing mature welfare state. The low-tax strategy is much easier in a country that has not developed its welfare services, where family and other networks bear much of the cost of adjustment, and where citizens and workers are ready to accept fluctuations in the individual and the social wage because they remember how dire things were before. There is no evidence that such a strategy has a political market in Scotland. Nor is it likely that such a policy could succeed, since there will always be jurisdictions prepared to cut taxes more and deregulate more than Scotland will, so that the nation will lose out in any such race to the bottom.

The other strategy, characteristic of the Nordic countries, is a high-cost and high-tax one. There is massive public investment in education, health and public services, seen as a contribution to growth rather than a cost. Labour market flexibility is assured not by introducing insecurity but by getting people back into work as soon as possible. Small countries cannot afford the cost of long-term unemployment unless they have a large emigration safety-valve, as did Ireland for such a long time. Even the United Kingdom managed to finance mass unemployment in the 1980s only by gobbling up the oil revenues that might otherwise have gone to long-term investment. We cannot, of course, generalise about successful small countries; their welfare regimes vary. Finland has achieved striking results in education. Denmark has a flexible labour market regime that makes it easy to fire workers but provides generous unemployment benefits and gets them back into work quickly.

What all the small social democratic countries have in common, however, is a mode of policy-making that incorporates interests and allows adjustment to change without serious social disruption. Social and economic interests were bound into national systems and condemned to co-operate with each other for mutual benefit. A shared national identity further brought interests together and provided a motif for social solidarity. The need for welfare provision encouraged high-grade public services, which in turn enhanced the quality of labour supply so that businesses, in the long run, benefitted from welfare policies. In the past, this has been described as corporatism and appeared to be on the way out in the 1980s as states were battered by externally-induced crises and at the mercy of footloose capital. National solidarity appeared under threat from marketisation and global change. There have indeed been significant changes in the Nordic welfare states, especially in Sweden. Yet corporatism, now relabeled social concertation or partnership, made a surprising come-back from the 1990s, precisely as a way of coping with uncertainty in the external environment. Since small states cannot control the environment, they must adapt to it in their own way and, as the most recent economic crisis has shown, they have done it very differently. Iceland and Ireland, having recklessly committed themselves to the world of footloose global finance, suffered meltdown, while other northern European states did much better. Generalisations about arcs of insolvency are thus as misleading as the arc of prosperity boast.

There has been little sign that politicians in Scotland have learnt this complex lesson about the fate of small nations. Unionists have gloated over the fate of Iceland and Ireland. The SNP, for its part, has tried to combine the neo-liberal and social democratic models of political economy, with blithe disregard for their inconsistency. The neo-liberal wing of the party has grown in recent years, but without cancelling the social democratic message and the SNP has been trumpeting low taxes with high public spending. They seek to square the circle with the argument that tax cuts will pay for themselves by stimulating economic activity, an argument famously derided by George Bush senior (running against Ronald Reagan for the Republican nomination) as 'voodoo economics'. Indeed, the experience after Reagan gained office was of ballooning deficits. By contrast, social democratic governments have historically been much more fiscally prudent; at least if one excepts the last few years of New Labour, which also sought to combine the economics of finance capital with social democratic levels of spending. If nationalists are committed to a social democratic road to prosperity, they must accept the wider consequences of this in the form of high costs but at the same time build a productive system that will support them. They must also ask hard questions about the form of welfare services and their beneficiaries, now that easy universalism is palpably unaffordable.

Independence in Europe

The debate on self-determination has also been transformed by the project of European integration. For many stateless nationalist parties, Europe takes care of the difficult externalities of independence, including market access, borders and national security, the latter through the wider North Atlantic community. It is perhaps surprising that it took the SNP until the late 1980s to rediscover Europe, to which it had been rather favourably inclined in the early post-war years. Yet the party has never really presented a vision for the Europe which it aspires to join. It has nothing to say about the competing neo-liberal and social democratic perspectives on Europe. It is officially pro-European but appears to favour a strictly intergovernmental Europe, with the ability to opt in and out of policies at will. This is simply not possible, as new member states have to accept the whole of the *acquis communautaire*, although existing states have sometimes negotiated opt-outs from new policies. An *à la carte* Europe would cease to be a community at all and amount to no more than a series of international treaties.

Denmark, with its multiple opt-outs, is often presented as a model but the Danish stance is rife with contradictions and pretences. Denmark is officially not in the Euro, but is in the European Monetary System in that its currency is tied to the Euro, Danish kroner notes having something like the status of Scottish banknotes in relation to sterling. Yet Denmark has no representation in the making of European monetary policy, including interest rates and the spillover into fiscal policy. It must simply accept what it decided in Frankfurt and Brussels. Denmark has opted out of various policy fields but in practice adopts the vast majority of directives. It refuses to participate in the common defence and security policy but is a member of NATO, which provides the overarching framework and is more constraining. The SNP, as far as one can gather, does it the other way round and would accept European defence but is still committed to withdrawal from NATO. Meanwhile, Danish and to some degree Swedish Euroscepticism has deprived Europe of strong social democratic voices in the design of its institutions and policies. Even now that neither state has a social democratic government, their social democrats do not seem to be looking to safeguard and rebuild social democracy at a European level. Yet we know that, as social democracy is pushed back to the margins, it becomes ever more difficult to defend there. Social democracy in one country may have been viable in the past; it no longer is.

Social Partnership in Scotland

Scotland has some of the prerequisites to become an adaptable, self-governing and social democratic nation coping with global markets and engaging positively in Europe. It is of the right scale, with short lines of communication and a sense of common political identity. In the past, it has mobilised itself in defence of its economic interests. There is a strong commitment to social solidarity and, indeed, this provided much of the impetus for devolution during the 1990s. Since devolution, there has been a stress on partnership in policy-making. There has been, at least until now, a stronger social democratic consensus among policy-makers than in England and an unwillingness to subordinate policy in all fields to the logic of markets and competition.

On the other hand, there is nothing like the social partnership or concertation found in other small European nations. Such ideas were driven out in the United Kingdom generally under successive Conservative and New Labour governments committed to neo-liberal ideas and unthinkingly taking a 'pro-business' line even when in the case of financial regulation, this was not even in the long-term interest of business itself. Scottish interest groups have adapted rather slowly to devolution, with the business community in particular taking time to realise that Scottish government is an arena in which it needs to be involved. Consultation and partnership tend to take place within sectoral policy communities without much opportunity to bring together the economic, social and environmental aspects of policy.

There are historic reasons for this. Scotland evolved during the 20th century as a dependent polity, with most policies handed up from London. The most important Scottish dimension to policy-making involved lobbying for more – a matter on which both sides of industry and everyone else in Scotland could agree. With devolution, Scotland suddenly became a policy arena in which groups compete for resources and are invited to find their own solutions, social compromises and trade-offs. The illusion of consensus, easy enough when Scots were overwhelming aligned with the Opposition, was broken once they had to come to agreement among themselves. The flood of money for public expenditure in the years after devolution merely postponed the hard reality.

A second reason for Scotland not developing a more sophisticated form of social concertation and debate is the absence of taxation powers. As long as the decision on taxes and aggregate spending is taken in London, big economic groups lack the incentive to engage in the policy process and government lacks the means to incentivise them.

A third reason is that labour market regulation and most wage-bargaining are conducted at a British or UK level, in both private and a significant part of the public sector (even in devolved fields). Again, there is less incentive for social compromise at the Scottish level than in states characterised by concertation and partnership.

Is Independence the Answer?

It has frequently been noted that national independence is not what it was in the past. European integration so attenuates it that many British Conservatives, not to mention UKIP, see it as incompatible with the independence of the British nation. Nationalist movements across Europe have widely accepted this, moving to a post-sovereignty stance that emphasises self-determination within wider forms of negotiated order (Keating, 2001).

The SNP Government, in successive phases of the National Conversation, retreated from swathes of traditional independence territory, accepting common policies and regulatory institutions. It even proposed keeping the Pound sterling at least pending a hypothetical entry into the Euro. The latter would happen only at the right time and following a referendum but, since this idea was not accompanied by a convergence plan (obligatory for all Euro candidates) it was effectively postponed *sine die*. There was much, albeit vague, talk of a 'social union'. Yet so far the party has not come around to abandoning independence officially in favour of the open-ended strategy favoured by, for example, Catalan nationalists.

Polling evidence shows that Scottish voters, like those in many other stateless nations, aspire to more self-government and believe in self-determination but do not want to push this to independence in the traditional form (Keating, 2009). They want more control over taxation and over social security, at present almost entirely reserved to Westminster. There are enormous technical difficulties about negotiating these matters but the result would be a form of Scottish social citizenship, encouraging an informed debate about priorities in welfare and public services and the social model for a self-governing nation.

So a modern form of self-determination, geared to a viable political economy as much as to old notions of sovereignty, is a possible route to a better future. It could unite Scots across the old unionist-nationalist divide and appears to be the most popular choice. Yet such a transition would require not only political will but important social and economic adjustment. The present interest group structure, largely echoing that at British (and sometimes UK) level, does not facilitate social partnership. Economic change necessarily involves dislocation and job losses in some sectors. This can be managed through mass unemployment as in the 1980s or through more intelligent forms of adjustment that bring people into new jobs and sectors.

Independence might provide a salutary shock that forces Scottish social and economic groups to work together, as happened in Ireland in the 1980s. On the other hand, they might not respond effectively and it took Ireland some 60 years after independence to learn new ways of adapting and break the emigration syndrome. An independent Scotland will not have its own currency and so will lack the superficially attractive option of devaluation to restore competitiveness. Monetary policy will thus be set by the European Central Bank or, more likely, the Bank of England whose concerns will no longer include Scotland. With the loss of monetary policy goes a swathe of macro-economic powers, since adjustment would have to take place by other means. So the SNP talk about gaining control of the macro-economic levers with independence is really beside the point. What will matter rather will be supply-side policies including innovation, education, training, research and active labour market policy as the key instruments. The same is true if we do not go for independence, suggesting that the constitutional obsession may be a distraction from the real task of taking control of our own destinies.

Self-determination is thus not just a legal category or a decision to be exercised once and for all. It is a strategy for gaining autonomy and control over a nation's future, which passes by policy as much as constitutional matters. The debate on external autonomy cannot be divorced from the debate about Scotland's internal order and whether it has the capacity to thrive and adapt in a turbulent world.

References

Keating, M. (2001), *Plurinational Democracy: Stateless Nations in a Post-Sovereignty Era*, Oxford: Oxford University Press.

Keating, M. (2009), *The Independence of Scotland: Self-Government and the Shifting Politics of Union*, Oxford: Oxford University Press.

Keating, M. and McGarry, J. (eds) (2001), *Minority Nationalism and the Changing International Order*, Oxford: Oxford University Press.

MacLeod, D. and Russell, M. (2006), *Grasping the Thistle: How Scotland Must React to the Three Key Challenges of the Twenty-First Century*, Glendaruel: Argyll Publishing.

Economic Self-Determination: Towards a Political Economy of Scottish Citizenship

DAVID DONALD AND ALAN HUTTON

Self-Determination: The Centrality of Political Economy

ANY ASPIRATION TO EXTEND and enhance the degree of self-determination of Scotland and the Scots must give a prime place to the role of political economy. Income and status—acknowledged legitimate and valued identities within the economic order—are clearly central to well-being and self-realisation. But is it feasible to achieve a Scottish political economy that would support greater national and individual 'self determination'? To what extent can we engender arrangements in which people have more capacity to determine their fate?

Ambitious schemes have featured through history, and central to many has been the image of a political economy of relative equality as a, more or less, attainable ideal. Frequently in these aspirational imaginings some minimal level of state activity establishes and maintains a community of freely interacting, self-actualising humanity that can be self sustaining through a homeostatic mechanism which appropriately harnesses human nature.

The myths of the 'free market economy' mobilise support for an ideology of commercialism that privileges certain powerful interests and legitimates particular patterns of investment and income distribution. The shortcomings and failings of this imagined world of self regulated exchanges, unencumbered firms and entrepreneurs, and 'free' individuals are apparent. It is defective in terms of both its predicted outcomes of opportunity for all and of its understandings of the workings of the economic orders of the contemporary world. It privileges and it divides.

The climate is now right for a challenge to this dominant narrative with its false images of globalist cosmopolitanism (Gray, 2002). Scotland, where many current settlements and priorities are inherently unstable, is fertile for such change. In common with others in Europe we must re-assert the roles of regulation, the rights, responsibilities and social obligations of economic actors to themselves and others and the importance and legitimacy of public purposes as countervailing forces to the logics of unrestrained capitalism. But Scotland could go further and institute a 21st century notion of a 'political economy of citizenship' (Sandel, 2005). For that we must re-image our economic world and its purposes, redevelop and restructure our economy, reassess the forms of economic incentives we support, and reform our economic governance.

Constraints: The Image of a Scottish Economy in a Capitalist World

Our starting point is the image of the Scottish economy that shapes our 'public philosophy'. How should we measure our relative successes and failures? What conceptual models of the economic forces that shape our lives should we promote? Notions of world, national and sub-national economies are socially constructed, politically negotiated and ideologically promulgated. Constraints, imperatives and priorities are 'real' but important elements of that reality are social facts, the perceptions of which can change. There are alternatives. We *can* act to shape our circumstances. But our first consideration must be the nature of the economic ideology at the centre of our public philosophy.

Effective economic ideologies become, necessarily, part of people's world taken for granted (Donald and Hutton, 2009). Narratives, symbols, idioms and, above all, myths and metaphors all become part of shared perceptions to such an extent that they are largely 'decontested' (Freeden, 1996). Human actions, motivated by particular interests, are bundled and presented as impersonal forces. At the same time they are given a collective persona with an implied rationality. A good example is how 'the Markets' react favourably or unfavourably; and we are ruled by our anticipations of their reactions. But the markets and global capitalism are continuously constituted and re-constituted by their reactions to our rules, regulations, understandings and behaviours.

Actors – policy makers, organisational elites and the general public – in the Scottish economy must be aware of the nature of this 'world markets' phenomenon, adjust to its vagaries to best secure the interests of Scottish citizens, and seek to associate with those who try to civilise the 'barbarous relics' (Keynes, 1924) of domestic and international economic exchanges.

This means a challenge to what has been a dominant theme in the world view of the Anglophone economies. It has been, with some success, promulgated and proselytised in other economic orders – particularly in Germany and, more generally, in the approaches of the European Union (Streeck, 2009). Its message was greatly strengthened by economic practices; those who resisted the gospel were disadvantaged in the market place. But liberal cosmopolitan 'globalism', despite its considerable influence, remains a far from complete guide – either to how the economic world actually functions or to prescriptions of how to promote the interests of the people whose rulers adhere to its precepts.

As a 'small state in world markets' (Katzenstein, 1985), we should eschew the brand of liberal economics developed in the context of Anglo-American imperial hegemony and consider the form of national political economy which best meets the security and aspirations of Scots in a changing world. This is the best position from which to make a positive contribution to the wider world. Our weakness and decline is unlikely to benefit others. As an aspect of our contribution we should select partners who share our values and aspects of our predicaments. As Asians 'look east' we should 'look north' – to the relatively successful 'smaller' economies of northern Europe.

Today's Scotland offers grounds for optimism in relation to reconstructing the image of our economy. As the Anglophone world globalised in its rhetoric, Scots have been thinking and acting more close to home. The notion of a *Scottish* economy is more readily and more widely accepted than it was three decades ago. Mere 'regionalism' no longer convinces. The processes which led to devolution have been reinforced by devolution. The perception of ourselves as members of a coherent political community is more widely acknowledged as realistic. Although, as we argue below, there are many limits to our freedom of action we are better placed to negotiate the pursuit of our interests and values than we once perceived. Aware of the exigencies of our memberships of the

United Kingdom and the European Union we are more willing to assert our separate interests and to attempt to negotiate outcomes more congenial to our temperament and traditions. We should take a similar stance in relation to our position in the world economy. For the most part those who live here identify with Scotland. We can now attempt to realise our own values rather than simply accept the values of our neighbours.

In summary, the 'Scottish economy' is a social construct predicated upon notions of Scottishness. It persists because of a shared perception of the existence of a Scottish political community. This community has retained a special identity even at the high points of UK unionism and regionalism. Devolution, the European Union and recent economic history have strengthened rather than weakened it. The majority who come to live in Scotland are willing to adopt or share in our identity. A concomitant of a growing sense of self is the recognition of the legitimacy and utility of Scotland as a valid political and economic entity. The set of traditions, interpretations and understandings of history and cultural symbols that sustains perceptions of Scottishness adds what Bronk (2009) calls a 'romantic' element to our political economy. This is a necessary component for fuelling separate Scottish institutions and motivating Scots. A yet more social political economy should be envisaged to support our strengthening sense of political community and, in the widest sense, enrichen our lives.

A Political Economy of Scottish Citizenship

Devolved government has further reinforced the formal contrasts to others in the UK. We can now begin to talk of a separate Scottish citizenship in which rights and responsibilities are, within limits and negotiated with the UK and the EU, different. We are shaping our citizenship into something we can be yet more proud of and something worthy of defending. Being Scottish should be desirable to all who live, or come to live, here. And some of these rights should be, wholly or partly, in the economic sphere.

Such an economy would operate to advance the rights and support the responsibilities of the population as a matter of citizenship. The negotiated articulation and integration of social and economic goals should be supported by the values of membership and the covenants implied by that. Such an approach to the economy requires a reconsideration of the appropriate forms of governance for different types of institution. Recent trends have 'managerialised' and weakened governance and accountability. An aspect of this is de-professionalisation. This dilutes the professional ethics that have become more, rather than less, imperative in a world of less face to face interaction. The advantages of specific professional, especially ethical, education and membership need restating. This is important for self-determination and self worth. The cult of 'management' and 'leadership' often results in unquestioned and unconsidered dubious ventures. Some of our European partners are more familiar with such practices than us. They have extended forms of rights of membership to workers rights; for example, German co-determination.

The resources necessary for organisations to function are not simply internal. Funds from grants, loans and shareholders are obvious sources, but other collective resource provision is also provided. The location of an entrepreneurial venture is usually crucial to its success. We should stress reciprocity and mutual dependence as a responsibility in the economic sphere and try to inhibit those who wish to squat in our economy and avoid paying the full rental. We should co-operate with the EU to prevent the 'beggar my neighbour' bidding down of taxation. Those who wish to manufacture and trade in Europe should pay their fair share for maintaining the market – and its related communities. An important starting point is to consider how unhelpful 'mainstream' economics is in a range of ways and particularly how it might undermine our efforts to re-structure our economy and manage our patterns of trade.

Beyond Mainstream Economics

As indicated above, consideration of the nature and possibilities of increased economic self-determination in Scotland must start with how 'the economy' is perceived. Those perceptions are heavily conditioned by the 'scientific' and ideological outputs of the conventional wisdom in economics. We wish to challenge those accepted approaches and images.

So we do not set out here to examine the prospects for Scotland's economy in a conventional way, considering the future levels and growth in productivity and GDP per head, in employment or unemployment, in exports and imports. For that we can look to the work of the Scottish Government Economic Service, the Council of Economic Advisers – along with University research units such as the FAI and the CPPR – in analysing and measuring economic activity and developing important bases for Scottish Economic Strategy. Valuable though such analysis is in its own terms, in a more thoroughgoing attempt to explore the chances of greater economic self-determination at every level in Scotland, the significant limitations of the way mainstream economics approaches the explanation of patterns of economic activity, and the measurement of its social impacts, soon become clear. It is an approach which narrows the vision of the 'economic' and concedes too readily many possibilities of shaping them through collective action. In important ways we *can* 'buck the market'. Indeed '(g)ood economic policy does not require good (orthodox) economics' (Chang, 2010). The remarkable economic development of Japan (from the 1950s to the 1980s), and more recently other south East Asian states, was founded on an approach that explicitly rejects liberal economic orthodoxy – a 'national political economy'.

The exposure of orthodox economics in the present international crisis simply highlights a long established situation. As a frame of reference for understanding, charting and forecasting the key institutions, processes and outcomes of our economic society, orthodox liberal economics is flawed. Its image is of an abstract market economy with stylised institutions, whose workings are explained through universal 'theoretical' models, founded on the assumption of individual 'rational choice' maximising behaviour in a cosmopolitan market world – apparently unaffected by differences of history, institutional evolution, culture or politics of 'real world' national economies.

But the *social* is the justification for economic arrangements and the *political* is a major, and ineluctable, component of such arrangements. Not so for the liberal economic orthodoxy which, initially in the Anglo-American market capitalist world and now – through the US globalist project – more generally, has dominated the contemporary view of economic life, serves as an ideological buttress to the 'great capitalist restoration' of the last 30 years (Stanfield, 2010). We cannot ignore the individual and the cosmopolitan levels at which mainstream economics operates. The wider international economy and the predicaments that it presents are significant for Scotland, and some understanding of individuals' 'economic behaviour' is vital. Even more importantly, however, we need a political economy that operates at the 'national' and 'community' levels where

Scottish economic self-determination must work. Orthodox economists, when they descend from the high plains of ideal-type 'economic theory' to the world of 'applied' economics, tend to see historically/culturally grounded social and political institutions as merely contingent factors which have to be accommodated in economic policy or, more often, as 'noise' in the machine or 'imperfections' which should, ideally, be ironed out in the pursuit of the over-riding value of 'efficiency'. This kind of economism and the values, policies, behaviours and outcomes that it engenders are damaging to the possibility of enhanced self-determination at every level within Scotland. Writing in the mid 1990s about Britain as a whole John Gray summed up the issues:

> Individualist market institutions ...detach individuals from localities and communities and weaken commitments to families. They do this by imposing unending mobility on people and by routinising high levels of economic risk, so that all relationships come to be perceived as revocable and transitory.
>
> Our...individualist economic and moral cultures will be defended by unreflective economic liberals... who promote individual autonomy. ... however, ... an anomically individualist society, such as ours has become, does not act to strengthen autonomy. That depends on the existence of a strong public culture, rich in options, and embodied in common institutions. Moreover autonomy is only one human interest, one component in individual well-being, even in a society such as ours; the satisfaction of needs for belonging and for stable relationships and attachments, is equally essential to our flourishing as individuals. (Gray, 1996, 49)

We agree with Gray that effective individual autonomy can only operate in a context of enhanced collective self-determination at community and national levels.

Economics need not be like this. In Scotland, to a greater extent and for longer than in the rest of the Anglo-American world, a different style predominated. The first object in the constitution of the Scottish Economic Society – now largely honoured in the breach – remains 'to advance the study of economic and social problems on the widest basis, in accordance with the Scottish tradition of political economy inspired by Adam Smith' (Hutton, 2006).

Recent work by many economists in fields like behavioural economics might be seen as rendering the discipline more eclectic in its vision (see Backhouse, 2010), and many economists would eschew the values of neo-liberalism. But its established liberal core retains an ideological hold through what Hayek, in his concern for the influence of intellectuals in promulgating a socialist climate of opinion 50 years ago, called the 'dealers in second-hand ideas': the civil servants, policy makers, think tanks, journalists and McKinsey and Company and their ilk. In the wake of the present financial crisis even such free market believers as Alan Greenspan and Richard Posner are admitting that deregulation has gone too far and 'we need a more active, and intelligent government to keep our model of a capitalist economy from running off the rails' (Posner, 2009). It is not, of course, Posner's model of a capitalist economy that we wish to advance here.

Important starting points for the challenge to the individualist, economistic, free market vision can be found in the work of a range of political economists who are concerned for the social and environmental impacts of economic orthodoxy in theory and practice – for 'the common good'. This includes the 'economics of happiness' (Layard, 2005) and of human well-being (Jackson, 2010); the importance of capabilities and functionings for human well-being (Sen, 1987); and a focus on socio-economic development rather than economic growth (Chang, 2010). Even if Jackson's strong version of the material limits to future growth for the world is not fully accepted, there is compelling evidence of some kind of overarching Malthusian predicament. And his argument is attractive: the possibility of 'prosperity' without significant growth of material production – at least for those of us who already enjoy high material standards – in which prosperity includes vital social and psychological dimensions.

Just as the way we envisage our economy affects our view of what is really possible, it also affects what we measure, and what we measure and the indicators used in turn affects what we do. Economic orthodoxy leads us to standard aggregate measures of economic performance: GDP and its growth; employment and unemployment, changes in the general price level, the balance of payments. As the Report of the President Sarkozy's Commission on the Measurement of Economic Progress and Social Progress (2009), chaired by Joseph Stiglitz and advised by Amartya Sen, states:

...for a long time there have been concerns about the adequacy of current measures of economic performance, in particular those solely based on GDP. Besides, there are even broader concerns about the relevance of these figures as measures of societal well-being... it has long been clear that GDP is an inadequate metric to gauge well-being over time particularly in its economic, environmental, and social dimensions, some aspects of which are often referred to as *sustainability*.

The Commission's central position is that 'the time is ripe for our measurement system to *shift emphasis from measuring economic production to measuring people's well-being.*' And well-being is multi-dimensional. In addition to material living standards (including wealth as well as income and consumption) the report lists health, education, and personal activities including work, along with political voice and governance, social connections and relationships, the present and future conditions of the environment, and insecurity (economic as well as physical).

A particularly significant recommendation is that 'quality-of-life indicators in all the dimensions covered should assess inequalities in a comprehensive way'. This picks up the importance of the large and growing economic inequality experienced in the UK/Scotland along with the other Anglo-American style economies, a phenomenon whose importance for human well-being is central to the arguments of Wilkinson and Pickett (2010) and Layard (2005).

Also of importance for policy is the Commission's emphasis on the need to assess the links between various quality-of-life domains for each person. The aggregate level of employment or unemployment is a standard indicator of economic performance but, whilst having a job and the resulting income is a benefit for an individual, the experienced security of employment, the quality of the job and the degree of self-realisation work experience offers, along with the income provided, have a major impact on well-being – for individuals, their families and communities.

The Commission concludes that: '(q)uality of life depends on people's objective conditions and capabilities. Steps should be taken to improve measures of people's health, education, personal activities and environmental conditions. In particular, substantial effort should be devoted to developing and implementing robust, reliable measures of social connections, political voice, and insecurity that can be shown to predict life satisfaction.'

Attempts to create well-being indicators have been underway in a number of places (eg UNICEF, 2010). In Britain development has been led by the New Economics Foundation (see Michaelson et al, 2009). NEF proposals for the development of 'National Accounts of Well-being' within a context of societal and environmental sustainability, along with Layard's 'economics of happiness', have led to serious consideration of the policy relevance of these dimensions in Whitehall, culminating in David Cameron's recent commitment to consult on the creation of an index of well-being for the UK to be established next April. This is a limited, but important initiative and if we are to advance the well-being of Scots, including their individual and collective capacities for self-determination, Scotland must do much more in this direction.

Development and Re-development Economics

Our economy, like that of the rest of the United Kingdom, has an imperative to re-develop and restructure. We accept that the funding of desirable public provision is reliant on private sector performance and, in particular, on the tradable goods and services sector. There is currently a wide acceptance that the scale and effectiveness of this private sector is inadequate – but little agreement of explanations for its failure. The obvious example of this is the catastrophe of the finance sector on which so many hopes rested. 'Back to normalcy' in that sector seems somewhat optimistic. A current mantra is that 'manufacturing matters' – but what industrial manufacture might be established, re-established or expanded? A 'fortress economy' seems neither desirable nor possible. So how might Scotland, with some degree of volition and security, fit into, benefit from and contribute to the world economy?

It must surely do so as part of a balanced and articulated pattern of economic development, led by strategic industrial policy which evolves through interaction between government and the other key economic interests. For a structure of economic activity in Scotland which better meets the multi-dimensional requirements of increasing well-being for all Scottish individuals and communities, developments must be characterised by strong attachment to Scotland. Such attachment can be reinforced in many ways. These should include: a growth of collective and community-based forms of economic organisation and governance; key productive activities based directly on Scottish natural resources; activities which depend on higher skills and education, and innovative technological developments that can be provided by well-resourced and highly valued school and higher education systems; finding ways of developing a commitment – a political economy of citizenship – not just for individuals but, just as importantly, for capitalist corporations; an increase in Scottish owned private businesses; more financial institutions geared to the funding of Scottish based projects and developments. Fundamental to future socioeconomic success is the development of key elements of network infrastructure of transport, communications, water and energy. Imaginative forms of co-operation between all levels of government and private companies may be needed here.

Scottish Government has made a useful start in some of these directions. Its approach is embodied in a Government Economic Strategy focusing on seven well chosen Key Sectors (Creative Industries; Energy; Financial & Business Services; Food & Drink; Life Sciences; Tourism; and Universities) – which offer the real prospect for the kinds of attachment that we list above – together with the 'social economy' of Education and Healthcare (Scottish Government, 2010).

In relation to the major economic challenges facing the world as a whole Scotland may be not too badly placed. We should be well placed to reduce our energy use and to increase our reliance on renewable sources and thereby our carbon footprint; we are far from overcrowded; do not face a water shortage; and the climate change which may now be an inevitable result of human economic activity is not likely to significantly undermine living conditions for Scots. We are, however, far from self-sufficient in food and in many essential raw materials and manufactured goods.

So the economy of contemporary Scotland is necessarily open. All seven Key Sectors offer the prospects of export growth. In reality, and in contrast to 'free trade' rhetoric, the international trade regime is negotiated environment of formal and informal treaties and understandings. In seeking ways to influence that environment – to manage trade as far as possible to sustain the extensive external relationships required to secure the 'standard of living' that we would associate with the capabilities and functionings required for satisfactory and fulfilling life for Scotland's citizens – the sub-nation state status of Scotland is an obvious constraint, as is our inability, even with the latest Calman-based proposals, to flexibly use fiscal powers to influence key allocation and distributional outcomes for Scots.

Space does not permit a more detailed consideration of policy options here, but a valuable menu of possibilities with a UK focus is offered in 'A New Political Economy' produced by the campaign group Compass (Shah and McIvor, 2006) and grounded on a similar analysis to ours.

Towards a Political Economy of Citizenship

Central to aspirations for greater self-determination for Scotland are the processes of political economy. Hopes for a revitalised Scottish political economy have, to some extent, to be grounded, practical, realistic – recognising a range of constraints. Yet they can be radical and aspirational. It has to be a bit romantic – to embody some rational myths – to capture the imagination of Scots, new and old, in order to engage their emotions and mobilise their energies. The contemporary predicament of a small population, slightly beleaguered, a sub-set of humanity and on the fringe of the challenged, less than unified semi-state that is the European Union, in itself creates imperatives for change.

In this chapter we have argued for the promulgation of a 'political economy of citizenship' as a prerequisite for the extension of 'democratic autonomy'. Specific economies are social and political constructs reflective of the specific political community which they serve. Change requires a re-imaging of how the economy works and what interests should determine economic arrangements and settlements. An economic order with changed priorities is challenged by the status quo. But there is cause to be more optimistic now than at any time in the last three decades of neo-liberal 'great capitalist restoration'. Scottish political identity is more secure and Scottish arrangements and interests recognised as legitimate. Mainstream economics is less secure in its dogmatism and more observers are conscious of its explanatory limitations, sceptical of its prescriptions and aware of the shortcomings of conventional economic metrics of well-being. In general, in the wake of the crisis, 'back to normalcy' is viewed with suspicion and resentment across the political spectrum. A wide set of interests is threatened by the insecurity of current arrangements. A new settlement is possible. Discontents with contemporary arrangements and their democratic deficits have a central economic element. The active defence and pursuit of Scottish interests is necessary in the context of European economic redevelopment, English economic restructuring and global change. We argue that the time is right to establish a new order for the negotiation of economic rights, responsibilities and priorities.

References

Backhouse, R.E. (2010), *The Puzzle of Modern Economics: Science or Ideology*, Durham, NC and London: Duke University Press.

Bronk, R. (2009), *The Romantic Economist*, Cambridge: Cambridge University Press.

Chang, H.-J. (2010), 23 *Things They Don't Tell You About Capitalism*, Harmondsworth: Allen Lane.

Donald, D. and Hutton, A. (1995), *Participation and Hierarchy in Firms and Other Organisation: A Communitarian Opportunity*, PARU Papers in Comparative Political Economy 6, Glasgow: Glasgow Caledonian University.

Donald, D. and Hutton, A. (2009), *Ideology and Intention: Moral Imperatives and the Practice of Economics* SCEME Working Papers: Advances in Economic Methodology 30, Stirling: University of Stirling.

Freeden, M. (1996), *Ideologies and Political Philosophy: A Conceptual Approach* Oxford: Oxford University Press.

Gray, J. (1996), *After Social Democracy: Politics, capitalism and the common life*, London: Demos.

Gray, J. (2002), *False Dawn* (Revised Edition), London: Granta Books.

Held, D. (1987), *Models of Democracy*, Cambridge: Polity Press.

Hutton, A. (2006), 'A Scottish tradition of applied economics in the twentieth century' in Dow, A and Dow, S.C. (eds) *A History of Scottish Economic Thought*, London: Routledge.

Jackson, T. (2010), *Prosperity Without Growth? The transition to a sustainable economy*, Sustainable Development Commission, http://www.sd-commission.org.uk/publications.php?id=914

Katzenstein, P.J. (1985), *Small States in World Markets*, Ithaca, NY: Cornell University Press.

Keynes, J.M. (1924), *A Tract on Monetary Reform*, London: Macmillan.

Layard, R. (2005), *Happiness*, Harmondsworth: Penguin.

Michaelson, J. et. al. (2009), *National Accounts of Well-Being*, London: New Economics Foundation, http://www.neweconomics.org/publications/national-accounts-well-being

Posner, R. (2009), *The Crisis of Capitalism: The Crisis of '08 and the Descent into Depression*, Boston: Harvard University Press.

Sandel, M. (2005), *Public Philosophy*, Boston: Harvard University Press.

Scottish Government. (2010), *Government Economic Strategy: Key Sector Reports*, http://www.skillsdevelopmentscotland.co.uk/knowledge/reports/government-economic-strategy-key-sector-reports.aspx

Sen, A. (1987), *The Standard of Living*, Cambridge: Cambridge University Press.

Stanfield, J.R. (2010), 'Some social economics concepts for future research' *Forum for Social Economics*, http://www.springerlink.com/content/0736-0932/39/2/

Stiglitz, J, et al. (2009), Report by the Commission on the Measurement of Economic Performance and Social Progress, http://www.stiglitz-sen-fitoussi.fr/documents/rapport_anglais.pdf

Shah, H. and McIvor, M. (eds) (2006), *A New Political Economy*, London: Compass in association with Lawrence and Wishart.

Streeck, W. (2009), *Re-forming Capitalism*, Oxford: Oxford University Press.

UNICEF. (2010), *Child Poverty in Perspective: An Overview of Child Well-Bbeing in Rich Countries*, http://www.unicefirc.org/publications/pdf/rc7_eng.pdf

Wilkinson, R. and Pickett, K. (2010), *The Spirit Level* (2nd edn), Harmondsworth: Penguin.

After Barnett, After Calman

DREW SCOTT

Financing Scotland's devolved government: the debate

IN THE SHORT HISTORY of post-devolution politics no issue has attracted more discussion and debate than the arrangements for financing Scotland's devolved government. At present, and at least for the lifetime of the Scottish Parliament elected in 2011, the overwhelming part of total public spending by the devolved Scottish administration will (continue to) be financed by an annual block grant from the UK Government. The amount of the annual block grant is determined by the previous year baseline amount as adjusted (under the Barnett formula) to account for any increase (decrease) in spending assigned to those Whitehall departments responsible for policies that have been devolved. The formula itself is based on the relative population shares of the devolved territories and is not directly based on a measure of relative public service 'needs' of the devolved territories. It is also worth recording that the block grant arrangement is not enshrined in any legislation.

Since 1999 the arrangements for financing the devolved administrations, particularly Scotland, have come under increasing criticism. Three critiques have been advanced. The first is that the current funding arrangements are overly generous to Scotland in per capita public expenditure terms. Indeed, per capita spending in Scotland is higher than in many English regions. However, rather than consider the relative public spending 'needs' of Scotland, critics instead point to specific policies that the Scottish administration has introduced since 1999 which are not available in England – including the provision of free personal care to the elderly, the abolition of tuition fees for Scottish (and EU) students, ending prescription charges and providing senior citizens with free travel. Although the UK Government has never conducted a comprehensive, needs-based review of the current arrangements in order to assess their fairness, the view that Scotland enjoys a privileged funding settlement was reinforced by the recent publication of the Holtham Report. This called for a new funding settlement for Wales (Holtham, 2010).

Second, the funding system is criticised because the Scottish Parliament, which is responsible for spending the block grant, has no responsibility for raising the revenues that finance its' spending. At present the devolved administration has virtually no competence over taxation and therefore plays no role in setting the taxes that finance expenditure. The upshot is that the Parliament has every incentive to spend the full block grant even if, at the margin, additional expenditure yields little or no economic or social benefits. Some argue that this is precisely what has happened in Scotland where excessive public spending has 'crowded out' more efficient private spending. It is argued that making the Scottish Parliament responsible for levying taxes that finance all, or part, of its spending would rectify this anomaly by providing the incentive (lower taxes) for public spending to be reduced. At the same time, if Scotland's parliament collected revenues from taxes it levied, there would be a positive incentive for ensuring public spending increased the rate of economic growth, as higher revenues would facilitate lower taxation.

The third criticism levelled against the present financing arrangement is that it is predicated on the centralisation of fiscal authority at the UK level and as such ignores the economic benefits associated with the devolution of fiscal policy levers (i.e. empowering the devolved administration to set (most) taxes and determine (most) public spending within its jurisdiction). Politically this argument has now become most closely associated with the SNP, although the 2006 report by the Steel Commission essentially advanced precisely the same proposition. The intellectual antecedents of the proposition that fiscal autonomy would benefit Scotland's economy are to be found in the literature on 'fiscal federalism' that dates back to the 1950s. Adherents to this view argue that fiscal autonomy increases economic efficiency by matching tax-raising authority with spending decisions, and delivers improved economic growth because the devolved administration is able to utilise a wide range of fiscal (tax) policy levers that were previously unavailable.

Convincing as each of these critiques might be, the debate in Scotland over the future financing of devolved government was triggered mainly by the changed political context that followed the SNP victory in the May

2007 Scottish Parliamentary elections. Shortly thereafter the new Scottish Government announced that it would conduct a 'national conversation' about Scotland's future constitutional position with a view to holding a consultative referendum on independence in the lifetime of the new Parliament. That exercise was launched in August. The national conversation was intended to elicit the widest range of views about the future course of devolution and was not intended merely to debate independence versus the status quo. For instance, an intermediate position described as 'devolution-max' was quickly identified which would involve a move to fiscal autonomy (comprehensive devolution of tax and spending policies) within an overall UK constitutional framework. Nonetheless the 'national conversation' was promptly derided by the main opposition parties who opted instead to launch a separate exercise in constitutional consultation.

On St Andrew's Day 2007 Wendy Alexander MSP, then leader of the Labour group in the Scottish Parliament, announced the establishment of a Commission on Scottish Devolution to be chaired by Sir Kenneth Calman. The initiative was supported by the main opposition parties as well as the then UK (Labour) Government. The Calman Commission's remit was:

> To review the provisions of the Scotland Act 1998 in the light of experience and to recommend any changes to the present constitutional arrangements that would enable the Scottish Parliament to serve the people of Scotland better, improve the financial accountability of the Scottish Parliament, and continue to secure the position of Scotland within the United Kingdom. (Calman Commission, 2009)

As it transpired the main part of the work of the Calman Commission revolved around the issue of increasing the financial accountability of the Scottish Parliament. By this means the whole question of the future of the Barnett funding mechanism as it applied to Scotland was now open for debate (House of Lords, 2009).

The Calman Commission and the devolution of fiscal powers

The final report of the Calman Commission was published in June 2009, with its centrepiece proposal a revised mechanism for financing the devolved Scottish administration (Calman Commission, 2009). The aim of the

Commission was to bring forward proposals that would increase the accountability of the Scottish Parliament for its expenditure decisions. The solution it proposed was to make the Parliament directly responsible for raising some part of its annual revenues by substituting a proportion of the block grant with revenues that would accrue instead from the application of a new Scottish income tax.

This new tax would replace the existing Scottish variable rate (of 3p) and would be made possible by a reduction of 10p in the rate of income tax applied by the UK Government in Scotland. The block grant would be reduced by an amount equal to the yield of the Scottish segment of income tax, and it would be for the Scottish Parliament to restore that amount by levying its new tax. Indeed, the Scottish Parliament would be empowered to set its income tax at whatever rate is wished. Therefore if it set a rate below 10p then its annual revenue (and so expenditure) would fall, while if it set a rate above 10p its revenue (and so expenditure) would increase. According to the Commission this arrangement would not only increase the financial accountability of the Parliament, it would allow Scotland to decide to set its own tax according to its own public spending objectives.

Unsurprisingly the publication of the Calman Commission's report was greeted enthusiastically by unionist parties in the Scottish Parliament as well as the UK Government, and its recommendation on tax devolution was immediately endorsed. The Scottish Government, on the other hand, adopted a more cautious stance for two reasons. The first reflected serious reservations about the workability of Calman's fiscal proposals and the implications these would have for the revenue flowing to the Scottish budget. Second, while accepting the proposition that the tax proposal would slightly increase the financial accountability of the Parliament, the Scottish Government pointed out, correctly, that the proposals did little to equip them the fiscal powers needed to tackle the deep-seated and, in the light of the financial crisis and associated recession, increasing problems of the Scottish economy.

Critics of the Calman Commission's tax proposal, the author included (Hughes Hallett and Scott, 2010) pointed to a number of defects in the scheme. First, it simply is not feasible to prepare a budget on the basis of in-year future tax receipts as these are subject to collection lags and variations that simply cannot be anticipated. The Calman Commission seemed oblivious to this basic point and offered no proposal as to how it might be tackled. In practice a post-Calman Scottish budget could only be set either on the basis of a forecast of the yield from applying Scotland's income tax, or by providing the Scottish Government with borrowing powers to enable it to raise finance in order to offset (or 'smooth') such unanticipated variations in tax receipts. However, either solution merely creates other problems. Economic forecasts of tax yields are notoriously inaccurate and so inherently contestable. And which government would produce the forecast? Further, any errors in the forecast would need to be corrected by adjusting (upwards or downwards) financial transfers to the Scottish administration in a later year. This would result in revenues from the devolved income tax being inherently uncertain – the uncertainty over in-year tax yields now being replaced with uncertainty over the requisite financial adjustment in later years. The alternative solution – providing the Scottish Government with borrowing powers to enable it to smooth any unanticipated shortfall in tax receipts – was summarily ruled out by the Calman Commission on the dubious assertion that these were not needed.

Second, the tax receipts accruing to the Scottish Parliament would be subject to change as a consequence of decisions made by the UK Government regarding the rules governing income tax (including the rate of tax and tax allowances) and/or the balance between different taxes in the overall fiscal policy mix.

Third, the Commission rejected giving the Scottish Parliament the power to apply their new tax powers differentially between income earners on the basic and higher tax bands. The upshot is that, if Parliament decided to use its new tax power, the marginal change in the tax rate would be equivalent to imposing a flat tax on Scottish income earners which – as with all flat tax regimes – would be highly regressive.

Fourth, the proposals would introduce a pro-cyclical bias into public spending in Scotland. A cyclical upturn in the economy would lead to rising incomes and higher tax yield thus increasing the expenditure of the Scottish Parliament, while an economic downturn would see the yield from falling income tax resulting in lower spending by the Parliament. The consequence is that government spending will accentuate rather than stabilise the economic cycle which, in economic terms, is precisely the wrong policy response.

Finally, and most surprisingly, neither the Calman Commission, nor the independent expert group which advised it, undertook any analysis of how the implementation of their proposal would have changed the profile of revenues accruing to the Scottish budget in the period since devolution. Authoritative calculations undertaken since the Commission published its report demonstrate that for the majority of the decade the Calman model of financing the devolved administration would have resulted in an aggregate shortfall of almost £8 billion compared to the revenues that did accrue under the current (Barnett) system – the shortfall for the year 2009–2010 alone being some £900 million (GERS, 2010). Of course, that the Calman reform would have lowered Scotland's budget by such an extent does not in itself undermine their proposal. Nor do these calculations provide any indication of the future profile of Scotland's budget resources going forward. However, they do demonstrate that implementing the Calman proposals would (and will) change the profile of Scotland's revenue going forward and, based on the evidence to hand, that this will necessarily lead to either public spending being lower, or income tax being higher.

Towards fiscal responsibility

The critique of the Calman Commission's proposals offered above focuses entirely on the defects in its preferred tax devolution model for financing the devolved Scottish administration. A more important criticism is that the Commission did not take the opportunity to consider how Scotland's economy might be 'better served' by devolving to the Scottish Government comprehensive responsibility for the conduct of fiscal policy – i.e. moving to a situation of fiscal autonomy.

The intellectual case for Scottish fiscal autonomy is rooted in the fiscal federalist school of thought in public finance. There are two aspects to this. The first revolves around the issue of financial accountability on the part of spending authorities – the issue that informed the work of the Calman Commission. However, unlike the conclusions of the Commission which proposed very limited transfer of tax raising responsibility to the Scottish Parliament relative to its spending powers, academic opinion suggests that only a comprehensive transfer of such responsibility will provide sufficient incentive to ensure the maximum efficiency in public spending.

Accordingly, while there is broad agreement between advocates of fiscal autonomy and the members of the Calman Commission that empowering the Scottish Parliament with fiscal powers is desirable, there is disagreement as to the extent to which such empowerment is necessary in order to ensure maximum efficiency in public spending.

The second aspect concerns the consequences of fiscal autonomy for economic management. It is beyond this chapter to detail how fiscal autonomy for Scotland would operate within the UK context (Hallwood and MacDonald, 2009); rather, we confine ourselves here to a basic outline of the central argument. The core proposition is that devolving full authority over virtually all taxes levied in Scotland (with the exception of VAT) and public services delivered in Scotland would provide the Scottish Government with the economic policy levers it requires in order to maximise the growth and employment performance of the economy. The Scottish Government would then be responsible for raising, through taxation, all the revenue required to finance Scotland's public spending and cover the net remittances required to pay for Scotland's consumption of those services that continue to be provided centrally – e.g. defence, foreign policy. Scotland's government would also be responsible for financing any deficit of income over expenditure by issuing debt instruments and, subsequently, of managing its own domestic debt levels. However, as we discuss below, this does not imply that Scotland would be fiscally independent. Various inter-governmental agreements and institutions would be required in order to ensure that Scotland's fiscal autonomy was consistent with macroeconomic stability for the UK as a whole.

Equipping Scotland's government with comprehensive taxation powers would enable it to construct a tax regime that was optimal from the perspective of the long-term management of the economy. Some of the likely effects of tax autonomy are well rehearsed – such as the impact of lowering the rate of corporation tax on inward investment. Other benefits have had much less discussion. Broadly stated, the more extensive control a government has over taxation and spending within its jurisdiction, then the better able it is to design a tax regime that is optimal from the perspective of both the economic challenges and opportunities it faces, and the broader societal objectives it seeks to realise.

Opponents of fiscal autonomy for Scotland tend not to dispute the proposition that it would add to the economic policy levers to which a government had recourse in order to better manage the economy. They object for other reasons – that Scotland could not afford to be fiscally autonomous; that fiscal autonomy is equivalent to political independence; that fiscal autonomy would be economically destabilising from the Scottish and UK perspective; that UK fiscal policy is in any event optimal from the perspective of the Scottish economy.

The first two propositions can be fairly easily refuted. Official statistics in recent years have demonstrated that Scotland's economy would be eminently capable of generating sufficient income to cover its expenditure on a sustainable basis. This does not mean that Scotland's finances would permanently record a financial surplus, but the data does demonstrate that the scale of the budget deficit associated with the current economic slowdown would lie within the range associated with the better performing EU member states. The argument that fiscal autonomy is equivalent to political independence can be equally speedily dismissed. There is no example anywhere in the world in which the decentralisation of fiscal policy has resulted in political independence on the part of the devolved administration. One can point to examples of very high levels of fiscal decentralisation – such as in Spain or Switzerland – to demonstrate this point.

The other two objections warrant closer attention. The extent to which fiscal autonomy might result in economic (and social) instability both for Scotland and the UK depends largely on the inter-governmental coordination measures and policy constraints that accompany fiscal decentralisation. As we discuss elsewhere, fiscal autonomy within the context of overall UK economic policy requires both the creation of a dedicated institution for inter-governmental macroeconomic policy (including tax setting) coordination and a specific debt protocol to ensure the requisite degree of financial prudence is exercised by the Scottish Government (Hughes Hallett and Scott, 2010). Moreover, we advocate the creation of an independent fiscal authority which would oversee, and if necessary publicly comment on, the fiscal policy decisions taken by the Scottish Government.

The proposition that the fiscal policy decisions taken by the UK Government are those most appropriate for Scotland's economic circumstances is not sustainable. It is clear from even a cursory review of the data that Scotland's economy has, persistently though not always, under-performed the UK average, and the current recession is likely to see a significant widening of this performance gap. The divergence between Scotland's economy from the UK average (and significantly from the performance of the UK's stronger performing regions) reflects a number of factors that could be addressed in the context of fiscal autonomy. Differences in economic structures, endowments and resources; differences in the way the economy responds to external economic shocks; differences in the economy's position on the economic cycle; and differences in preferences or public service needs, all contribute to explaining Scotland's relative economic underperformance over many years. Each of these factors requires specific interventions and in each case fiscal policy would constitute a significant economic level.

Going forward

On 30 November 2010, St Andrews Day, the UK Government published a Bill setting out its legislative intentions in the wake of the proposals made by the Calman Commission. The Government's intended arrangements for financing the devolved administration adhered closely to these proposals although, if legislated, the new arrangements will not enter into force until 2015 at the earliest (2018 now seems a more likely date). A new Scottish rate of income tax will be created as set out in the Calman Commission report, and the yield accruing from this will form a new funding stream for the Scottish Parliament – the block grant being reduced accordingly. Limited borrowing powers will be assigned to the Scottish Parliament (similar to those already enjoyed by local authorities), although Scotland will not be able to issue its own bonds in order to raise capital.

The UK legislative proposals recognise, although certainly do not resolve, many of the defects in the original Calman proposals. The over-riding message is that the UK Government is fully aware of the difficulties associated with the prospective new arrangements – as we set out earlier – but that for the moment it has no clear idea how these can be addressed. Accordingly, extensive transition arrangements (possibly lasting to 2018) are provided for in order to 'assess' the operation of the new financial arrangements. The proposals offer no comment either on what criteria will be applied to judge the success of the proposed regime, or indeed what will happen if the problems that are clearly identified in fact cannot be resolved. In that regard the proposed legislation take us little farther forward in answering the critics of the original Calman Commission proposals.

Conclusion

It is evident that we are now inhabiting a 'post-Barnett, post-Calman' world with respect to financing Scotland's devolved administration. In one respect this is to be welcomed. Thus far, the debate has focused almost entirely on the recommendations made by the Calman Commission. Despite the fact that these have been shown to be deeply flawed in economic terms – as implicitly recognised in the 2010 Scotland Bill – narrow political considerations seemed to militate against them being scrutinised with the diligence they warranted. Indeed, an utterly erroneous view emerged from the debate; that only if the proposed new tax-varying powers were used would the net budget of the Scottish Parliament be changed from the status quo ante. However, as is now clear, if these measures are implemented then some part of Scotland's annual budget will directly depend on income tax yields in Scotland. If the profile of this yield does not track exactly the profile of UK public spending, and there is no reason to expect it shall, then the profile of Scotland's public spending will be unavoidably different than otherwise. If tax yields rise faster than UK public spending then Scotland's budget will be higher than otherwise under the new arrangements; if tax yields lag UK public spending growth, Scotland's budget will be lower. Historically the latter case has predominated and, as already noted, would have resulted in an £8 billion shortfall in Scotland's budget over the period 1999–2010.

It can be argued that the economic arguments support a shift to fiscal autonomy for Scotland. Only by equipping Scotland's government with the full range of fiscal policy levers is it likely that Scotland's economic performance will improve significantly and the potential for economic growth over the longer term be maximised. And rather than undermined the case for fiscal autonomy, the current recession has made achieving fiscal autonomy more urgent.

References

Calman Commission. (2009), *Serving Scotland Better: Scotland and the United Kingdom in the 21st Century*, Commission on Scottish Devolution, Edinburgh: Scottish Parliament.

GERS. (2010), *Government Expenditure and Revenue Scotland*, Edinburgh: Scottish Government.

Hallwood, P. and MacDonald, R. (2009), *The Political Economy of Financing Scottish Government*, Cheltenham, Camberley and Northampton: Edward Elgar Publishing.

Holtham, G. (2010), *Fairness and accountability: a new funding settlement for Wales*, Independent Commission on Funding and Finance for Wales, Cardiff: Welsh Assembly.

House of Lords. (2009), *The Barnett Formula*, Select Committee on the Barnett Formula, House of Lords, 1st Report of Session 2008–2009.

Hughes Hallett, A. and Scott, A., (2010), *Scotland: A New Fiscal Settlement*, Edinburgh: Reform Scotland.

Mapping the Context
of Public Sector Reform

JOHN MCLAREN

FOR AT THE LEAST the next decade, public sector reform will become a crucial element in helping to reduce the impact of spending cuts on the quality and quantity of public services available to the Scottish people. While there was little pressure to improve efficiency in the post-devolution public sector (as the Scottish Budget rose by an average of over five per cent a year in real terms), that situation has now changed and there will be cuts over the next four years, at least. How can we best introduce reforms? And what are the outcomes that such reforms are aiming to achieve? This chapter concentrates on the first of these two questions, but before doing so it is worth outlining the principal outcomes that are assumed to be the most desirable from such changes.

Successful reform of public sector services should result in both greater efficiency and greater equality of outcomes for those in receipt of such services. On the latter point, let's take the example of education. Each student should have, as near as possible, the same opportunities available on leaving school, even if they involve different skill sets. However, we need to be realistic as well as idealistic. In the same sense that it is almost impossible to eradicate child poverty in any society (the lowest rate amongst OECD countries are between 2½ – 5 per cent in the Nordic nations), we will never be able to achieve complete equality of opportunity on leaving school. Complete equality is probably both unmeasurable and unrealisable, so the best that can be hoped for is near equality of standards across schools. With this in mind the remainder of this chapter considers where reform is most needed; does ideal policy exist; how to improve innovation; how to measure success; and the impact that politics has on all this.

Before we reform, how are we doing?

This seems a pretty obvious question to ask, yet Scotland's comparative standing with respect to its provision of public services is seldom looked at in any real depth.

The Centre for Public Policies for Regions (CPPR) has undertaken two major studies in recent years to better understand how well Scotland performs, within the confines of the four constituent countries of the UK. These studies looked at health (CPPR, 2010) and at schools (CPPR, 2009), arguably the two most crucial areas of public service provision. The results were not very encouraging in terms of understanding Scotland's relative performance, or in understanding the causes for its under, or over, performing other parts of the UK.

Schools spending and performance across the UK

The data available on schools suggests that Scotland spends more per head than any of the other three UK countries, but has no better performance levels in terms of equivalised exam grades at 16 years old. Not only that but this position has worsened over the decade since devolution as, in 1999, Scotland's performance was significantly better than that of England and Wales. This seems to present a clear enough picture across the UK and this is often as far as cross-country analysis goes. However, after further investigation worrying issues emerge.

For example, the official spending figures per pupil in Scotland are over 50 per cent higher than in Northern Ireland (NI) (over 80 per cent for Primary School pupils). Almost certainly an exaggeration, there could be many reasons for the figures. The most important is likely that some administrative costs, included in the education budget for Scotland, are found elsewhere in the NI breakdown. The same may well be true for England and Wales, but on a lesser scale which means that we cannot properly compare these figures. If this is the situation within the UK, imagine the problem of trying to get like for like figures on a wider international basis.

In both the above examples, the ultimate problem is unreliability regarding the true comparability of statistics. Given that the performance levels of our schools and pupils is one of the most important outcomes to emerge from spending on public services, one might have thought that greater efforts would have gone into ensuring reliable and comparable data was available. It has not.

Health spending and performance across the UK

A similar, though even more complicated, picture emerges over the performance of health services in the UK. Scotland has a higher spend per head than any other country, while it is difficult to find evidence of associated higher need or of better outturn performance in terms of efficiency. As with the data on schools, after further investigation this finding becomes difficult to explain, for in terms of the main spend item – staff costs – staffing per person is almost 30 per cent higher. These figures are so different that they are unlikely to be truly comparable, and yet again, this is the best information we have available to compare countries different health systems

A similar cross-UK comparative study of health by the Nuffield Trust's (Nuffield Trust, 2010) came to firmer conclusions than CPPR's. However, there were issues with Nuffield's data checking that makes the conclusions they reached on health productivity questionable. Simple collection of the data in these circumstances is not enough. Each data series has to be considered critically and any unusual data queried further. Despite all the caveats on the quality and comparability of the data, what emerged from the two studies, in a general sense, was that for schools and health it would be difficult to make a positive case for Scotland's post-devolution performance relative to the rest of the UK, whereas a negative case could be easily constructed.

Therefore, the main lessons that have been revealed by CPPR's work in this area so far are; the lack of high quality analysis of public services spending, in both absolute and relative terms; the lack of robust data to carry out such high quality analysis if required; and the lack of interest by representative bodies in knowing the true position over the quality of the services they provide. This results in a poor evidence base from which to try to devise best policy initiatives. There is no doubt that accurate and comparable data is a strong tool in comparing outcomes from different policies and attempting to determine what factors affect any different outcomes. However, if even measuring the differences in inputs accurately is too taxing, then it is virtually impossible to measure any improvement in outputs and to extract any policy lessons that might apply.

Does 'ideal' policy exist?

Most governments only pay lip service to 'evidence based policy making', preferring instead to disseminate partial evidence that bolsters their existing policy preferences. This may be due to reasons of political expediency but there are also deeper issues of concern.

Take the example of school education policy. There are a variety of international comparison sources available, including the OECD's PISA data and IEA's PIRLS and TIMMS data. These show that the countries emerging at the top of the rankings can be very different in nature. For example, both Finland and Singapore do very well but their means of achieving high performance differ greatly. Some similarities, such as the cultivation of high quality teachers (Whelan, 2009), are common but emerge in different ways. This suggests that there may be a number of ways to reach a good outcome and that the quality of implementation is as important, if not more so, than the policy itself. The best policy, poorly managed may not be as successful as a well managed, secondary solution.

A case in point might be the political obsession with class sizes. Apparently this is evidence based, but little such evidence actually exists (OECD, 2009). The reality is that it is a commonsense policy. Smaller class sizes should improve results; however, if such a policy were implemented through an expansion of classes which were staffed by less qualified, lower quality teachers, then standards may overall drop. Improving the quality of teachers is generally found to be a more cost effective policy (OECD, 2009).

This is relevant to on-going policy debate in Scotland. It is also relevant to the outcome of the post-devolution expansion of schoolroom assistants and the benefit that accrued versus what might have been delivered using different policies.

This is not easy, which is why current attempts at collecting and analysing the evidence fall woefully short of properly contributing to finding the most effective policies.

How do you improve innovation in the Public Sector?

Post-devolution, it could be argued that a lack of innovation-led effi-ciency gains has hampered progress in improving public services. This has been due to the large real terms rises in the Scottish budget that have obviated the need for greater efficiency, alongside strong producer side interest groups that have been conservative in their approach to intro-ducing new practices, or reorganising existing ones. Hence, possibly the greatest challenge is how to make the Scottish public sector more inno-vative. Some of the difficult issues that need to be addressed with regards to achieving and sustaining such innovation include:

- clarity over objectives
- motivation levels of public service workers
- recognising and rewarding good performance
- leadership and management abilities
- skills and competency levels of public sector workers

This is a daunting list. Many in the public sector will have their own per-sonal anecdotes with regards to a lack of personal initiative, poor manage-ment and delegation of responsibility, resulting in low motivation and little feeling of responsibility. But they tend to be just that – anecdotes, and many similar stories could be found in the private sector. In recent times, the most pursued avenues to improve public sector productivity have been increased monitoring through performance targets; and increased contestability in the provision of services. Both approaches have draw-backs as well as advantages, made clear in the rather mixed results that have emerged in the UK and elsewhere. Problems in interpreting these mixed results are compounded by the difficulty in achieving accurate, compa-rable, results that fully take into account, and monetise, the costs and benefits of different policies.

Performance targets can fail to attack the culture of underperformance, instead moving to a more command and control model. Greater compe-tition often means that more well-informed users (usually the wealthier), benefit most, risking greater inequality even if standards in general improve. A more subtle shift in working practices might be introduced that improve incentives and encourage innovation, although this will always have to be centrally guided and assessed to ensure no localised failure.

For example, in education, the introduction of better teacher evaluation techniques could result in higher quality teaching. Some of these techniques are already used in countries like Singapore and Finland (see Whelan, 2009), where screening tests look at leadership potential and emotional suitability to be a teacher alongside technical ability. This should improve the quality of new teachers and is more efficient than the alternative strategy – replacing underperforming fully trained teachers who fail to deliver in the classroom. A complementary measure might involve the use of incentives to encourage the best teachers to work in schools in the most deprived areas. This example still uses both competition and targets as routes to refining processes that improve the education sector.

The preceding discussion is not intended to propose moves into a more private sector, us-style direction. The answer could lie just as easily in the Nordic countries who exhibit strongly innovative public sectors and high taxes. These countries cannot afford such a large part of their economy to be inefficient and experience low or no productivity gains. If they do, they will soon start to stagnate.

How do the Nordic countries achieve this? A recent inquiry into global wealth and well-being – the Legatum Prosperity Index (LPI) – found that Norway, Denmark and Finland occupied the top three spots, with Sweden coming sixth. The report (Legatum Institute, 2010) explains this finding – 'the size of the public sector and levels of taxation tend to matter less than the incentives that individuals face when deciding whether or not to engage in productive activities'. Thus, in terms of 'entrepreneurship and opportunity', all four countries emerge in the top six. They are joined in the top ten by lower tax and lower public sector countries like the us, Ireland and Singapore.

Scotland needs to be more open to different types of reform or building on existing successes. Scottish Water, through use of benchmarking, monitoring and regulation, is considered to have been successfully reformed (Armstrong, 2008). There is also a need to ensure that reform is suitably ambitious. So, while reduced class sizes (relatively straightforward to achieve) may do some good, improved teacher quality (a more elusive goal) would lead to greater achievements.

How do we measure success?

Measuring success in the public sector is a very tricky business. The traditional productivity measure used for private sector industries does not work as well for the public sector (see Crafts, 2005). The problem with measuring the productivity or contribution to GDP of the police is a good example. But equally the value added of teachers is not straightforward. Even health, where there are sometimes quantifiable outputs, is by no means uncontroversial.

Until recently, most public sector output in Scotland was estimated by measuring the number of people working in that service. This makes it very difficult to achieve productivity gains because the numerator, output, is very closely correlated with the denominator, the staffing level. But if there is no commonly accepted measure of success, how can we know if we are getting better or worse? How can individuals be incentivised to do more if there is no agreement on what this looks like? Alternative measures to GDP, which better capture the value of public services, might be created. These could be partially based on surveys of customer satisfaction – although such surveys would need to be carefully undertaken to avoid bias, and to attempt to inform interviewees of the potential output of alternatives systems of provision.

But does revealed preference and user satisfaction actually help measure changes in productivity? We need more concrete ways of understanding how and where progress has been made. Inevitably, in order to compare across services, that will involve some attempt to monetize benefits. However, if that includes issues like costing increased life expectancy from preventative health spending, then it could significantly adjust and improve the distribution of scarce funds. Building further on the 'new economics foundation' (nef) work for NHS Health Scotland (nef, 2008) might be a good staring point on this.

The Politics of Change

There are important political considerations involved in implementing change that will improve the quality and equality of public services outcomes. Using the worlds of education and health, perhaps the best examples are Early Years Investment (EYI) and investment in health prevention.

Considerable evidence exists that greater investment in these two areas would reap a greater return than for some existing policies. There is growing support for the potential of EYI in terms of its payback, not just in education but in terms of reducing criminal activity, improving health and employment prospects, and for the parents as well as for the child (see Heckman and Masterov, 2005). However, the funding that is being invested in children under five is still relatively small. By way of comparison, the effectiveness of post-school training is consistently found to be low but funding sources remain (McLaren, 2005).

This brings us to two political dilemmas that continue to hold back effective reform. The first is how to move funding from a relatively in-effectual initiative, but which has strong pressure group support, to one which appears to be much more effective but, because it has little funding attached to it, has fewer powerful supporters. The second dilemma is how to move funding away from the treatment of existing problems and towards the prevention of those problems in the first place. This dilemma is strongly related to the short-term mindset of political parties, and occurs regardless of the type of political system that exists. If the benefits of EYI do not give a quick pay-back, say within five years, then that counts against it in terms of political attractiveness.

There is currently a big debate around this subject in Scotland and the UK (Alakeson, 2005), but the outlook is not good. If one considers the balance of power with respect to funding of health preventative initiatives over treatment ones, a much older debate than the EYI and one where the evidence again strongly favours more investment in pre-ventative initiatives, there has been little progress made in rebalancing funding towards prevention in recent decades.

How do we go about changing the dynamics of this debate? Clearly greater leadership would be beneficial, involving more belief in prosec-uting the case for longer term investments. Greater social cohesion, both across the current population and across generations, would also be beneficial; an attitude that is perhaps expressed more strongly in Nordic countries. But it is not clear how either of these changes might come about.

Considering additional measures to complement the GDP might help. If certain traits are recognised as being positive, and therefore their growth as signifying a form of success, then it might prove easier to persuade the electorate to support parties that put forward policies which promote and fund them. For example, improvements in quality of life measures (life expectancy, education or the environment), might be considered prices worth paying for a more slowly growing standard of living (Stiglitz, 2010).

A greater role for academia might also be hoped for; one in which they act as the arbiter of what the existing evidence tells us is more effective in terms of policies. Of course, it will always be up to politicians to make hard choices over limited funds in the final event and academics will rarely be in complete agreement over the impacts of different policies, but the present position leaves voters at the mercy of subjective prejudices which are given the same respect as a policy that has been evaluated and can be backed up by reasonably hard findings.

Perhaps greater definition of the benefits of such policies would lead to a more compelling case. For example, on EYI most evidence comes from the US and involves highly deprived, non-white, urban samples, relating to policies initiated back in the 1960s or 1970s (by necessity, to some degree, as the rewards of these policies can best be measured over a lifetime). This evidence base may not be very satisfactory to a European government in the 21st century. More evaluation needs to be done, but it must be thorough and so may be expensive. Capturing the full effects, across all areas of potential benefit for both parent(s) and child, involves considerable effort, and involves working out the true counter position. However, it may turn out that significant returns emerge quicker than expected and so the rate of return is higher, or the break-even point comes quite quickly. Then a much stronger case can be made to the general public for funding to increase and it can become a central part of political manifestos, rather than a fringe issue.

Conclusion

The basic outlook for public services in Scotland and the UK over the next decade, and probably much longer, is that the supply of government money to fund them will, in real terms, be either falling or rising well below the historical average, while the demand for these public services (in particular in relation to health, pensions and social care) will continue to rise and the pace may increase. Within this context, continuing with the status quo of service delivery, even if it was currently viewed as efficient and effective, could lead to greater rationing of existing services. A better model is needed which reduces existing inefficiencies; one where there are fewer people of working age on incapacity benefits, or other sources of income support, that drain public sector funds but contribute nothing; one where public sector staff possess the skills that allow them to show greater personal initiative and to enlarge workforce capacity without necessitating any increase in its size.

This is not an easy task and made more challenging in that the first decade of devolution has allowed strongly entrenched conservative forces to set the pace, to lower expectations and minimise innovative practices. We cannot afford to continue like this in the next decade. If construction of a new model is to be aided by the evidence available, it is necessary to ensure that such evidence is robust. Traditional alternatives to this betterment option would appear to be repeating either successive waves of decentralisation followed by recentralisation and/or, persistent tinkering that satisfies more of a political than an actual need for change.

At present, the best answer that can be given to the original question of how to introduce reform can be stated thus: do not repeat past mistakes where ideology has driven policy, but try to understand the problem(s) and the possible solutions too, before moving in a direction that will hopefully lead to repeated benefits over time. This is opposed to another attempt at total success through radical new practice.

References

Alakeson, A. (2005), *Too Much Too Late: Life chances and spending on education and training*, London: Social Market Foundation.

Armstrong, J. (2008), *Improving Productivity in Scotland's public services*, Glasgow: Scottish Policy Innovation Forum.

Crafts, N. (2005), 'High-Quality Public Services', in Coyle, D., Alexander, W. and Ashcroft, B. (eds), *New Wealth for Old Nations: Scotland's Economic Prospects*, Princeton, NJ: Princeton University Press.

Centre for Public Policy for Regions (2009), *Scottish Government Budget Options Briefing Series No 1: Spending on School Education*, Glasgow: CPPR, University of Glasgow.

Centre for Public Policy for Regions (2010), *Scottish Government Budget Options Briefing Series No 3: Spending on Health*, Glasgow: CPPR, University of Glasgow.

Heckman, J. and Masterov, D.V. (2005), 'Skill Policies for Scotland', in

Coyle, D., Alexander, W. and Ashcroft, B. (eds), *New Wealth for Old Nations: Scotland's Economic Prospects*, Princeton, NJ: Princeton University Press.

Legatum Institute, (2010), *The Legatum Prosperity Index: An Inquiry into Global Wealth and Well-Being*, London: Legatum Institute.

McLaren, J. (2005), *Improving Soft Skills in Scotland*, Glasgow: Scottish Enterprise.

nef, (2008), *An Index of Sustainable Economic Well-Being*, Edinburgh: NHS Health Scotland.

Nuffield Trust, (2010), *Funding and Performance of Healthcare Systems in the Four Countries of the UK before and after Devolution*, London: Nuffield Trust.

OECD, (2009), *Education Today: The OECD Perspective*, Paris: OECD.

Stiglitz, J. (2010), *Mis-measuring our lives: Why GDP doesn't add up.* New York: New Press.

Whelan, F. (2009), *Lessons Learned: How good policies produce better schools*, Fenton Whelan/MPG Books.

Health, culture and society: a Scottish-Nordic conversation

PHIL HANLON AND FREJA ULVESTAD KÄRKI

Dear Freja,

The idea of a dialogue between Scotland and our Nordic neighbours is interesting because there is no doubt that in Scotland there is a strong belief that we can learn from places like Sweden, Norway and Finland. From our perspective, Norway and Sweden have enviable health outcomes and our perception is that this is through creating two of the most open and equal societies in the world. Low levels of inequality in income and high levels of welfare expenditure are particularly viewed as key factors.

My first question therefore is 'Are these views shared in the Nordic countries?' Do you see your own societies as fair, equal, mutually supportive and a model to the rest of the world? Or do you, like us, concentrate more on problems and less on successes? One of the reasons I say this is that Finland has an international reputation for work it did in the 1970s and 1980s to combat heart disease. Yet, although Finland is seen as successful in this respect, improvement in Scotland has been similar – in fact, identical for working age men. So why do we feel a lack of success while Finland celebrates and is congratulated around the world?

I think the main reason is that health is the area of policy in which Scotland performs least well. If the countries of the United Kingdom were regarded as separate entities, then life expectancy in Scotland would, for women, be the lowest in the European Union, and for men, the second lowest after Portugal. Scotland is only now achieving levels of life expectancy which the best performing European countries achieved in 1970. Yet, Scotland has not always performed so poorly. In the first half of the 20th century, life expectancy in Scotland was actually higher for both men and women than in other Western European countries such as France, Spain and Italy. In the mid-20th century however, while other countries improved (many of which had once lagged behind Scotland), we began to slip down the table of European life expectancy.

To understand this, it is necessary to look at differences in deaths at different ages, among men and women, and from different causes. This shows that Scotland's position is not exceptional in infancy and childhood mortality. At older ages, while worse than the European average, it is not the worst; although improvements among elderly men parallel the European average, among elderly females, Scots are slipping further behind. Scotland's overall poor position is driven, to a considerable extent, by the very high mortality of working age adults, where both men and women lag well behind European counterparts. The main causes are the chronic diseases of mid life (heart disease, cancer and respiratory disease) and increasingly deaths from alcohol, drugs, suicide and violence (particularly among younger men).

The most frequently cited reason for Scotland's poor health is post-industrial decline, with associated features such as socio-economic deprivation. Part of the evidence to support this theory comes from the observation that, within Scotland, the poorest health is found in the West-Central belt – a region that experienced the effects of profound deindustrialisation in recent decades. As other parts of the UK and Western Europe have also suffered deindustrialisation and are charac-terised by social deprivation and relative poverty, work has been done to discover whether they too experienced adverse health effects and how they compare to Scotland; particularly, West-Central Scotland.

Ten regions were selected: the Ruhr area and Saxony in Germany; Katowice in Poland; Northern Moravia in the Czech Republic; Nord-Pas-de-Calais in France; Wallonia in Belgium; Limburg in the Netherlands; Northern Ireland; Swansea and the South Wales Coalfields in Wales; and Merseyside in England. The investigation found that post-industrial decline is associated with lower levels of prosperity and higher mortality, but mortality rates of comparable, post-industrial regions elsewhere in Europe are improving at a faster rate than the West of Scotland. At the same time, the West of Scotland's current socio-economic status is better than most of the other regions.

So, I begin this dialogue with a conundrum. Scotland is a wealthy Western European country that seems to be performing less well than it should in heath outcomes. We blame deprivation and post industrial decline but these factors, while important, do not seem to be the complete answer. It will be interesting to know your perspectives on these and other matters.

With all best wishes,

Phil

Dear Phil,

Firstly, thank you very much for starting this dialogue! It as a useful way of exchanging and developing ideas about historic and current states of health and wealth in our respective societies. We share many cultural and historical features yet differ in a number of aspects. Introducing myself will help explain my perspectives. Born in Finland, I moved to Sweden in the 1980s and then emigrated to Norway – considering myself a kind of 'atmosphere refugee' – as I held strong views and observations about Swedish society in transition that were not necessarily positive.

I find your question – whether we perceive our society as fair and equal, mutually supportive and a model to the rest of the world – very stimulating, and to explore it we need some history. As you know, there was a major change in wealth in Norway thanks to the discovery of seemingly unlimited natural resources in the 1960s. This, to a large extent, changed the world's (stereotypical) perception of Norway, and had a substantial impact on Norwegian self-perception. The balance between the Nordic countries then changed. Norway, from being a kind of adjunct to Sweden, substantially improved its status which translated into a large number of Swedes moving to Norway to work in trades unpopular amongst Norwegians.

Finland, from the Norwegian perspective, is seen as successful in educational terms, with good pupil outcomes which Norway cannot match. In our schools, children and youngsters perform relatively poorly by international comparison, and the long-standing explanation has been that our school system fosters social competence not academic performance. The Finnish school system is traditionally more focused on discipline and performance. The latter evokes pressure, and issues about performance, that can translate into anxieties and later mental health problems – perhaps unsurprisingly Finland tops the suicide statistics among the Nordic countries.

To turn to the Norwegian self-perception, the stereotypical image of a Norwegian used to be an outdoor, mountains type, living the simple life. It would be a good thing for public health if this were still true, as much work is being done by Norwegian health authorities to combat sedentary life styles. Having a humanistic/humanitarian approach to one's life and neighbours is also important in Norway, linked to a very high awareness of human rights including reducing social inequalities, welcoming refugees and so on. It is important to add gender equality, as the Norwegians have achieved a very good level of equality between the sexes. Of course, in wages and public representation we have some way to go but, both relatively and comparatively, Norwegians are performing nicely. Individuality is also a praised characteristic, demonstrated from numerous Norwegian Antarctic adventurers to Norway choosing a strategic political position outside the European Union

It is also important to recognise widespread notions about balancing ideals of modesty with wealth, which can be seen as guilt about being privileged and also links to ideas of wanting forgiveness. The media, in exposing histories of victimisation through documentaries and narratives, plays a significant role in this collective search for reconciliation, and regularly presents state child care or health services as perpetrators.

During the last decade or so, there has been an explosion of people applying for compensation for a 'lost childhood', sometimes because the care system intervened in a negative way, but mostly for not intervening. The current trend is dichotomous, as while the scientific paradigm supports an evidence base, society itself increasingly trusts the subjective experiences and disclosures of its citizens.

One area where this notion can also be observed is the number of people on disability pension: Norway is the only country in the world where the level of public health has no correlation to the number of people receiving disability pensions! Of course, the welfare structure influences this to a large extent, as does the status and role of general practice.

To summarise, the Norwegians perceive themselves as a model for others whilst reminding themselves of the need to be humble. Welfare institutions have increasingly become receptacles for contemporary hopes and disappointments – a position not very different from that of the God of our ancestors.

Best wishes,

Freja

Dear Freja,

Thank you for your thoughtful and interesting comments. I was struck that you considered yourself a kind of 'atmosphere refugee' and would like to hear more about the 'atmosphere' in Sweden and the detrimental transition that you perceive in that society. To explore further, I will draw on the work of Richard Eckersley (2004), an Australian writer, who observes that there are a series of 'isms' that afflict many modern societies. They are certainly evident in Scotland. These are:

Economism: The tendency to view events through the prism of economics, skewing society and politics away from other goals and towards growth. Economic development and its concomitant growth have yielded many benefits, but there is now an unquestioned reliance upon Gross Domestic Product as the measure of success, even though this is simply a measure of the volume of transactions – desirable and undesirable. Economistic perspectives are now highly influential in areas like health and education where, until quite recently, other values pertained.

Consumerism: The belief that fulfilment and happiness comes through the acquisition and ownership of material goods. The new religion seems to be shopping with huge shopping centres the new cathedrals. Although people report temporary satisfaction from shopping, it does not bring them lasting happiness.

Individualism: The idea that the individual, individual rights and fulfilment are the most central dimension of life.

Scientism: The belief that the kind of science that helps explain the physical world is the only legitimate approach – and applicable to all spheres. Taken to its logical conclusion, scientism teaches that only science and rationality can provide meaning and explain the world. Scientism delivers a world in which knowledge is narrow cast with limited connectivity. This has led to another characteristic of modern culture – technocracy – in which specialists have high status and make the rules.

The consequences of these influences and 'isms' are evident in our society. Arguably, the most widespread set of dysfunctional activities are 'space-filling' activities. A large number of people experience contemporary life as insecure, uncertain, difficult and risky with no deeper meaning. They try to suppress these unpleasant feelings in a variety of ways; they overeat, overshop, overindulge, overwatch television; they engage in much activity (being busy is a virtue in modern culture) or use sex or drugs (legal and illegal). These behaviours often lead to obesity, addiction, mental health problems, alcohol-related damage and sexually transmitted diseases; the very health problems prominent in Scotland today.

Living in a society that prizes economic growth means constant pressure to contribute by performing harder at work, to conform to the values of economic growth, and to consume as much as possible. Indeed, we are encouraged to consume more than we can afford by incurring debt. It is probably no coincidence that the amount of credit card debt in the UK is greater than the whole of the rest of the EU. I wonder if this is what you were observing in Sweden? And are these trends emerging in Norway?

The oil wealth of Norway will have solved many problems, but what you say about the relationship that Norwegians have with their 'welfare institutions', which you say have increasingly become a receiver of high hopes and deep disappointments, is interesting. Wealth on its own does not seem to satisfy. The 'ism' of modern societies can undermine a deeper sense of purpose and meaning in life. You seemed to be hinting that in Norway these tensions are also being experienced by ordinary people. It is certainly true of Scotland.

With all best wishes,

Phil

Dear Phil,

Thank you for your most interesting and thought-provoking reflections! I forgot to mention previously that I also briefly lived in Denmark while working for the WHO, an experience also giving some insight into Danish society. The circumstances for my emigration from Sweden did coincide with some of the emerging features in the atmosphere mentioned in the list of –isms. In my subjective opinion, Sweden was corresponding to various idealised national characteristics – an old and free civilisation, still reflecting the cultural glow of ancient heroism, invincible in wars long ago (true to some extent) – yet demonstrating a current deep devotion to political neutrality and a social democratic value system.

Furthermore, Swedish society was able to afford freedom of speech and thought for its citizens. To reflect upon how it was possible to create a burgeoning welfare system, and openness and hospitality, in a country with originally scarce resources on the outskirts of Europe, some historical interpretations should be made. During World War II Sweden received a number of 'war children' from Finland, and continued to welcome foreigners from different countries through labour immigration and refugee reception. As early as the 18th century a flow of Finns were welcomed to inhabit and cultivate under-populated areas in the Swedish forests. (Finland, then, was part of the same kingdom, though considered a cultural and historic backyard).

A cornerstone in Swedish self-understanding is 'The Peoples' home' ('folkehemmet'). The construction itself was a political and societal reform intended to ensure every member of Swedish society equal rights and welfare in the framework of solidarity, but without giving up the capitalistic economy. Adherence to this idea was demonstrated when the social democrats finally lost to the right wing in the 1970s and the latter ruled the country implementing the former's politics! However, changes came, and the originally Swedish homogenous society went through a transition in the 1970s to 1980s, when these social democratic ideas, implemented in a large scale since the 1930s, were tested. They no longer had the same legitimacy, and commitment to shared values and collective responsibilities were gradually pulverised. The Swedes would probably say even today that the 'good old principles' still reign, and the economy does still work in line with them – but the glue in the system no longer exists to the same extent.

One hypothesis could be that, due to integration challenges, the population no longer has access to the same historic value system. Sweden increasingly found its new ideals from European contexts at the cost of nation-specific political ideas and its own identity. Urbanisation proceeded and the countryside was more or less emptied (in Norway this development has been deliberately restricted, through Governmental subsidies, to the least densely populated areas) leaving behind the sense of continuity embedded in the earlier self-understanding.

That was when I moved to Norway. In Norway too, the –isms are emerging gradually, and for a number of years the general discourse has been individual rights over the collective sphere, however the latter is defined. The classless society has been realised more than in Sweden where the upper classes never lost their privileges. In Norway, a new upper class – through inherited or self-made wealth – has been growing, but the nouveau riche are strangely not considered a threat to equality.

Another big question was, at least before the financial crisis, whether Norway should join the EU. Some voices supported membership, arguing for more influence internationally, others because of a solidarity principle. The majority has always been against. The contemporary economic situation has contributed to silence these discussions.

But to return to your question about the –isms and whether they are experienced by people in a large scale: indeed they are. One of the consequences is the growth of small groups that could be characterised as aspects of the new age-movement, as spirituality sought through alternative medicine, healers and spiritualist teaching. Norway was recently selected as the Number One country in terms of good living conditions. At the same time, alcohol consumption increases and free time is so packed with activities that reflections about the meaning of time itself leave us stressed and frustrated.

Paradoxically, while being 'connected' to whoever, whenever, we gradually lose connection to ourselves. The ideal of being a global individual suppresses the fact that the only way of living one's life is to live it locally. This is the contemporary trend, supposedly shared with both Scotland and other western societies.

Best wishes from Freja

Dear Freja,

I was fascinated by your most recent letter and am learning that the countries in which you have lived have profoundly changed. You drew attention to the history of Sweden and how wider influences from beyond its borders combined, with a growing national solidarity, to create a society which in many ways was a model for others. Yet, Sweden has felt the impact of modernity – individualism, consumerism, materialism, urbanisation and inequalities in wealth have to a degree eroded some, but by no means all, of that spirit. More recently, globalisation and the relocation of investment and jobs to developing economies have added to political tensions.

My impression is that Norway has been more successful in resisting these pressures. It has a cosmopolitan and global outlook, while being intensely local in the way it acts. I was interested that Norway maintains a strong regional policy which incentivises the maintenance of larger populations in rural areas. At best, this sounds like an application of the maxim popularised by the Greens – think globally and act locally. At worst, might it become parochial or even nationalistic? It seems to me that many in Scotland aspire to the Norwegian ethos described. I am convinced that the ecological challenge the world faces means that we will all either have to develop a global consciousness (albeit expressed and manifested locally) or face collapse. It is the greatest challenge of our times.

However, I will return in more depth to this issue later, as I would like to explore the problem that our countries seem to have with alcohol (and in Scotland also with illegal drugs). Scotland is sixth in the world rankings for illicit drug use – only Afghanistan, Iran, Mauritius, Costa Rica and Russia have worse problems! This is new. As recently as the 1970s, official reviews concluded that we had no major drugs problem. The situation with alcohol is similar. The rise in deaths from alcohol took off during the early 1990s, since when male death rates from alcohol have quadrupled and female rates more than doubled.

Throughout history, addictions are less problematic when societies are more stable and cohesive. Modern, free-market societies like the UK create wealth but also subject people to irresistible pressures towards individualism and competition, tearing them from the social and spiritual ties that normally constitute human life. People adapt to their dislocation by finding the best substitute for a sustaining social and spiritual life, and addiction can serve this function all to well. Currently, drugs and alcohol are being confronted by linked policy initiatives – prevention, harm reduction, treatment and law enforcement. Each component has value but despite all these efforts, the problem is growing.

In the past half century, Scotland has become a post-industrial society. Post-industrial decline is important but, as I explained, Scotland's mortality trends compare badly with other, post-industrial regions of Europe, including in Eastern Europe, which are characterised by higher levels of poverty. Importantly, drugs and alcohol are major contributors to Scotland's additional mortality. This finding challenges any simplistic explanation of Scotland's poor health being caused by post-industrial decline alone. It begs the question as to what other factors may be at work.

Many in Scotland see Norway and Sweden as having resisted some of the worst manifestations of modernity. They argue that if we were more like you (less inequality, more support for children, greater community solidarity, more meaningful work) there would be less addiction in Scotland. What they are responding to is the realisation that many in Scotland seem to lack a sense of purpose and meaning, and this is at the heart of their addictive behaviours. Others call for a radical shift in our acceptance of alcohol and drug misuse in our families, communities and country. Most recently, this has led our government to try (without success) to raise the price of alcohol. My feeling is that price is important, but we need a change throughout Scottish society and not just among those who are struggling with 'overwhelming involvement'.

There is a yearning for change, yet, there is also denial over the scale and severity of the problems we face. We look to the Nordic countries for inspiration but, from what you say and from what I have read elsewhere, you also have a problem with alcohol – and you have very expensive alcohol. I would be really interested to hear more about your understanding of why this problem has developed and what you think might be done about it?

Best wishes,

Phil

Dear Phil,

Thank you very much for your letter! It is interesting how attitudes towards alcohol and drug use and abuse change in different time periods. In Finland, Sweden and Norway, there is (or was until the EU regulations somewhat altered the praxis for Finland and Sweden) a state monopoly for trading alcohol. There is also a history of combating negative consequences of alcohol abuse, but with modest outcomes. Strategies and plans have been developed to control the problem, but rail against seemingly insurmountable industrial unwillingness, and deep rooted beliefs in individual free choice and determination. Drug abuse is a growing concern too, and a few years ago there was a heated discussion among Norwegian politicians about whether regular heroin users should be granted their daily dose financed by the state. One topic discussed was which measures to use to guarantee a 'worthy life' for all the citizens in the Norwegian society.

The change in drinking habits in the Nordic countries has mostly been towards urban wine drinking, adopted from the more Southern latitudes in combination with traditional binge drinking, especially during weekends. Finns would be (as they have always been) the leading nation here but the others also qualify. The wealthy drink more expensive and more sophisticated choices – the less wealthy stick to their ancestor's choices and patterns. A special issue is that of districts near national borders with access to inexpensive alcohol – Denmark (Germany), Norway (Sweden) and Finland (Estonia). European approaches to alcohol taxation don't consider public health priorities as much as trade and economic aspects!

During the last decade, the consumption of alcohol has increased most in Finland, Iceland and Norway and decreased or remained the same in Denmark and Sweden. Finland tops the list of alcohol-related deaths, liver dysfunctions and intoxications, and arguably the Finnish melancholic mind-set, social patterns and family structures, combined with influence from Russian drinking traditions, greatly affect the attitudes and practices of its population.

So in terms of societal changes reflected in increased use and abuse, increasingly we perceive the abdication of the middle generation, the one which the younger ones previously turned to for supervision and advice. In our society the three generations conduct very separate lives in their respective cultures, and the exchange between them can often be characterised as alienated rather than fruitful. The ideals and idols for each are to be found outside the traditional value systems. TV, of course, has had an enormous impact on our relationship to alcohol since the 1960s, and liberal American habits have been adopted accordingly.

The combination of more leisure time, beliefs in freedom of choice for all and disappearing parenting skills have resulted in an unhappy situation: the cornerstone in reframing the life of next generation is replaced by an army of so-called experts, giving advice about things that previously where a part of normal life experiences.

Speaking about the specific Norwegian situation (because I think that, even if high level of alcohol consumption are the same across Nordic countries, the mechanisms behind each might be slightly different), the special conditions in Norway reinforce a strong belief that everybody can become whatever she or he chooses, and that life choices are virtually unlimited. Everybody should take higher education (high school at the very minimum), and everybody is entitled to a good life with handsome rewards, quite independently of their efforts or abilities. Practically this means that initial differences should be compensated for (by society) or denied. I think that the trend has been a state of denial now moving rapidly towards compensation.

School drop-out is a problem, and, as mentioned before, Norway has many people on disability pension (only 0.5 per cent of those return to work). But the employment climate in our country is no worse than elsewhere and we embrace work migrants from other countries. However, Norwegians increasingly see themselves as fragile creatures and implant this attitude in our children – and this is one of my main points: we don't think that pain or sickness should be a part of life. We give a great amount of pain killers to children and youngsters; alcohol can be used for the same purpose, it can compensate for discomforts minor or major, and is also part of the urban, cosmopolitan life that we want to embrace; elderly people in care homes too are given tranquillisers to make them more easy to manage for the busy and stressed staff. This condition is not that different from in Huxley's *Brave New World*.

To return to reflections about the causes – I think that primarily imaginary choices and frustrated hopes make us vulnerable, rather than the burdens of our postmodern lives. This does not deny vulnerable groups that need special attention, but I'm referring to the majority. Addiction is a rising concern, whether the Internet, food, alcohol or shopping. We are allergic to feeling bored, and need to be compensated with new stimuli that is ready-made and entertaining. Alcohol is expensive in Norway but everybody can afford it. Decadence, originally reserved for the selected few, is now within everyone's reach!

Promotion and prevention is the key from very early on. Champions should be used to give children healthy ideals; parents should be re-connected to their parental ability; parents and schools should collaborate to a much greater extent; and we should all learn to post-pone gratification to give the growing generation a good example.

But if we ourselves are unwilling to speak and think, making these suggestions is a moral issue. Culture is gradually changed through introducing a set of attractive values that compete with the ruling negative ones. For example, refusing alcohol in company should boost identity rather than foster shame. At the end of the day, adults must lead the way.

With best wishes,

Freja

Dear Freja,

This is my final communication in what has been a fascinating dialogue. I have learned that Scotland is not really so different from Norway and Sweden. We face similar challenges and seem to be employing very comparable approaches when it comes to devising solutions. Norway and Sweden have a great deal to teach us in Scotland, as I think some of your social and economic policies have softened many harsh impacts of the competitive market economy. We can learn from these specific examples but, more importantly, all the countries that face these problems can learn from each other.

I identified strongly with your use of the term 'three generations' to better understand what is occurring in our societies. As a member of the middle generation, my observations of the other generations confirm much of what you said in your last letter. The older generation was born into the great depression and the Second World War. Personal resources were often scarce and they had to learn resilience when young. It was a harsher world in which family and community solidarity were strong, but it was also intolerant of outsiders and minorities, and women often suffered from discrimination. We must not fall into the trap of imagining that things were better in the past.

After the war, that generation were determined to build a better world. The idea of progress and economic growth were embraced, as was the ideal of creating universal (individual) human rights. My generation (the baby boom generation) have enjoyed the positive fruits of that project. We have more economic resources than our parents and had more opportunities for education, travel and personal development. We have been idealistic and energetic, have supported many important causes and have helped to make more tolerant societies. At the same time we can be accused of being too self absorbed and the great ecological threats to humankind have escalated 'on our watch'. We have also been intolerant of boredom and have increasingly used drugs / alcohol / work / shopping / sex for stimulation or to address psychological pressures. The younger generation (our children) have inherited the advantages and disadvantages of coming after the baby boom generation. The younger generation are easy and open with each other, friendships matter to them and there seems to be a comfortable coexistence between the sexes. They are less inclined to march and protest but are often individually committed to personal causes. Yet, I fear that many have been damaged by the drive among our generation to promote self-esteem – irrespective of self-efficacy. In part, this accounts for a lack of resilience and an even greater intolerance of boredom and distress. The younger generation no longer believe in 'progress' as a simple and inevitable future for us all.

So, where does this take us? My own thinking is that we are entering what might best be called a 'change of age'. That is, we are already in a process of change as revolutionary as the transition from agriculture to industry: from the pre-modern to the modern world. Human history has been characterised by change, and we can identify a number of historical ages, each with a distinctive outer world (social structure, economy, ecology and culture) and inner world (belief, motivation, consciousness). Resource and population pressures have catalysed each change of age. To cope, our ancestors developed new outer worlds (technologies, social systems and cultures) and inner worlds (beliefs, consciousness). The modern age followed this pattern: resource and population pressures catalysed change and, over an extended period, our current outer and inner worlds emerged. This is the 'modern world' of which we have been speaking in this dialogue and it is clear to me that the similarities between our countries come from this common experience of modernity.

The ability of modern people to understand, predict and control the natural world has brought many undoubted benefits, such as health and material prosperity. However, evidence is also steadily accumulating that the methods and mindset which were successful in the early period of modernity are now subject to diminishing returns and adverse effects. One manifestation of this is the rise of new forms of 'dis-ease' (rather than disease): obesity, alcohol related harm, loss of well-being, rising rates of depression. For these challenges, the tools of modernity have proven largely unsuccessful.

This prompts me to suggest that a new approach is needed. As yet, however, there is little evidence that many people are responding to modernity by embracing a new mindset. At the end of your last letter you called for adults to lead change. By this I assumed you meant the middle generation I refer to above. This would be wonderful, but instead we seem to observe denial, resistance or – at best – passive adaptation. Whilst we might be able to ignore or deny the effects of these dis-eases there are still other threats that we cannot ignore, because of their massive potential to effect our lives. Climate change, peak oil and resource depletion (amongst other problems) provide convincing evidence that there are limits to conventional ideals of economic growth. If we are to avoid a total collapse in our civilisation (I think some collapse is inevitable and some dimensions may even be desirable), profound change will be needed.

None of us can predict what will happen next, but radical change is surely coming. If change is inevitable, then we urgently need to identify opportunities as well as threats: we need to find the 'upside of down'. Although daunting, I honestly believe that the fundamental nature of the emerging 'change of age' is hopeful. The reasons for hope include the obvious resilience of all human beings and our ability to reach out to each other. Thank you for being so willing to share your insights.

With all best wishes, Phil

Dear Phil,

It has been a great pleasure to correspond with you around some of the most burning societal topics of our time! I very much liked the hopefulness at the end of your final letter, even if the challenges are massive.

Indeed, there are many signs of awakening, not least in the youngest generation, even if hope must be nurtured continuously. Scottish experiences are, to a large extent, shared by us Nordic countries. The days of escapism are definitely over and realities have to be faced. Your description of the middle generation's dilemma was pertinent, and it is easy to recognise the features you are mirroring.

We also speak about the egocentrism of the ageing population group (and now I am addressing those who are still in charge but on their way to retirement). The Norwegian pension system has recently been altered so that the ageing generation will have to work significantly longer to maintain the standard of living they have been used to. The middle generation, once radical and now enjoying their quite conservative lifestyle, will not be economically affected. We see a growing concern for the countryside while services are concentrated in densely populated areas, an important example being health services. There are protests from people who wish to maintain ecologically responsible lifestyles, and this is not only a nostalgic longing for past days.

Things were not, as you mention, better in the old days, but the choices seemed more clear-cut and controversies more explicit. This goes also for generational controversies. A friend once asked, looking at youngsters enjoying themselves – 'What do they have that we don't?' and I answered 'The knowledge about how it is to be part of the next generation'. This is pretty much what I mean by an interpretation problem – we are really conducting separate and parallel lives as generations, and struggle to make ourselves understood by each other.

Technical achievements, and the obstacles for large parts of the oldest population in sharing them, are some of the most visible signs of this. And yet, we have to – and want to – take part in each others lives, and extract the knowledge necessary to pass to those to come.

Economic growth is not unlimited, and the age of becoming aware of this is undoubtedly present in our countries. At the same time, societies such as China and India are just starting to enjoy the economic 'Wheel of Fortune' perceived as their share. The world is divided in age zones as well as time zones, and to find a shared agenda under these circumstances is as demanding as it is to understand that we are mutually responsible for challenges and opportunities, present and future.

The crisis will force a change, as you underline. In organisations, as well as for individuals, the crisis provides the opportunity to re-organise thinking patterns and to challenge value systems. The start is often an individual and inspirational one. To turn a whole nation demands strong and strategic leaders. Yet grass root movements have shown their potential before. The world starts at home!

There are two mythological creatures in Norwegian folklore – Peer Gynt (Ibsen) and Askeladden (a popular adventure). The first one is manically convinced about his invincibility, and ends by recognising the existential emptiness in all his opportunistic fortune seeking. The second one creatively uses everything he finds for practical purposes, independent of other people's opinion – and eventually wins the princess and half of the kingdom. I think that we must make our way from the false premise of Peer Gynt to the practical wisdom of the fairy tale. We also have to find the holistic approach to change of age, even if we are being bombarded by both quality time and junk food, and by easily adapted face value solutions to serious problems.

All the best,

Freja

References

Eckersley, R. (2004), *Well and Good: How We Feel and Why It Matters*, Melbourne: Text Publishing.

Who are Scotland's schools accountable to in an age of educational innovation?

KEIR BLOOMER

Introduction

THE GOVERNANCE OF SCOTTISH state schools has remained largely unaltered for almost 90 years. The current split of responsibilities between local and central government dates back to 1929 when the ad hoc parish school boards handed over their responsibilities to councils. However, now both educational and broader democratic considerations seem to call for change.

In November 2004 Peter Peacock, then Scotland's education minister, approved a brief document entitled, 'A Curriculum for Excellence' (Scottish Executive, 2004). Despite the title, it was not a curriculum in any conventional sense but rather a mission statement, setting out a number of long-term aims for Scottish education. It defined the purpose of schooling as being to enable young people to develop as 'successful learners, confident individuals, effective contributors and responsible citizens'.

Curriculum for Excellence is typical of many educational policy frameworks produced throughout the world in recent years. UNESCO, using a high-powered international commission chaired by Jacques Delors, produced a report entitled 'Learning: The Treasure Within' (1999) that described the purpose of education as helping young people 'learn to learn, learn to be, learn to do and learn to live with others'. These aims are, of course, identical to those of Curriculum for Excellence. In many individual countries these common elements of better learning, personal development, economic competitiveness and citizenship appear in the national 'vision' for schools.

All of this suggests a broad international concern that these critically important aspects of education are not, in practice, being realised, in practice or at least not to the extent that the circumstances of the contemporary world require. Perhaps Governments are most concerned about the economic aspects. School systems do not seem to be raising standards to the extent that is required. There is insufficient emphasis on developing skills, especially advanced intellectual skills such as critical thinking and problem solving. The focus remains firmly on the conveyance of a fairly traditional range of curriculum content. Creativity – widely seen as the driver of modern economies – is not being promoted or developed. The social dimension of the problem is significant too. Schools are not seen as addressing the issues that confront young people growing up in a world where traditional support systems (including the family) are under pressure and the influence of modern consumerism can be destructive.

The pace of educational change

Many of the participants in Scotland's National Debate on education in 2002 suggested that Scotland's schools have great strengths but need to change because the world is changing around them. This view, that the pace of change in education is too slow, would be widely shared. Furthermore, the effects of change are often superficial. Despite successive waves of curricular and organisational reform, the schools of 2010 would still be recognisable to a visitor from 1910.

There are, no doubt, many reasons for the resilient conservatism of school systems. Intrinsically, the task of passing on the heritage of the past is a backward looking one. Teachers are sometimes characterised as a conservative profession, although one that has always contained its fair share of radicals; however, it is difficult to avoid the conclusion that an important part of the problem lies in the way that school systems are governed. Although the details vary greatly from country to country, everywhere schooling is predominantly provided by a state near-monopoly. Two levels of political accountability are usually involved. There is a high level of centralisation of policy making. Curriculum development, inspection and the organisation of examinations and qualifications are frequently in the hands of the government ministry or of government controlled national agencies.

Scotland, of course, fits into this pattern. Strategic control is now almost entirely exercised by the Scottish Government, while schools are under the immediate management of the 32 local councils. National agencies – Her Majesty's Inspectorate of Education (HMIe), the Scottish Qualifications Authority (SQA) and Learning and Teaching Scotland (LTS) – are highly influential. HMIe is generally viewed by schools as the body to which they are most accountable despite the management role of local authorities.

This kind of structure reflects a particular view about how policy should be created and implemented. It embodies a top-down notion of governance, in which the key strategic decisions are made by a relatively small group of people in the most senior centralised positions. An important aim is to secure the uniform implementation of these decisions across the system. There can be limited autonomy at school level and individual teachers may have significant discretion within their own classrooms, but this latitude extends to how policy is implemented rather than to the policy itself.

This model is very different from the kinds of management to be found in the most creative and successful parts of the private sector. There it is understood that progress depends on using the skills and ideas of the whole workforce (and by frequently co-opting the ideas of customers, and even competitors).

Curriculum for Excellence – the need for a new model

To an extent, this understanding is beginning to have influence in Scottish education. In important respects, Curriculum for Excellence is in important respects a highly decentralised programme. Although strategic advice has been issued from the centre, individual schools are seen as having a key role in taking the programme forward. The Scottish Government has creditably resisted pleas from less confident teachers for higher levels of specification and direction. It seems to have understood that the new curricular approaches can be taken forward successfully only by releasing the creativity of the teaching profession, encouraging innovation at school and classroom level, fostering diversity in practice, and enabling the whole system to learn from the richness of its collective experience.

However, the institutional framework of Scottish education was designed with a top-down, command-and-control model of management in mind and does not easily accommodate itself to the new thinking. In general, local authorities do too little to encourage initiative at school level and tend to focus on promoting common practices across their areas rather than the experiment, diversity and mutual learning that is required. At the same time, there are important questions to ask about the functioning of the main national agencies. HMIe, whether by design or not, has helped to create a climate of compliance and risk aversion. LTS has done too little to meet the needs of both schools' and individual teachers' in taking forward *Curriculum for Excellence*. SQA appears to have difficulty in moving in the direction of 'measuring what matters': the essential requirement of ensuring that examinations function as a sound proxy for what the education system is seeking to achieve.

In seeking alternative models, a useful starting point might be to question whether all of the activities that are traditionally lumped together under the heading of 'governance' might not be better dealt with separately. These activities might be broadly categorised as 'funding', 'support' and 'accountability'. Each of these is dealt with below.

Funding

Funding is one of the few areas in which local authority control of schools continues to have genuine significance. Although roughly 80 per cent of councils' resources come in the form of grants from central government, they retain the capacity to adopt funding priorities that can make a real difference at the frontline. One council may attach a greater priority to schools than most others. Similarly, within the education budget, another council might wish to tilt its funding more towards early years at the expense of, say, curricular choice in upper secondary. As a result, there can be quite substantial variation in funding between two schools which are in similar circumstances but in different parts of the country. Thus, among secondary schools serving similar catchments and being of comparable size, the difference can be as great as £2000 per pupil per year (at a time when the average expenditure per head is £6665).

This kind of variation is not generally seen by teachers or by parents as the legitimate expression of local political priorities, but rather as a 'post code lottery' with no underpinning rationale. Thus, there is a strong case for trying to achieve equitable funding arrangements across Scotland. Equitable does not, however, mean identical. Account needs to be taken of factors such as deprivation, rurality and additional needs, as well as simple learner headcount. The way in which these factors are quantified should not vary according to local authority whims and preferences.

This does not necessarily imply that schools should be funded direct by the Scottish Government (although one school, Jordanhill College School in Glasgow, does receive direct funding for historical reasons). Indeed, there are good reasons for wanting to place funding issues at arms length from direct political involvement. Furthermore, the task of creating equitable funding mechanisms, especially in a country with the varied geography of Scotland, is an enormously complex one that calls for specialist expertise.

The best course of action, therefore, might be to set up an ad hoc body with a specific remit for funding school education. This body might be called the Schools Funding Council. It would operate in a way not dissimilar from the Scottish Funding Council that funds FE colleges and universities but would not have the policy role that SCF exercises. It would deal with both revenue and capital funding, and would have powers to intervene and/or assist when exceptional circumstances required. Such special powers would be more necessary in relation to schools, many of which are small and have little capacity to cope with unusual financial demands, than universities and colleges that have much greater capacity to redeploy existing resources.

A significant advantage of such an approach is that it would make it possible to fund schools other than those currently administered by local authorities. Scottish school education is remarkable for its homogeneity. With few exceptions, the system consists entirely of seven-year primaries and six-year secondaries. All are comprehensive in concept, although differences in catchment area create major differences in practice. The only variation in the system relates to religious denomination, with many parts of the country offering Roman Catholic schooling as an alternative to the non-denominational schooling that is the norm. Although religion is a significant matter to some parents, it hardly seems appropriate that it is the only basis of choice that the state sector offers.

For this reason, governments have occasionally flirted with the idea of offering funding to, for example, the small group of Steiner schools.

There certainly seems to be logic in offering the possibility of choice based on educational philosophy. Furthermore, at a time when there is an urgent need to increase the pace of change in education, encouragement of innovators seeking to put new ideas into practice seems sensible, perhaps even essential. Providing the possibility of access to public funding would be a useful step forward.

The recent approach initiative in England, inspired by the Swedish 'free school' model is also intended to make public funding available beyond the local authority sector. However, what is being suggested here is not specifically directed towards giving parents the opportunity to set up schools (although it does not exclude this possibility). It is more likely that individual schools or small groups of schools would be established by charities or trusts aiming to offer a distinctive form of schooling based on a particular pedagogy or philosophy. Any body could access funding provided it; subscribed to certain minimum educational requirements (such as acceptance of the objectives of Curriculum for Excellence), could demonstrate efficiency and viability, did not charge fees, and was not profit seeking.

Support

It may seem surprising to include support functions as part of the governance framework. Surely it is for schools to choose their own forms of support? Aren't support providers – almost by definition – accountable to schools rather than the other way round? The reality is that schools have little freedom in these matters. They are obliged to make use of a range of in-house services provided by the local authorities. These cover professional areas such as law, finance, human resources (HR) and ICT; services relating to the infrastructure of the school, such as cleaning, catering and maintenance; and educational support services, such as curriculum advice, teachers' CPD and educational psychology. (Somewhat different arrangements apply in the growing number of PPP schools which receive services such as cleaning and maintenance from a private sector partner as part of the long-term contract).

The distinction between support and control is often blurred. Councils see schools as requiring to use in-house services such as finance and HR as much to ensure compliance with corporate policies as to receive assistance tailored to the school's particular needs. Explicitly, educational support, such as that provided by quality assurance teams, is intended to meet the objectives of the council as much as the school. In addition, schools effectively subscribe to some national services, especially those provided by LTS and HMIe, in that funding that might otherwise be devolved to schools funds these agencies direct.

However, there are strong reasons to suggest that all these services are best provided through an open market. There is currently no mechanism to ensure that the existing monopolistic local authority services provide either best quality or value for money (although some may do both). On the other hand, markets have proved effective in improving both quality and price in an almost infinite range of circumstances. Furthermore, schools with the power to select their own sources of support can more legitimately be held to account for the consequences of their choices.

It will be argued that schools do not wish to be involved in, for example, buying the central heating oil although they certainly want greater freedom in relation to educational support. In practice, schools would be able to sub-contract the decision making on a whole range of practically important but not essentially educational matters to bodies that would be accountable to the schools for the quality of their services. This issue is explored in the next section.

Accountability

Accountability is, of course, the core of governance. Schools receive large sums of public money and are expected to serve societal as well as individual needs. They cannot be answerable only to themselves. To whom do schools consider themselves accountable... and for what? This seemingly simple question reveals a significant difference between perception and reality. Asked the question, most teachers and headteachers would undoubtedly talk about their responsibility to parents and young people. They might mention the local community, particularly if the school served a small town or some place with a clear sense of identity. Perhaps there might be an acknowledgment of some broader accountability to society as a whole. All of these – parents, pupils, community and broader society – would be generally regarded as having a legitimate stake in the school and a right to expect that it will do its job conscientiously.

Undoubtedly, there would also be a recognition of the position of
HMIe as the main external quality assurance mechanism in Scottish education. Opinions might differ about the legitimacy of this mechanism,
particularly in relation to the second part of the question. Are schools
accountable to HMIe for the way in which they carry out their mission
as they see it or for adherence to an externally imposed template?

Some teachers would also refer to the position of local authorities,
but it might well be an afterthought despite the fact that, in law, it is
councils that are the bodies charged with ensuring the availability of
school education. Relatively few school staff would see local political
accountability as significant, helpful, or even legitimate. Headteachers
would see the director of education as their line manager, but even they
would probably consider their accountability as being to national as much
as local government, and quite possibly to parents and young people
before either.

All of this contrasts sharply with legal reality. Despite the periodic
efforts of governments since the late 1980s, schools have little formal
accountability to parents, young people or the local community. Any
individual with serious concerns about a school can certainly put them
to the headteacher, but more formal redress requires the intervention of
local or national government.

The question 'what are schools accountable for?' also raises some
difficulties. When teachers talk about being responsible to parents or the
learners themselves, they are normally thinking about the young person's
welfare at school and educational progress. There is room for disagreement
over how closely these concerns relate to compliance with official policy
or performance in measurable outcomes, such as certificate examinations
that are often the main focus of more formal channels of accountability.
Also, it has to be remembered that a large part of accountability is concerned with legal compliance and financial propriety and solvency. These
matters seldom figure in schools' thoughts on their own responsibilities,
and are discharged through a range of services provided by the local
authorities. They tend to be taken for granted by schools that currently
have little capacity, and possibly little inclination, to undertake them. In
the funding model suggested above, financial accountability would be from
the school to the funding council.

Schools and the community

As matters currently stand accountability to local authorities, although in some respects supportive, does comparatively little to develop strong links between schools and the key groups such as learners, their families and local communities to whom they feel most immediately responsible. Traditional lines of accountability have often operated in ways that have reduced the responsiveness of schools to their immediate stakeholders, while simultaneously discouraging educational initiative in order to promote a uniformity of approach across the council area. The argument that local authorities provide local democratic accountability is often found unpersuasive. Education is seldom a key area of debate in local elections and the validity of councillors' mandates in relation to schools is open to serious question. This opens up bigger questions about the nature of local democracy in the 21st century.

When considering changes in the governance of schools, the primary consideration must be educational. Will the new arrangements promote greater attention to the needs of the individual learner? Will they make schools more responsive to changing circumstances? However, ideal forms of governance would also help to promote a healthier democracy at community level. As Scotland gradually adjusts to the implications of a Scottish Parliament and Government, discussion of governance below national level becomes more important.

Therefore, there is a strong case for schools becoming accountable to bodies with stronger local roots and a clearer focus on education than councils achieve with their numerous areas of responsibility. Charitable trusts could be established and could draw members from a wide range of groups with legitimate interests and relevant expertise. These could include parents, local business, community representatives, co-opted members with relevant expertise and local councillors.

A real possibility exists for building grassroots democratic structures. While this would obviously be easier in some areas than others, mechanisms such as co-option would offer the prospect of bringing in public-spirited expertise from outside. Schools are of genuine interest to many. They offer an important, perhaps a unique, possibility of enabling communities to shape local institutions that they value.

Trusts would have the powers and responsibilities that currently lie with local authorities. They would receive funding direct from the funding council and would be the employer of all teaching and other staff. As well as guiding educational strategy, they would require to approve budgets, scrutinise accounts and satisfy themselves in relation to a host of other obligations such as equal opportunities, risk management and disabled access. Management would be the responsibility of the headteacher, who would be a member of the trust board in the same way as college and university principals act as both chief executive and board member. Such an approach would bring the formal arrangements into alignment with schools' existing feelings of responsibility to their communities.

The 'bottom-up' education authority

Schools could make the transition from the local authority to trust status on a staged basis. Responsibilities could be passed from the council to the trust as it acquired the experience and the competence to discharge them. It would not be essential that all schools moved at the same pace.

Although former local authority schools would obviously constitute the overwhelming majority of publicly funded schools, the financial arrangements outlined above would make it possible for other schools, probably mostly newly established, to have access to state funding. The public education service would thus not only contain trust schools but others run by charities, educational interest groups and possibly parents or not-for-profit companies. These bodies would have similar accountability regimes as well as similar funding arrangements.

While many people acknowledge the case for greater school autonomy, reservations are often expressed about the ability of the individual school to take on the responsibilities involved. A critical issue, therefore, is whether the unit of organisation should be the school or some larger grouping. Given the opportunity, schools would almost certainly join together to achieve economies of scale and provide for themselves a variety of support services. This is the approach that has been taken by the independent sector in Scotland through the Scottish Council for Independent Schools, and by the academies in England through the Specialist Schools and Academies Trust. In effect, both of these represent successful attempts to construct something like the local education authority, but with the difference that it is the 'authority' that is accountable to the schools and not the other way around.

These federations might take one of several forms. The most obvious would be a geographical one, but other possibilities could include educational philosophy, sector or faith. Furthermore, there is the option that, even within a federation, the unit might be larger than the individual school. Particularly within distinct communities, it might be preferable to see the school 'cluster' as a single entity. In many areas, clusters consisting of a single secondary school, a number of associated primary schools, and any other educational centres such as free-standing nurseries or special schools, already act in close partnership. The cluster would have much greater organisational capacity than the individual school but would retain a close identification with a locality and community. The concept of the cluster also reinforces the continuity of education through from pre-five to upper secondary and into lifelong learning.

The role of inspection

An important strand of existing accountability arrangements lies in the role of HMIe. It provides the main external quality assurance role in Scottish education. Although individual local authorities maintain their own quality improvement teams, their activities do not command the same level of public credibility as those of HMIe. Although the Inspectorate has been active in promoting self-evaluation by schools, it is still widely regarded as enforcing compliance with a national policy agenda. This perception means that external inspection has negative as well as positive effects. It may stimulate improvement (although there is little research evidence to support this), but it can also encourage unthinking compliance and risk aversion. It is worth noting that Finland, the country that regularly emerges best from international comparisons, has abolished its inspectorate and now has no quality control mechanism of this type.

It would be possible to combine features of the Finnish system with the approach that is already taken to the audit of commercial undertakings. A core inspectorate could be retained along with a power to inspect in situations where there is reason for concern, but routine regular inspection of all schools should cease. However, it would be open to schools to commission audits of educational functions, and there could be an obligation on schools to secure such audits on a regular (perhaps annual) basis. They might look either at the whole school or take a more targeted approach. The audits would require to be carried out by registered persons or bodies – just as commercial audits need to be undertaken by qualified auditors.

Conclusion

Current governance arrangements for schools have ceased to serve Scotland well. It is clear that educational innovation is not being sufficiently encouraged and that the pace of change is falling behind what is required. At the same time, schools' real stakeholders are being held at arms length. Both practical and democratic considerations now combine to mean that this is the time for a rethink.

References

Scottish Executive (2004), *A Curriculum for Excellence: Curriculum Review Group*, Edinburgh: Scottish Executive.

UNESCO (1999), *Learning: The treasure within : a report to* UNESCO *of the International Commission on Education for the 21st century*, Paris: UNESCO.

Why the early years matter:
Growing up in Scotland

SUE PALMER AND ALAN SINCLAIR

Dear Alan,

We'd better start by explaining why you, with a background in business, and I, a literacy specialist, are going to have a 'conversation' about child development in the early years – not a subject that often raises its head in political discussions.

In my case it starts with an H.G. Wells quote I found in my teens: 'Human history becomes more and more a race between education and catastrophe.' It seemed a good reason to become a teacher, and since education depends on being able to read and write I ended up concentrating on that. By the late 1990s, I was working for the National Literacy Strategy in England, telling teachers about the importance of phonics in early reading instruction.

But everywhere I went (especially in disadvantaged areas) teachers told me that an increasing number of children were arriving at school with poor language skills and behaviour difficulties. So they couldn't teach phonics till they'd taught the social and attentional skills that a few years ago had been taken for granted. Then the *Times Educational Supplement* sent me to interview a speech and language therapist called Sally Ward. She was conducting a long-term study in inner city Manchester of nine-month-old babies' listening skills – the capacity to single out their mother's voice from all the other noise going on around them. In 1984, 20 per cent of the infants she tested weren't developing this skill on schedule; by 1999 it had doubled to 40 per cent.

Dr Ward was alarmed at this rapid deterioration in a basic human skill that had previously been expected to happen 'naturally'. She reckoned it was due to steadily increasing background noise – traffic outdoors, all-day TV indoors – accompanied by a serious decrease in parent/child face-to-face communication. With the proliferation of electronic media, we all (including babies and small children) spend more and more time interacting with screens and less and less interacting with each other. This may not matter for adults who know how to communicate and control the focus of their attention, but it matters a lot when you're learning the ropes of human behaviour.

Having been brought up in the same back streets of Manchester where Dr Ward conducted her research, my own experience had convinced me that access to education was the route to greater social justice – and the way to avoid Wells' catastrophe. It seemed reasonable to assume that, as society grew healthier and wealthier, we could expect all children to arrive at school in a fit state to learn. But I now started wondering whether the technological and consumerist revolutions that drove economic growth in the latter half of the 20th century had also spawned unintended side-effects that were just as bad for children as old-fashioned poverty.

This was the time when nutritionists were first drawing attention to the effects of junk food on physical development – and it was depressingly obvious that kids (especially those from the poorest homes) were growing larger by the year. What if aspects of an increasingly sedentary, screen-based, consumer-driven existence were having a similar effect on children's social, emotional and cognitive growth? If so, relying on schools to educate them wouldn't be enough – we'd have to ensure they all had the right sort of early experiences to fit them to learn.

That's why, for the last decade, I've been far more interested in the developmental factors underpinning literacy acquisition than the teaching of literacy skills. I've interviewed scores of experts on various aspects of child development, and every one expressed deep concern about young children's changing lifestyles. Depending on their individual disciplines, they cited lack of 'real' play, changes in eating and sleeping habits, lack of first-hand experience and interaction, and continual exposure to screen-based entertainment that's been linked in recent years to ADHD, autism, language delay and long-term problems with social skills.

And over those ten years – despite endless educational initiatives – the achievement gap between rich and poor in our schools has grown steadily wider. So I've come to the conclusion that human history now rattles along at such a relentless pace that, by the time children are developmentally ready for education, an increasing number of them are already on a catastrophic trajectory. Since cultural change is unlikely to slow down, we need to take urgent action to tackle its unintended consequences in the early years of children's lives.

Yours,

Sue

Dear Sue,

Forget the business about not being an early years expert. Six years ago, when I was a senior executive in Scottish Enterprise, I was asked to appear with the Minister to talk about economic development and child-care. For the life of me, I could not see the relevance or what could be said. Now I see early years – and by that I mean from pregnancy to three years of age – as critically important to the society we want to create and the single most important economic investment we could take.

So, let me start with a personal story. In 1983, I started a company called Heatwise Glasgow. Our aim was to insulate homes by employing long-term unemployed adults and to then get them a job in the mainstream job market. I did this for 18 years. The company grew into the Wise Group, operated in several parts of Scotland and England, and got about 2,000 people into work. It was, and is, a leading social economy company. Typically, we got six out of ten of our long-term unemployed recruits into work. Perhaps we could have done better, but there was a reality that a very large slice of those who did not get a job were close to being unemployable and when they did turn up they would spend the day staring into space. I am not blaming them but commenting on how far they were from possessing the characteristics that an employer would rightly expect – from punctuality, to attitude, to clothing and speech.

At Scottish Enterprise, while I was Senior Director for Skills and Learning, we conducted the largest and most systematic survey of Scottish public and private employers. We asked employers about their experience of recent recruits. Generally they were happy, but three groups of employers were dissatisfied – employers of lower skilled people, deciles nine and ten of the labour market (e.g. care, call centre and retail workers), employers of school leavers and workplaces that were growing in size. Employers told us that the people they took on were not good at talking and listening, at dealing with customers, working with one another or with their supervisor, and poor at elementary planning (turning up on time) and problem solving.

This lack of basic or soft skills or attributes was the single most revealing insight from the survey. I played this issue to the Scottish Enterprise Board and to the Education Department in Scotland. I also set in motion an exercise to find out how you got these skills of talking, listening and working with others. To my surprise the answer came back that you either have these attributes before you get to school or likely do not get them at all. I had spent 20 years working with unemployed people on skills issues and I found this answer surprising. Over time, however, I began to realise that it fitted, both with my own observation and with research findings. When I left Scottish Enterprise, the challenge presented by this understanding of the need to get skills and attributes right first time remained unresolved.

Best wishes,
Alan

Dear Alan,

I'm really interested in the 'soft skills' that employers in your survey identified – speaking, listening and social skills, self-management and problem-solving. The roots of all these can be traced back to early childhood, and infant teachers have noticed a steady deterioration in every one of them by the time children start school.

I've already mentioned the significance of face-to-face interaction between babies and their parents, essential for developing language and social skills. When the only way to comfort a fretful infant (or entertain a happy one) was to pick it up and talk or sing to it, this happened naturally many times a day – developmental psychologists call it (rather delightfully) 'the dance of communication'. But once video became available (then baby DVDs, then dedicated 'baby channels' on TV), it became increasingly unnecessary – you could just park your little one in front of an electronic babysitter.

When young children spend hours every day staring at a screen, it easily becomes their default activity. And when there's no reason for regular emotional engagement between generations, parents find it increasingly difficult to build the close relationship that helps them shape their children's behaviour. So toddlers aren't initiated into very basic self-management skills, like dressing themselves – it's easier to do it for them. Dependency then becomes a default state too.

Early screen-gazing also undermines children's capacity for problem-solving, which is developed through the real-life play (building, making, pretending) that children used to dream up themselves. If they grow up relying on someone else to entertain them, they become less creative and more passive.

Around 75 per cent of brain growth happens in the first three years so, if things go wrong at this early stage, it's progressively more difficult to sort out. As a society, we've failed to notice the endless small changes in children's lifestyles that impact on their development. We've taken it for granted that the ability to focus attention, control behaviour and get along with other people just happens 'naturally'. Meanwhile, the 'natural' aspects of early nurture have been steadily eroding away.

What's happening is a sort of 'unintentional neglect' that slows down children's social, emotional and cognitive development. In the majority of cases, it's still possible for schools and employers to compensate for the problems this causes, but it, too will become more difficult as socio-cultural change accelerates. And change *will* continue to accelerate – constant advances in digital technology mean we're living in exponential times. If we don't wake up to the unintended consequences for child development, there are serious long-term implications.

One obvious effect at the moment is the widening gap between rich and poor. Material poverty ratchets up the impact of unintentional neglect, so each generation of disadvantaged children starts from a lower developmental baseline than the rest of the population, making them less able to benefit from education, and gradually wiping out the chances of social mobility. The problems are particularly acute with the growing numbers of teenage mothers.

However, a project that's recently started in Edinburgh offers some hope. It's based on a programme devised by Dr David Olds of the

University of Colorado, with a 30 year track record of improving disadvantaged children's chances. It matches teenage mums with experienced nurses who become their mentors during pregnancy and for the first two years of their baby's life. In effect, the nurses mother the mothers, helping them care for themselves and their babies, and modelling the sort of talk, play and positive interaction the girls never got themselves. The Edinburgh pilot – called the Family Nurse Project – is the first ever city-wide application of Olds' idea and early results suggest it could have a big impact.

For me, this sort of early, personal intervention appears the only way to break the cycle of social and emotional deprivation that underpins severe developmental delay. It's also a way of drawing attention to the significance of all children's developmental needs. If policy-makers were to shift their attention from mopping up the social consequences of poverty, and on to the significance of 'unintentional neglect', it could alert everyone – across the social classes – to what children need in the preschool years.

Our culture may be evolving at a fair old lick, but human evolution is a long, slow process. Today's children still need what small human beings have always needed to grow up bright, balanced, and able to survive and thrive in the real world. In a complex society rattling into an uncertain future, we have to respect the aspects of nurture that can't be left to chance.

Best wishes,

Sue

Dear Sue

I am pleased that you see the connection and significance between the soft skills that children pick up, or fail to pick up, in the years before they go to school and the type of skills that employers need. Now that I understand more about the fundamental significance of 'birth to three' on school attainment, behaviour and entanglement in the criminal justice system, mental and physical health, teenage pregnancy, alcohol and drug abuse, and of course employment; I feel a deep sense of wonder and bewilderment as to why we place so little value on young children and supporting struggling parents.

How can this be put right? Much of it is cultural – what we do in hugging or hurting babies, talking to them or ignoring them, playing with them or plugging them into a screen. Holland has one of the highest scores for child well-being in Europe and Scotland has one of the lowest, scoring next to ex-Soviet states and satellites. I was reflecting on this with a Dutch woman in her forties who spent the first half of her life in Holland and the second half in Scotland. 'It seems obvious to me' she said, 'In Holland we love children – in Scotland you tolerate children'.

Changing culture would make a big difference, but finding that switch would have us groping around in the dark for a very long time. However, we do know how to change public policy and make structural changes. This could provide better health and development support to new parents, and help to improve what they do and what they see other parents doing. Ironically, I see this time of reduced public spend as an opportunity to put early years in the top league of political issues. At the moment early years is spoken of well, but lingers in the lower leagues. Good as they are, Getting It Right for Every Child (introduced by the Labour/ Liberal-Democrat coalition) and the Early Years Framework created by the SNP and COSLA, do not command the high ground of spend or decision making.

When money is tight you need to stop spending on peripheral issues and focus on the forward march of where you are going. What is it that makes the difference? How do we get what we do right first time, like the lives of our people, instead of all sorts of piecemeal interventions when they are on the skids? How do we create a society with less intergenerational failure, and one where people are connected and contribute?

You use the phrase 'unintentional neglect' to refer to parents who, through lack of understanding or life style, do not do enough to care, love and play with their children. Politically or institutionally in Holyrood, in Health Boards and in local authorities 'unintentional neglect' is played out in spades. Instead of repairing the tile on the roof we rush around to the point of impact – locking more youths and adults up, increasing our accident and emergency provision to cope with weekend 'social' crime, and watching the disintegration of communities by alcohol and drugs. There are concrete steps that we can take to remedy the situation, start the fight back and prepare our people for today and help the next generation. Like you, I am much taken by the work and success of the Nurse Family Partnership and it would definitely be in my top five practical steps we should take.

But before giving you my other four, I would like to iron out an issue that you raise and I think is formulated in a way that does not help which, to a lot of liberal minds, does not help. You say that the widening gap between rich and poor ratchets up unintentional neglect. In conversation we say that families are failing because they are poor. My own observations and conversations with nursery staff and primary school teachers tells me that failing our babies is not just the preserve of the poor. Many middle class parents are, in their more confident way, struggling.

In post war Britain many people, me included, grew up in 'poor' households. I hesitate to use the word, but we had little in material goods and lived in (what would now be demolished as) substandard housing. But something about our parents' love, care, nurture and stimulation, combined with growing up in a meritocracy, meant that we 'got on'. I believe that this is more about what parents do than who they are, and reflects a lot of the post war British experience. It is also one of the big conclusions of the Effective Pre and Primary School Study (EPPS). They have followed a cross section of 3,000 children from the age of three and have now tracked and tested the children at five and 11 years of age across various measures including numeracy and literacy. For age three, they collected lots of information about what went on in the home, who looked after the children and what they did. They also checked out the type and quality of child care provision and of the primary school experience.

At age 11 the three biggest effects on literacy and numeracy in growing importance are socio-economic status of the parents (poverty), the educational status of the mother and, most significant of all, the home learning environment. What do they mean? The researchers have found that parents who read, sang, played, took their children to the library, drew with them etc, had the single greatest effect on how that child would perform by age 11.

One other very hopeful lesson they draw from their data is that a child who comes from a low socio-economic group but has a good home learning environment, good child care and a good quality primary school experience, performs as well as children from higher socio-economic groups at age 11.

Next time I will share with you the four big things I would do – along with the Nurse Family Partnership type intervention – to make sure that we engage with parents and children in a way that is good for them and good for the society we want to create.

Best wishes

Alan

Dear Alan,

I couldn't agree more that modern lifestyles affect children from every type of home background, not just disadvantaged ones. The global electronic village in which children are growing up is based on the 'winners and losers' ethic of competitive consumerism, and it's easy to become fixated on the plight of the 'losers' without considering the contribution of 'winners' to the steady erosion of social capital.

As you say, the EPPS study shows that socio-economic status and mother's educational background are key indicators of educational success. They also affect the sort of 'home learning environment' parents provide for their offspring. Middle-class parents tend to recognise the importance of nurturing language and cognitive development, so their children arrive at school ready to take advantage of education. But, especially in the early years, social and emotional development is just as important as cognitive development. Scotland needs future citizens who are not only bright, but well-balanced and socially responsible. Middle-class parents are often unaware of the effects of a hyper-competitive, screen-based culture on the values they communicate to their children.

A mass of research shows that, in western democratic systems, the most effective type of parenting is 'authoritative', balancing warmth and firmness. But a market-driven culture encourages parents to confuse warmth with indulgence, so a growing number of children grow up thinking that love = stuff. Meanwhile, media-fuelled anxiety about safety issues means that instead of setting firm boundaries for children's behaviour (and expecting them to take increasing responsibility for their actions within these boundaries), many parents resort to over-protection.

In the not-too-distant past, it was widely acknowledged that indulgent, over-protective parenting produced 'spoilt' children. And spoilt children tended to turn into selfish adults, who often had difficulty sustaining relationships, were unconcerned about the welfare of others and clung to a narcissistic belief that 'the world owed them a living'. In her recent book, *The Selfish Society: how we forgot to love one another and made money instead*, psychologist Sue Gerhardt makes a powerful case for the links between early childhood experiences and western society's current culture of 'selfish individualism'.

So, it's not just the 'children of the poor' whose childhood needs detoxing. 'Unintentional neglect' of children's emotional and social needs happens across social classes. To ensure that all our children grow up to be 'successful learners, confident individuals, responsible citizens and effective contributors', it's not enough to have a Curriculum for Excellence in our schools. As a society, we have to focus on what children need for all-round healthy development from the moment they're born.

After trawling through the research, I reckon that – given the basic material requirements of nutrition, warmth and shelter – it comes down to the following:

- *love*, which isn't measured in 'stuff', but in time and responsive attention from the loving adults in children's lives;
- *discipline*, which means that adults set sensible boundaries for children's behaviour, and encourage them to take increasing responsibility for their actions and relationships with others;
- *language*, which involves frequent first-hand interaction from birth, including songs, stories, and chat around the day-to-day experiences they share with mum and dad (such as shared family meals, learning essential life-skills and getting out and about in the world beyond home);
- *play*, which is the natural learning mechanism programmed from birth. This doesn't mean sedentary screen-based entertainment, but real play that lucky children have enjoyed through the millennia. In the early stages it usually amounts to messing

about with whatever's handy in the home environment, and playing games like Peek-a-Boo with parents. But as they grow older, they need to play outdoors, with other children and without too much adult supervision.

It's not exactly rocket science – indeed, most people recognise it as 'common sense'. It's just that the technological and consumerist revolutions of the last few decades temporarily blinded us to the blindingly obvious.

I'm really looking forward to reading the Four Big Things you think could put things right. Personally, I think public policy has to help everyone – not just parents but the public in general – to recognise that providing a 'good childhood' for all Scotland's children is the best way to create a healthy society in the future. As well as personal targeted help for the most vulnerable parents and children, as in the Family Nurse Partnership, I'd like to see:

1 A concerted effort to inform all adults about the essential ingredients of a healthy childhood, and its social significance. This could start in secondary school with child development as part of education for citizenship. It could be continued through universal ante-natal and post-natal classes, and updates when children start each stage of education (nursery, infant, junior, secondary).

2 A change in early years education policy. Nordic countries have long recognised that, by stressing play-based learning rather than formal education to the age of seven, they enhance educational and social outcomes in later years. (Wales last year introduced a play-based 'Foundation Phase' between three and seven, based on the Nordic model.)

3 A national campaign to raise the profile of outdoor play, not just at school but in the community, and real political commitment to turning rhetoric about play in our Early Years Framework into actions. (Wales is ahead here too, having already introduced a statutory requirement for local authorities to provide open-access play opportunities for all children.)

4 Political attention to the dangers posed to children by a market-driven screen-based culture, especially in the early years. This could take the form of advice and awareness-raising (Australia

recently issued guidelines to parents that children under two shouldn't watch TV) and/or regulation (France has banned broadcasting to children under the age of three and Sweden has banned marketing to the under-12s).

It's been a salutary experience for someone who spent her adult life obsessing about the importance of education to find that early child-care is just as (if not more) significant in the great scheme of things. But I've amended that quotation pinned to my office wall. It now reads: 'Human history is more and more a race between catastrophe and universal understanding of child development.'

Best wishes,

Sue

Dear Sue

Swapping notes with you has been rewarding. How many books about politics in Scotland in the past thirty years have addressed child development or intergenerational failure? I do not know of any. How many political parties over the same period of time have campaigned to improve the early year experience? Early years seems to be thought of as mums and children playing while men discuss the constitution, tax powers, targets and efficient public services.

There is a need to see early years appreciated as a top line social and political issue. If it was important but there was nothing we could do to improve parenting and early years we would be tilting at windmills. However, there are very practical steps we can take. You offer a range of largely cultural prescriptions: love, language and play. I sincerely agree with these, as what we need is cultural change and change in politics and policy aimed particularly at parents from pregnancy onwards till the child is three years of age.

So here are my five key approaches, all based on policies and practices that have small footprints here but have been demonstrated to work in other countries.

1　Support all teenage mothers from early in their pregnancy for a two year period, either using or adapting the Nurse Family Partnership, as we discussed earlier. To run a universal programme in Scotland would cost around £38m per year.

2   Maternity grants are provided in Finland to all mothers and
fathers who attend sessions on understanding the health and
behavioural implications of having a baby. They do not have to
attend these sessions but, in the tradition of rights and responsibilities, attendance results in the grant or package of baby
goods. If you do not attend then you get neither. The whole
aim is: to build upon the technical health checks received during
pregnancy; to build on the 'golden moment' that pregnancy and
child birth brings; to help parents form peer groups and to
understand the changes that will come in their own relationships;
and to help them have a healthy pregnancy. There are 57,000
children born in Scotland each year. This service could be
provided by community organisations and health workers.

3   In the Netherlands mother and well-baby clinics provide
immediate support to parents from birth to school age. They
provide comprehensive coverage in ensuring that children are
safe and being properly looked after, attention is given to both
health and development. Visits are more frequent in the first
weeks and months of life, spacing out as school approaches.
Clinics are staffed by doctors who attend to social and
emotional development, motor skills, language and general
health, and nurses concentrate on baby care, parenting, feeding,
toileting and sleeping. Back up is provided by walk in surgeries.

4   Children and family centres that straddle the first year of life
through to school age are already found in some of the most
challenging communities in Scotland – some run by local
authorities and others by voluntary organisations. Under one
roof they provide parent and child groups, child care, speech
therapy, therapeutic support and parenting classes, and out-
reach services to reach the most vulnerable families. Children
and Family centres are one of the cornerstones of family
support in Holland and the Nordic countries, and we could
have more here.

5   Safe families, fostering and adoption have become all the more
important as a result of the epidemic of alcohol and drugs
across Scotland. Substance abuse has accelerated the breakdown

of families and rendered parents incapable of looking after their children. Young vulnerable children need the attachment and care of a steady relationship, but the institutional arrangements we have mean that the most vulnerable children commonly have four or five different 'domestic' arrangements each year. There is a need to look at how the legal and care system can be more child centred (making decisions in the interests of the child), how fostering can more easily become adoption and how therapeutic support can be given. Perhaps we can learn from the American experience where, within the last decade, two different pieces of legislation have come in; one concentrating on the rights of the child, setting an 18 month period for supporting parents and resolving the final destination of a child; the other improving the route through fostering and adoption.

All of the above prescriptions are very practical and cost effective and work. So, how can early years and parenting become a more significant and weighty issue in Scotland? The arguments and evidence, and practice in other countries, is overwhelming.

I find it very revealing that you started out as a literacy expert and became an advocate for early years through direct experience. Earlier I explained how I came to early years, having tried to improve the lot for unemployed people, skills in the workforce and economic development. Neither of us expected to be an early years champion. Yet in each of our fields, we saw that the arrows pointed to improving parenting. And it's not just us. Other people across a range of fields feel the same.

Thank you for the exchange, the next few years could be very rewarding.

Best wishes

Alan

References

Gerhardt, S. (2010), *The Selfish Society: How we forgot to love one another and made money instead*, London: Simon and Schuster.

Determined to Punish?
Scotland's Choice

FERGUS MCNEILL

Introduction

DECIDING WHO, WHEN, how and how much to punish is (or should be) a central concern for any community, any society and for any polity. Necessarily, penal politics is concerned both with the proper purposes of punishment and with the intended and unintended effects of its administration. But as Durkheim (1984) argued, punishment is also deeply symbolic, expressive and communicative; for better or worse, who, when, how and how much we choose to punish says at least much about the punishing polity, about its passions, fears and beliefs, as it does about the punished. Though industrialisation placed the state centre-stage in the administration of punishment, and allowed punishment to become less corporal, less severe and less intense, punishment still serves the same expressive functions, solidifying social values.

As Page (2004) has argued, Durkheim's theory has been increasingly questioned, not least when applied to a late-modern context which makes any claims about the existence of a monolithic 'collective consciousness' ever less convincing; contemporary societies, Page argues, are pluralistic and highly ordered. However, this is not to say that such societies lack a 'dominant moral order which is historically established by particular social forces' (Garland, 1990, 53); such a moral order may be better understood as the expression of a particular, dominant consciousness rather than a collective consciousness. Garland also argued that punishment does not merely reflect particular social values and the social order; rather, it helps to constitute and construct them; and that politicians use punishment to 'connect with the fears, insecurities and prejudices of their intended audience' (Garland, 1990, 252).

Neither Durkheim's theory nor these refinements of his argument necessarily imply any particular form of penal politics. But if contemporary societies are more pluralistic in terms of their values, it follows that we should expect penal politics, cultures and practices to be more contested. We should not be surprised, therefore, to find different and sometimes contradictory values being expressed simultaneously – penal communication can be progressive and repressive, understanding and condemnatory, inclusive and exclusive, cerebral or visceral. To borrow a famous example of a more progressive voice, one eminent 20th century politician argued thus:

> A calm and dispassionate recognition of the rights of the accused against the state, and even of convicted criminals against the state, a constant heart-searching by all charged with the duty of punishment, a desire and eagerness to rehabilitate in the world of industry all those who have paid their dues in the hard coinage of punishment, tireless efforts towards the discovery of curative and regenerating processes, and an unfaltering faith that there is a treasure, if you can only find it, in the heart of every man, these are the symbols which in the treatment of crime and criminals mark and measure the stored-up strength of a nation, and are the sign and proof of the living virtue in it. (Winston Churchill, Home Secretary, House of Commons, 20 July 1910)

With this in mind then, rather than providing an academic analysis of the 'problems' of crime or justice in the devolved Scotland, and lacking the resources to seriously interrogate the nature of penal-political discourses in Scotland, this chapter aims simply to speculate from the perspective of an interested and concerned observer, about the 'strength and virtue of the nation' in 2010 (at least insofar as this can be discerned from political and public debates about the punishment of 'offenders'). I want to ask what kind of penal polity we are, and what kind of penal polity we might aspire to be. Necessarily, this involves some looking back to look forward.

Devolution and De-tartanisation?

For those interested in Scotland's criminal justice institutions, cultures and practices, devolution has been something of a paradox. The 1707 Act of Union ensured the maintenance of separate legal jurisdictions; in that sense, a distinctly Scottish criminal justice existed long before devolution (Duff and Hutton, 1999). Indeed, some have claimed that Scottish legal institutions and traditions had 'come to represent and carry the burden of Scottish identity, culture and privilege' (Munro, Mooney and Croall, 2010).

A strong case can be made that while 'the constitutional question' remained unresolved, successive Conservative Secretaries of State in the 1980s and 1990s lacked a mandate to interfere too much with the structures, cultures and practices of Scottish criminal justice; instead, 'real' power circulated amongst civil service and professional elites, many of whom were committed to the maintenance of Scotland's distinctive traditions and practices (see McAra, 1999, 2008). These peculiar dynamics perhaps insulated Scotland from the 'heating up' of the politics of crime and justice that affected other English-speaking jurisdictions in this period (on which see Loader and Sparks, 2010), and enabled the survival of a welfarist ethos. Though this philosophy is most clearly associated with the Children's Hearings System that followed from Lord Kilbrandon's famous report (1964), these reforms of juvenile justice and child welfare also served to locate probation and parole services firmly in local authority social work, ensuring that welfarism penetrated adult criminal justice too (McNeill, 2005; McNeill and Whyte, 2007).

The significance of this insulation is probably hard to overstate. David Garland's influential analysis of the emergence of a 'culture of control' in the USA and the UK rests in part on his claim that, in the latter part of the 20th century, the combination of rising crime rates, declining faith in penal welfarist strategies, and the apparent failure of criminal justice to deliver security, conspired to create a crisis of sovereignty for the state (Garland, 2000). The resulting 'schizoid reaction', according to Garland, involved recasting crime and criminals as problems to be rationally managed (rather than cured), *and* to use institutions of punishment symbolically — as a means of flexing muscles that re-affirmed the state's capacity to govern on behalf of its citizens. Jonathan Simon, an eminent American penologist, has gone so far as to suggest that states came to govern *through* crime (Simon, 2007).

Prior to devolution, Scotland's crisis of sovereignty was constitutional rather than governmental; it was less concerned with the state's *capacity* to act than with its *entitlement* to do so. With the constitutional question addressed (however imperfectly) by devolution, this layer of insulation was removed and the Scottish Parliament, the Scottish Executive, Scottish politics and Scottish criminal justice became much more exposed to the dynamics referred to above and thus to *greater* English (and American) influence.

Examining these changes in more detail, Lesley McAra's thoughtful analysis of developments in Scotland between 1999 and 2007 (2008) highlights four sets of related changes that together represent the 'de-tartanisation' of Scottish criminal justice. These include the scale and extent of managerial and institutional transformation (she reports the creation of over 100 new institutions since 1998); the reshaping of systems and practices associated with emerging discourses of public pro-tection and risk management; the development of a community safety agenda that blended social inclusion priorities with the more punitive and exclusionary dynamics of tackling 'anti-social behaviour'; and the emergence of victims as key stakeholders in youth and adult justice.

McAra contends that this de-tartanisation can be explained as the result of a civic and political culture cut adrift from its cultural history and welfare traditions by an increasingly febrile domestic politics, and by greater ideological convergence between the Labour/Lib Dem coalitions in Scotland and their New Labour sister administrations in the UK. In this context, welfarism lost its cultural purchase just at the moment when political actors in the new Parliament needed to build their capacity and their legitimacy. As McAra observes 'weak governments often turn to crime control as a ready mechanism to overcome crises of legitimacy' (McAra, 2008, 493). Put in simpler terms, being seen to be doing some-thing about crime and anti-social behaviour appeared to be a useful way of shoring up the authority of the new political institutions and classes. As in other jurisdictions – and perhaps continuing and accelerating a process that had begun before devolution – the disciplines of manageri-alisation (Clarke and Newman, 1999) provided the mechanisms through which professional and civil service resistance could be undermined or marginalised.

Nationalism and Re-tartanisation?

The 2007 election changed Scottish penal politics. Perhaps this was partly a result of the particular stance on crime and justice taken by the

SNP administration; perhaps it was the result of their minority position. The two influences were reflected, respectively, in changes to the tone of penal-political discourse and to the pace of change in the criminal justice system. In sum, the tone became more moderate, and the pace became much more measured.

Leaving aside the detail of his policy programme, as Cabinet Secretary for Justice, Kenny MacAskill's analysis of Scotland's crime problems locates them in cultural and structural contexts, regularly invoking the 3 'd's of 'drink, drugs and deprivation', or to two 'b's of 'booze and blades'. But while he laments these cultural and structural problems, much like his colleague Fergus Ewing's statements (and silences) in relation to youth crime and young people, he always balances sober analysis of Scottish *problems* with an upbeat message about Scottish *potential*. Thus he bemoans our rising prison population (more of which below), questioning why we seem determined to lock up so many more of our people than our Celtic cousins to the west or our Viking cousins to the east (note the direction of the comparative gaze). He questions the sense in providing 'free bed and board' to those on short prison sentences, when they could be 'paying back' for their crimes. Most famously of all perhaps, he insists that Scottish justice is tempered with mercy.

This may be a penal politics based on conviction, but it is also arguably *politically* necessary for the nationalists. Re-opening the constitutional question, and building the requisite confidence that the Scottish people might be able to govern themselves, will be harder to do in a context where fear of 'feral' youth, lawlessness and institutional impotence abounds. Nationalist politicians must balance sober assessment of Scotland's problems with an upbeat confidence in her resources and capacities: for them, better a *constitutional* crisis of sovereignty than one related to fear of crime and disorder. The converse may be true for at least some of the unionist parties. Thus MacAskill's Conservative shadow, Bill Aitken's preferred sound-bite is 'soft touch Scotland', whereas his Labour shadow, Richard Baker, prefers 'the criminals' charter'. For them, talking up problems of crime and justice makes sense, both as a way of connecting with voters' anxieties and, perhaps more cynically, as a way of undermining Scottish self-confidence.

As the brief analysis of the impact of devolution above suggests, MacAskill's position is, in some respects closer to Scotland's historical traditions and represents, fittingly, something of a 're-tartanisation' (to adapt McAra's term) of Scottish penal policy. Indeed, it might be argued that his penal ideology reflects a much longer tradition of collectivist corporatism in Scotland. His efforts to reform community sentences and to reduce the use of short-term imprisonment echo similar initiatives from the early part of the last century. A history of the first 50 years of the probation service in Glasgow, published by the City of Glasgow in 1955, notes how that service was created because its progenitors (and the corporation's leaders) were worried that high rates of imprisonment for fine default constituted a *social* problem:

> ... in view of the admittedly demoralising influence of imprisonment, the serious consideration of all was demanded concerning the welfare of the community. (City of Glasgow, 1955, 9)

Note that the serious consideration of *all* was demanded because this 'demoralisation' represented a threat to the interests of the *whole* body corporate. In 1905 there was at least some recognition that harming one entailed harming all.

I risk lapsing into the kind of penal-historical romanticism that Munro, Mooney and Croall (2010) have challenged in their call for closer scrutiny of claims that welfarism (and corporatism) has been engaged in a heroic struggle for survival in Scotland, resisting the chill winds of punitiveness blowing in from the South and from the States. Rather than trying to unpick the many strands of evidence for and against this proposition, I turn instead to an examination of one particular penal drama, in an effort to dig a little deeper into the question of where Scotland now stands in relation to punishment.

Penal Self-Determination: Scotland's Choice

Though the decision to release Abdelbaset Mohmed Ali al-Megrahi might seem the more obvious drama to examine in an analysis of Scotland's penal character, instead I focus here on 'Scotland's Choice', the report of the Scottish Prisons Commission (2008). In doing so, and returning to his revision of Durkheim's theory, I draw on the work of Joshua Page, though do not aim to offer the sort of empirically grounded and fine-grained analysis that he does. Page's (2004) case-study concerned a more ordinary aspect of American penality; the US Congress's 1994 decision to deny grant funding to prisoner education. Drawing on Durkheim, Page's analysis of congressional debates and popular media reporting shows how a 'legislative penal drama' was created through which politicians spoke to key (white, working and middle class) audiences, tapping into and legitimising collective sentiments, shoring up particular support for punitive policies.

As a penal drama, 'Scotland's Choice' was of a different sort[1]. It might be read as an attempt to re-engage key audiences in serious debate in an effort to undermine penal populism, or as an attempt to shore up welfarism – or at least a commitment to penal reductionism. In other words, it aimed not to *play* penal politics but to *change* them.

The Commission was established by the Cabinet Secretary for Justice in late 2007. Faced with unmitigated growth in the prison population over the past decade, MacAskill charged the commission to consider the proper use of imprisonment in Scotland and to raise the public profile of this issue. Chaired by former Scottish First Minister, the Rt. Hon. Henry McLeish, and comprising a mixed group of criminal justice (a sheriff, a chief constable and an Austrian prison governor) and civic leaders (a writer and broadcaster, a businessman, and a leader in the voluntary sector), the Commission reported in July 2008.

The title of the report – 'Scotland's Choice' – of course makes it an irresistible focus for a discussion of penal policy in the context of a collection about self-determination. The title signalled the Commission's attempt to eschew a discourse of crisis in favour of one of opportunity, conceiving criminal justice as a field in which thoughtful planning might replace the reactive management of seemingly insuperable problems.

---

[1] In this part of the chapter, I draw heavily on a short paper co-authored with my colleague, Dr Sarah Armstrong (Armstrong and McNeill, 2009), and am grateful to her for permission to use the material here. We were involved in the Commission's work in its final stages, drawn in to provide research support and advice as the Commission was concluding its collection of evidence. It is fair to say that we are supportive and assisted development of the plan set out in the report, but at the point of our involvement with this work, the Commission had already identified a set of priorities which provided the basis for making specific findings and recommendations.

In the aftermath of the report's publication, media coverage, particularly in the few days following publication (which ensured journalists had not been able to thoroughly read the document) focused narrowly on a few lines in the report: specifically, the target of reducing the prison population by as many as 4,000 (or half the current population) by increasing the use of community sentences. In a sense, these (mis-)representations and repetitions managed to convey a report that was both more radical and less interesting than it actually was.

The radical edge in 'Scotland's Choice' was less in the detail of its recommendations and more in its attempt to change both how penal change is managed and how the public is engaged. Firstly, the report argued that prisons are inescapably linked to national well-being. The first objective in the Commission's remit was 'to consider how imprisonment is used in Scotland and how that use fits with the Scottish Government's wider strategic objectives' to make the nation wealthier and fairer, safer and stronger, smarter, healthier, and greener (Scottish Government 2007). This encouraged the Commission to consider prison in relation to all of these objectives, and to compare how imprisonment fares against other forms of civic investment (as well as other forms of punishment) in achieving broad social goals.

Secondly, the Commission argued that punishment and prison are not interchangeable, and the purposes and limits of each must be separately considered. Typically, policy makers and academics alike have confused (and as a resulted inverted the purposes of) punishment and prison: the minimalist institutional function of prison to hold people securely has been back-defined as the purpose of punishment to incapacitate. The accumulating evidence that prisons fail to deter, rehabilitate or punish retributively has led to doubts about these as purposes of punishment generally. The Scottish Prisons Commission's holistic perspective in considering the place of punishment in society led it to consider *first* what it wanted from punishment, and *then* whether prison as an institutional form was well-placed to achieve this. This was an important conceptual distinction to make and allowed for the development of an integrated package of ideas directed at improving the outcomes of punishment rather than adapting to the limitations of prison as punishment.

Thirdly, the report produced a compelling case that criminal justice practices themselves drive up prison populations. The Commission's review of crime and imprisonment data shows that no matter what crime rates have done – whether rising, falling or remaining stable, the prison population has grown (Scottish Prisons Commission, 2008, 16). It also showed that two of the main drivers of Scotland's high prison populations are system-led: rates of parole recall increased 900 per cent over less than a decade and more people entered prison in 2006/07 to await a trial or sentence than to serve one (there has been disproportionate growth in the part of the remand population waiting to be sentenced, suggesting the impact of heavy paperwork burdens on the sentencing process).

Fourth, the Commission recognised that the public is able to participate knowledgeably and with maturity in crime and justice debates. Around the middle point of its tenure, the Commission was asked to include a review of the prison's open estate in light of a recent prisoner's absconding from an open prison and subsequently raping a schoolgirl. This issue had the potential to derail the Commission's measured deliberations about the balance between community and prison based sanctions. Instead, the Commission believed in a public that could understand that a tragic but rare event should not necessarily drive policy decisions about the use of prison in the long-term future, and it enshrined this belief in the report's aims to 'take crime seriously, engage the public in rational debate and make evidence-informed policy' (Scottish Prisons Commission, 2008, 2). The Commission's belief was supported by evidence, presented in the report, that more people in the country feel drug and alcohol abuse are major problems than crime. In fact, few people fear being a victim of a serious violent crime (Scottish Prisons Commission, 2008, 20).

Finally, the Commission argued that a plan of action should integrate a normative vision, practices supported by research, and institutional capacities. The Commission presented 23 recommendations as an interconnected package linking changes in prosecution and court processes through to sentencing, community justice and prisons and to resettlement of offenders. Taken together, the plan de-centred imprisonment as the main form of punishment in Scotland (where currently it is frequently used for very short sentences), and developed an overall plan for targeting the use of prison for serious offenders, increasing the use and credibility of community-based sentences.

There were two critical elements of this plan – establishing the idea of *paying back* as a core principle of punishment and establishing a *progress court* to oversee community sentences. These two recommendations took account of the need for policy to be inspired by vision and connected to evidence and also reflected striking differences with the direction policy is currently taking in England and Wales. Louise Casey's report for the Westminster government on 'Engaging Communities in Fighting Crime' (2008) has lent the concept of payback renewed salience. For Casey, the idea of payback represented a solution to perceived problems of public confidence in criminal justice and community penalties. Recognising that public attitudes reflect emotional responses to crime, her prescription for building public confidence was yet another re-branding of community service as 'community payback'. For Casey, two features were critical to the re-branding: firstly, paying back had to hurt and secondly, offenders doing payback should wear bibs identifying them as such, ensuring that payback involved the pains of public shaming.

The emphasis on payback in the Commission's report reflected a similar concern about public confidence, but the nature of the payback proposed was quite different:

> Payback means finding constructive ways to compensate or repair harms caused by crime. It involves making good to the victim and/or the community... Ultimately, one of the best ways for offenders to pay back is by turning their lives around. (Scottish Prisons Commission, 2008, 33)

A three-stage process of sentencing was proposed to deliver this payback. Stage 1 would determine *how much payback* (ensuring proportionality), and was to be determined by the judge alone. Stage 2 would determine the *form of payback,* and required a dialogue between judges, social workers and offenders themselves. Stage 3 of the proposed sentencing process would involve a 'progress court', the function of which was both to deal with non-compliance and to recognise progress. The emphasis was on the constructive management of reparative community sanctions rather than their rigid enforcement. But stage 3 had another function, too, as fulfilling the public's 'right to know – routinely – how much has been paid back and in what ways... [It] should mean that much greater effort goes into communication with the communities in which payback takes place' (Scottish Prisons Commission, 2008, 36–37).

This model of payback contrasted sharply with Casey's. It rejected the emphasis on exacting pain and shame from offenders as passive subjects of punishment. The Commission's version of payback engages with offenders both as the perpetrators of previous harms and as potential authors of reparation and reform.

The inevitable moderation of the impact of the Scottish Prisons Commission's report in the development and passage of the Criminal Justice and Licensing Act 2010 leaves its longer term impact far from clear, but whatever legislative changes and policy outcomes 'Scotland's Choice' has contributed to, its more lasting contribution may have been in offering up new ways of understanding and talking about punishment and imprisonment. If nothing else, the report has signalled that Scotland does have a choice to make, and the capacity to determine its penal future.

Conclusions

If it is true that welfarism in Scotland – something perhaps approximating a more Scandinavian than an Anglo-American approach to punishment – endured in Scotland because of now weakened civil service and professional elites, should we regret the opening up of penal policy to political engagement and public debate? This question begs several others.

Firstly, has elite-sponsored welfarism been 'a good thing'? Certainly, there is no straightforward, inevitable or historical symmetry between Scottish penal welfarism and progressing towards social justice or a more equal society (Munro, Mooney and Croall, 2010). Despite the restraining influences of penal policy elites, Scotland still deals very severely with adult offenders, at least by European standards (see Scottish Prisons Commission, 2008), and shows no signs of letting up. Those who suffer the consequences are not just highly stratified populations of predominantly disadvantaged and disaffected young men from our cities' housing schemes (Houchin, 2005), they are the families and communities of these prisoners of inequality; families and communities compelled to carry the burden of the uneven geographical distribution of imprisonment (Breen, 2010). Well-intentioned attempts to reduce the prison population by introducing alternatives have too often served only to increase the reach of the carceral state, bringing more marginalised people under the supervisory gaze of the state, and drawing them further into the wider and finer-meshed nets (Cohen, 1985) with which it dredges up for punishment the 'flotsam and jetsam' to whom the current Cabinet Secretary repeatedly refers (see McNeill and Whyte, 2007; Munro and McNeill, 2010).

That said, it is clear that increased political and public engagement in penal policy carries risks of exacerbating these forms of inequality and disadvantage. Zimring and Johnson (2006), for example, suggest that greater leniency tends to be found in jurisdictions where crime and justice have low salience as political issues (leading to their delegation to 'non-responsive' arms of government), where trust in government is high, and where systems of justice are characterised by norms of discretion exercised in individualised judgements by professionals. In similar vein, Lappi-Seppala (2008) has suggested that Scandinavian penal restraint owes much to the absence of bi-partisan politics and a hostile tabloid media, as well as to higher levels of trust in society and in its institutions, and to the maintenance of higher levels of welfare provision.

But can it really be desirable, practicable or even democratic, to try to sneak progressive penal policy and practice under the radar of political and public engagement, leaving it to professional determination rather than national self-determination? To do so would be to deny Scotland the means to build the collective autonomy, shared competence and mutual connectedness encouraged by self-determination theory (Deci and Ryan, 1995, 2002). A better way might be to work towards a closer examination of the *kinds* of public debates and penal politics that are the pre-requisites of genuine penal self-determination. As Habermas (1990) suggests in his discussion of discourse ethics, there are important differences between a 'rationally motivated consensus' and 'mere agreement'. Creating the right sort of dialogue in penal politics is far from easy, but perhaps it is not impossible (see Weaver, 2009). However, there are circuits of power and influence – commercial, corporate and global – as well as local, professional and political – that need to be exposed to critical scrutiny in determining and developing the conditions for genuine democratic dialogue (Wacquant, 2009).

Loader and Sparks (2010) recently argued that the de-politicisation of crime and penal policy is neither feasible nor desirable and that academic criminology needs to fashion itself as a 'democratic under-labourer', contributing to a 'better politics of crime and regulation' (Loader and

Sparks, 2010, 117), partly by cultivating 'greater humility in the face of democratic politics' (Loader and Sparkes, 2010, 119); by understanding the circumstances of politics; and by better appreciating the need to build consensus and support collective decision making. This is not, they argue, to cede too much to the multiple problems of contemporary politics (and the threats to democracy that these problems bring); rather, it is to play a part in addressing and challenging them, not by arguing that criminologists (or any other professional 'experts') know best and should be left to get on with the job, but by bringing criminological knowledge to the negotiating table. Leaving the particular merits and demerits of criminology (or even of the academy) aside, the same argument might be applied to other legitimate interests and other forms of penal knowledge.

In their analysis, Loader's and Sparks' (2010) notion of democratic under-labouring involves three 'moments'; the moment of discovery (of new knowledge about and constructions of 'problems' and 'solutions'), the institutional-critical moment (which generates new knowledge that challenges existing systems, cultures and practices), and the normative moment (which engages with the moral dimensions of and value judgments at stake in criminal justice). All three 'moments' are potential sites of exchange and dialogue in the development of the autonomy, competence and connectedness required for genuine penal self-determination.

How far are we from this kind of dialogue in Scotland? The central argument in this chapter is that we are closer to it than we were just a few years ago. Partly, this is the consequence of the exigencies of nationalist politics in a minority administration, which have required the current administration to pursue both a more progressive and a more consensual penal politics. On an optimistic reading, it might be argued that Scottish penal politics is showing some signs of maturing beyond populism and towards a richer, deeper and more open dialogue about whether we remain determined merely to punish, or whether our aspirations rise a little higher than that, despite the late-modern insecurities and neo-liberal forces that conspire to hold them down.

References

Armstrong, S. and McNeill, F. (2009), 'Choice versus crisis: how Scotland could transform thinking about prisons and punishment', *Criminal Justice Matters*, 75(1): 2–4.

Breen, J. (2010), 'Secondary Effects of Imprisonment: The New Direction of Prison Research', *Irish Probation Journal*, 7: 46–64.

Casey, L. (2008), *Engaging Communities in Fighting Crime*, London: Cabinet Office.

City of Glasgow (1955), *Probation: A Brief Survey of Fifty Years of the Probation Service of the City of Glasgow 1905–1955*, Glasgow: City of Glasgow Probation Area Committee.

Clarke, J. and Newman, J. (1997), *The Managerial State: Power, Politics and Ideology in the Remaking of Social Welfare*, London: Sage.

Cohen, S. (1985), *Visions of Social Control: Crime, Punishment and Classification*, Cambridge: Polity Press/Blackwell.

Deci, E. L. and Ryan, R. M. (1995), 'Human autonomy: The basis for true self-esteem', in Kemis, M. (ed.), *Efficacy, Agency, and Self-Esteem*, New York: Plenum, 31–49.

Deci, E. L. and Ryan, R. (eds), (2002), *Handbook of Self-Determination Research*, Rochester, NY: University of Rochester Press.

Duff, P. and Hutton, N. (eds) (1999), *Criminal Justice in Scotland*, Aldershot: Ashgate/Dartmouth.

Durkheim, E. (1984), *The Division of Labor in Society*, New York: Macmillan.

Garland, D. (1990) *Punishment and modern society: A study in social theory.* Chicago, IL: University of Chicago Press.

Garland, D. (2000), 'The Culture of High Crime Societies: Some Preconditions of Recent 'Law and Order' Policies', *British Journal of Criminology*, 40: 347-375.

Garland, D. (2001), *The Culture of Control: Crime and Social Order in Contemporary Society*, Oxford: Oxford University Press.

Habermas, J. (1990), *Moral Consciousness and Communicative Action*, Cambridge: Polity Press.

Houchin, R. (2005), *Social Exclusion and Imprisonment in Scotland: A Report.*, Glasgow: Glasgow Caledonian University.

Kilbrandon Report (1964), *Children and Young Persons (Scotland)*, Cmnd 2306, Edinburgh: HMSO.

Lappi-Seppala, T. (2008), 'Trust, Welfare and Political Economy: Cross-comparative perspectives in penal severity', http://www.rsf.uni-greiswald.de/fileadmin/mediapool/lehrstuehle/duenkel/LappiSeppala_Penal Severity.pdf

Loader, I. and Sparks, R. (2010), *Public Criminology?*, London: Routledge.

McAra, L. (1999), 'The Politics of Penality: An Overview of the Development of Penal Policy in Scotland', in Duff, P. and Hutton, N. (eds), *Criminal Justice in Scotland*, Aldershot/Ashgate/Dartmouth, 355–80.

McAra, L. (2008), 'Crime, Criminology and Criminal Justice in Scotland' *European Journal of Criminology*, 5(4): 481–504.

McNeill, F. (2005), 'Remembering probation in Scotland', *Probation Journal*, 52(1): 25–40.

McNeill, F. and Whyte, B. (2007), *Reducing Reoffending: Social Work and Community Justice in Scotland*, Cullompton: Willan.

Munro, M. and McNeill, F. (2010), 'Fines, community sanctions and measures', in Croall, H., Mooney, G. and Munro, M. (eds), *Criminal Justice in Scotland*, Cullompton: Willan.

Munro, M., Mooney, G. And Croall, H. (2010), 'Criminal justice in Scotland: overview and prospects', in Croall, H., Mooney, G. and Munro, M. (eds), *Criminal Justice in Scotland*, Cullompton: Willan.

Page, J. (2004), 'Eliminating the enemy: The import of denying prisoners access to higher education in Clinton's America', *Punishment and Society*, 6(4) 357–378.

Scottish Government (2007), *The Government Economic Strategy*.

Scottish Prisons Commission (2008), *Scotland's Choice: Report of the Scottish Prisons Commission*, Edinburgh: Scottish Prisons Commission.

Simon, J. (2007), *Governing through crime: How the war on crime transformed American democracy and created a culture of fear*, New York: Oxford University Press.

Wacquant, L. (2009), *Punishing the Poor: The Neo-liberal Government of Social Insecurity*, Durham, NC and London: Duke University Press.

Weaver. B. (2009), 'Communicative punishment as a penal approach to supporting desistance', *Punishment and Society*, 13(1): 9–29.

Zimring, F. and Johnson, D. (2006),'Public Opinion and the Governance of Punishment in Democratic Political Systems', in *The ANNALS of the American Academy of Political and Social Science*, 605, May, 266–280.

Social Justice, Aspiration and Autonomy

JIM MCCORMICK AND KATIE GRANT

Dear Katie,

My first job was with the Commission on Social Justice, an opposition inquiry set up by John Smith and reporting to Tony Blair in 1994, whose aim was to take a detailed look at how to advance social justice. Its final report offered a revealing snapshot of the UK at that time: tired, divided, unequal. It was not short of policy ideas to change matters. More interesting is the Commission's go at defining an ideal of social justice – a hierarchy of four related notions:

- The foundation of a free society is the equal worth of citizens, expressed in political and civil liberties, equal rights before the law against discrimination and so on.

- Everyone is entitled, as a right of citizenship, to be able to meet their basic needs for income, shelter and other necessities. These basic needs can be met by enabling people to acquire them for themselves or by providing resources and services.

- Social justice demands more than this: improved opportunities and life chances are needed so people can fulfil their potential. How opportunities are made in the first place, as well as how they are redistributed, should be a concern for social justice.

- Unjust inequalities should be reduced and where possible eliminated.

There's a lot here that people of different political beliefs might agree on; namely, the suggestion that we should be concerned about discrimination, homelessness and worklessness as well as poor experiences of education and inadequate training. To these elements of social justice, we might add a fifth – what some would call justice between the generations, expressed in how the decisions we make now (on energy, pensions and housing, for example) will affect others in future.

Inequality is perhaps the most difficult element of social justice. There's plenty of evidence that Scotland remains strongly divided by income, social class and working status. In Scotland, a complex mix of economic, social and cultural factors yields a population marked by a number of factors: slower improvements in health than in northern England, let alone the UK or EU average; big health inequalities; and better-off Scots faring worse than their peers elsewhere. Even if inequality isn't bad for *everyone*, it's bad enough for enough people to merit action. But what kind of inequalities offend an ideal of social justice?

The fourth element above is helpful in pointing us towards the target of *unjustified* inequalities, not all inequality. It's not unjust that the life-time earnings of most graduates are higher than most semi-skilled workers. Nor is it unjust that some people clean offices, flip burgers or do other jobs we might think unattractive. Someone will always need to do these jobs – but it doesn't always need to be the same people. In terms of life chances, what's unjust is if people get stuck in these jobs without opportunities to improve their skills and move to jobs with better pay and prospects. Within organisations, huge gaps in pay and benefits are usually bad for morale and productivity, especially where these can't be linked to performance.

We might focus in on the *duration* of experiencing disadvantage. Unemployment would still occur but we might bear down hardest on long-term unemployment. Poverty would still occur but would affect fewer. Witness the case of Denmark having cut its poverty rate to less than half of Scotland's without having notably more economic success. And no-one should have to live long-term without adequate resources: typically poverty would be a temporary state.

We might also aim to disrupt patterns of inequality. There is no law of nature that says a poor start in one part of life – such as housing or family income – must lead to disadvantage in others, like education or health. And we should place *capacity* at the heart of our endeavour. Social justice cannot be only for government – though we shouldn't underestimate the role of policy. It must also involve employers, service providers and citizens in developing a more resilient and capable population. This starts to touch on the theme of 'self-determination' that seems to have been largely absent from political debate in Scotland since devolution (leaving the constitutional debate to one side). I mean the role for each of us to influence what happens in the times we find ourselves. There is certainly evidence of foresight and innovation – we can look to work on community assets, emerging dementia care and volunteering to see how much people contribute. Too often, these cases thrive at the margins of systems which the most vulnerable depend upon.

Let me finish by reflecting on progress in recent years. The decade up to 2008 saw sustained economic growth, rising employment and unprecedented growth in public spending. The scorecard across that period shows:

- *Sustained progress* in housing standards; young people gaining 'standard' qualifications; and rates of poverty among older people.
- *Little or no change* in the average scores of the lowest-attaining 20% of young people at school; the proportion of people on low wages; and long-term worklessness.
- *Steady deterioration* in the proportion of low-income households having to pay full Council Tax; and the value of benefits for workless households without children.

Overall, the first half of that decade saw faster progress than the second. Things got better for some: worklessness fell by 20 per cent in the Scottish neighbourhoods which had started with the highest share of people claiming out-of-work benefits. But many gains left the very poorest untouched. Meanwhile, the fall in family poverty was accompanied by an increased risk for people without children, whether low-paid or out of work.

If this was the story after ten years with a fair wind behind government action, we will need to be much more creative in tougher times. I think the five elements of social justice referred to here are a decent basis for action, But we certainly need to re-think how to apply them.

Yours,

Jim

Dear Jim,

Your definition of the elements of social justice makes sense, but let me make an early admission: I have a problem with Commissions on Social Justice. Set up with the best intentions, they nevertheless follow a drearily predictable pattern, with earnest meetings, moving to solemn statements that outline the problem yet again and culminating fat reports to balance on top of previous fat reports on top of previous ... you see where I'm going here. Such reports are not blue-prints for action, they are substitutes for action, mainly because, amongst their other failings, social injustice is usually assumed to be something that 'they' do to 'them' and which 'we' could fix if only 'government' had the political will. As reports emerge, commissioners probably feel they have done a good job. Certainly, they will be asked to contribute to discussions on TV. Ministers may even give them a call. But will social justice improve? Unlikely.

Let's go back to the beginning. Your definition of social justice makes sense but actually has become part of the problem. How could it not, when it conveys the clear impression that if you're disadvantaged by the lack of social justice, you've got to wait to be rescued instead of helping to rescue yourself? This ability to help rescue yourself should surely be at the heart of our debate because to me, self-determination (in a non-constitutional sense) means that Scots as individuals should be the primary agents of social change. By this I mean that, although some people certainly need help, Scots as individuals should understand that to be as healthy, well educated, successfully aspirational and at ease with the world around us as our individual constitutions combined with our abilities can manage, our own efforts are key. In a country where self-determination is working well, men and women feel that their efforts at self-help are assisted and rewarded by a government whose main function is not to create 'clients' for the social security system but to remove the blockages individuals encounter along the way to self-determination. Poor quality education, hiccups in the health service and malicious discrimination are three such blockages.

Perhaps this isn't so different from when you talk about 'the role for each of us to influence what happens in the times we find ourselves', but after decades of state-fostered passivity that's too large a canvas. People must regain the confidence, and the impetus, to influence their own lives before they can even start to influence the times.

What role can government play in this? Perhaps we should not, as you say, 'underestimate the role of policy', but policy has a habit of seeing the wood but not the trees. I'm not suggesting that self-determination means rampant individualism. I simply suggest that, ideally, the quest for social justice involves both acknowledging the importance of self-motivation, and supporting that motivation rather than smothering it in statism. When people are motivated, they usually achieve. When they achieve, they feel powerful. When powerful, they can talk about self-determination and know that their voices, and the voices of the communities in which they live, will be heard. How many such voices do we hear in Scotland today? Gae few, as they say.

However, without an improvement in the education system, social justice can go sing. Education, I believe, is both where social justice started to go right and where it has all gone horribly wrong. Scots used to appreciate that education is the key to every door. This appreciation has vanished, and its disappearance is, I think, Scotland's biggest catastrophe. In an area over which Scotland has always had control, after ten years in school: more than half Scotland's pupils fail to get any decent exam grades; the job opportunities of roughly a quarter of Scots are diminished because of poor literacy and numeracy, and these poor literacy rates are directly related to where you live; truancy rates are unacceptably high; and some classrooms are battlegrounds. At the bottom of this dismal litany lies one awful fact: that many Scots – parent and children alike – no longer see education as an escape from their problems; they see it as irrelevant to their problems.

Scots should be hungry for education, particularly those growing up in deprivation. Why is this not so? The answer is partly that, although free state education is a splendid ideal, anything free very quickly becomes devalued. In addition, ideology took over from education towards the end of the 20th century, and particularly in Scotland, was less concerned with teaching a child how to aspire and achieve and more concerned with promoting political agendas and building political empires. Teachers were conscripts in this enterprise: some willing, some less willing. But there was no room for dissent.

The result has been thirty years of Scotland sneering at the well-educated as, by definition, 'snobs' and deriding as 'pushy' and 'elitist'.

It's not new policies we need in education: it's a new attitude. Perhaps, after the teething problems are ironed out, the Curriculum for Excellence will begin the slow process of restoring education to its rightful place in our society – a place of respect. It is, of course, stating the obvious that schools should produce 'successful learners, confident individuals, responsible citizens and effective contributors', as outlined in CfE's voluminous bumph. However, if we can take this as an admission that too many children are emerging from the Scottish state system without these attributes, that's a step in the right direction.

A refusal to admit to shortcomings is, perhaps, one of Scotland's worst characteristics. In education, we see this writ large. Successive devolved governments unthinkingly laud Scots education as 'the best in the world'. I'm sure it could be. But if we are to achieve self-determination both as individuals and as a nation, we need to hear a bit more self-criticism and a little less self-congratulation.

Yours,

Katie

Dear Katie,

Let's get to the heart of the matter: education *should be* a powerful route to self-determination. This involves much more than schools. Learning in all its forms – pre-school, further and higher education and training through work – offers the chance to develop. But let's focus here mainly on children's education. I think you over-egg the pudding a bit – appreciation of education hasn't vanished – but we agree on some fundamentals: for many, education is viewed as largely irrelevant to their lives; and unlocking personal motivation is the key to changing this. Your framing of this is elegant: '*When people are motivated, they usually achieve. When they achieve, they feel powerful*'.

Where to begin? Before school years, the roots of disaffection are found in the early years. If we are to break the cycle that can create such a bleak environment for home learning, we need to first ask why education isn't seen as a priceless opportunity for improvement. That means recognising the poor educational experience of parents whose children are on course for little better, even before they can talk. Working with parents is more likely to help their children thrive when they start nursery and reach the school gate. It's resource intensive but better than flogging the current system.

What about the picture of learning at school? Attainment is measured too narrowly as exam passes. This leads to an annual ritual of slowly improving pass rates being equated with 'success' only to be attacked by those who believe the system is being dumbed down. Even if more young people are clearing the hurdle of five Standard Grade passes – or whatever standard – a sizeable number don't achieve much at school. So, the average attainment of the bottom 20 per cent has barely risen in a decade and Scotland's overall progress for the same period was slower than in the rest of the UK. Not much to get complacent about there.

We can't see the full picture without looking at how schools relate to the world outside, as well as to families. There have always been some young people who fail to gain much from school. Previously that was masked by plentiful jobs for those with few qualifications. But as the number of manual jobs with skills training declined, their options shrunk. Over time, there's been a steady shift towards service jobs needing the now familiar set of soft skills employers say they prize. This is precisely where the schools system has so far failed to adapt. It remains stuck in delivering a curriculum dominated by imparting academic knowledge when the research evidence tells us we should be nurturing the full set of multiple intelligences (technical, sporting, artistic, musical, graphical). *Curriculum for Excellence* makes the right noises – but it resembles angels dancing on the head of a pin as long as this point is lost.

School should be preparation for adult life. What's going to persuade young people to stick with education when it would be easier to switch off and drop out? Experiences of learning that motivate. Secondary education is focused almost exclusively on teaching to boost exam passes to enable young people to get to university. Fine as far as it goes, but for too many, it doesn't work. And even if it does, it's a restricted view of learning.

People with the lowest qualifications had only a 50:50 chance of being in work even before the recession. The number in this group is falling, but casualties keep coming and the risk of detachment for those affected is growing. We need action on all fronts: better contact with families to challenge disengagement; better leadership in secondary schools; and a focus on high quality experiences to develop life skills as well as academic skills.

It's striking that the proportion of young people who left school without a positive destination barely changed during the years of employment growth and the expansion of tertiary education. Consistently about one in eight young Scots are in this group, slightly above the UK rate and higher than virtually every other OECD country. Contrast this again with Denmark where average education attainment is slightly below ours, but the rate of young people failing to move on when they leave school is lowest of all. That has much to do with the close links between employers, education providers and active labour market programmes.

For all the problems with state education in Scotland, I don't think they are the result of it being free. Of course, some things become devalued or over-consumed if there's no cost to the user, but in this case I think the devaluation results from the simple lack of benefit, both perceived and real, experienced by a sizeable minority. The priority is to change that equation. Education systems in other countries deliver notably more for children growing up in poorer families – including the Netherlands and Germany, Canada and Australia. There's plenty of room for innovation within the state system. Now, what would it take to motivate our leaders to really grasp the nettle?

Yours,

Jim

Dear Jim,

On education, we agree on something very important: that what happens at home has a crucial bearing not just on educational attainment, but on attitudes to education. Working with parents is vital. I also agree that education should involve multiple intelligences as you describe them. However, to encourage policy-makers to define education as 'preparation for adult life' or its purpose as inculcating 'life skills' is dangerous, since it both offers encouragement to teachers to abandon hard learning altogether and reinforces young people's belief that if something isn't immediately 'relevant', it isn't worth learning at all. Education is not about that grim catch-all 'relevance', it's about access to and understanding of things that make life worth living. In this respect, 21st century education is surely as much about unemployment as employment; about ideas, artefacts, activities and stories that can lift you out of the slough of despond, often for free. In the modern world, is this not the truth?

Yours,

Katie

Dear Katie,

Welfare reform is the most controversial part of the UK Coalition Government's spending review. A raft of changes will scale back the support people can expect out of work, while a new Universal Credit aims to make work pay more. No welfare-to-work programme can do much to boost weak labour demand. The harsh truth is the current set of reforms is being introduced while Scottish unemployment continues to rise. But rather than speculate on where we're heading, let's first consider how Scotland fared up to the eve of recession.

Work should be central to any social justice strategy. This encompasses unpaid work but here I'll focus mostly on paid work.
The assertion made by politicians of all parties – that work is the best form of welfare – is broadly true. However, a decade of employment growth up to 2008 reveals something more complicated. On the surface, Scotland had a decent story. The employment rate grew to more than three-quarters of the workforce by 2006. Unemployment dropped faster than most of the UK, falling below the English rate at the same time. Employment rose across the population, including those with typically less chance of being in work like single parents and disabled people. Scottish women were among the most likely in Europe to have a job.

We heard much about worklessness during those years – a catch-all term for people claiming out-of-work benefits for sickness and disability as well as unemployment. This fell by about one-fifth as people got jobs, even in places with high rates of worklessness. By 2008, about half households in poor neighbourhoods had someone in work and a majority of children were above the poverty line. Devolution appeared to make only a modest contribution.

Although work cuts the risk of poverty, it's still true that about one in eight working Scots are too low paid to escape poverty. Iain Duncan Smith didn't invent the mantra of making work pay, but the sheer complexity of transitional support and tax credits means in-work support is inadequate. Nor does it keep up with the pace of change at the lower end of the jobs market. People moving from benefits into work are more likely than other workers to lose their job within six months, and the odds of returning to benefit quickly have grown. This experience makes taking a job risky when it should be a further step to self-determination. Being stuck in a revolving door from low pay back to benefits with little prospect of improving skills, or only a little better off in work, attacks motivation.

The standard rate of *Job Seeker's Allowance* (JSA) pays less than £10 a day – not generous but relatively secure set against the kind of jobs likely to be available. As with education, the biggest issue is to improve the risk/reward equation. So we should start by treating even 'mini-jobs' – a few hours a week – as a stepping stone, with clear incentives to move on in terms of childcare support, pay and training. Moreover, we need to take particular care to help young people. In 2009, fully 40 per cent of jobs lost in Scotland were among the under-25s.

But what about those who remained workless? This is one measure where Scotland's progress was much slower during the 'good' years. Take long-term sickness, Incapacity Benefit and its successor Employment Support Allowance. In Glasgow, about one in six people of working age are on the sick, falling slowly as eligibility rules tightened and programmes like *Pathways to Work* gradually helped some claimants back to work. What do we know about the profile of claimants in the city? Most have been on sickness benefits over five years, half claim due to mental health problems, and female claimants are more likely to have a poor work history. We know that you're more likely to move off sickness benefits if you're under 30, been claiming for less than two years, are better educated and have a better work history. The 1980s profile of an ex-manual worker on sickness benefits due to a physical injury has changed substantially. While most people recover from mental health problems, some conditions fluctuate. That means having good days and bad days. And that's a very challenging proposition for employers.

In places where labour demand is weak or where a significant number of public sector job cuts is likely, people moving off sickness benefits after a long time aren't about to skip the jobs queue in any great number. To address this, we'll need a broader approach rather than a singular focus on full-time jobs. Let's start with those claimants (about one in three) who say they would like to move back to work soon. Few of them ever expect to. That gap can be closed. Then let's equip GPs to signpost claimants towards short-time work, without putting their income at risk, until they are able to do more. For others, let's encourage volunteering without affecting benefit. If people aren't fit to work or can't find a suitable job, we should be promoting other forms of being active which can also contribute to recovery.

It's the duty of government to address the culture of fear and fatalism that affects this area of policy. Shuffling people onto other benefits may save money, but won't do much for people's ability to find sustainable work. How about putting wellbeing at the heart of a social justice strategy for recovery? The goal would be to encourage the individual's desire to contribute, provide for themselves and their family, and to do meaningful work. Addressing low pay, the long-tail of low skills and taking a more flexible approach to work would do for starters.

Yours,

Jim

Dear Jim,

Your facts and figures are compelling. Yes, work is central to any social justice strategy since work pays, not just financially but socially too. It's through work, after all, that self-determination as we've described it, i.e. as the capacity of individual Scots to take charge of their own destinies, is most likely to flourish. But apart from that, you'd need the imagination of a stone not to see how demotivating, dispiriting and destructive long term joblessness is. This is why I support Iain Duncan Smith's efforts to simplify state support so that getting back into work is a hayfield, not a minefield.

There's a conundrum, though. You speak of some employees having 'good days and bad days'. This is more than a 'challenging proposition' for employers already half strangled by rights legislation: it's potentially disastrous. I'm not saying that employees don't need rights – of course they do. And certainly, those with mental health problems should not be excluded from the jobs market. But though employers must play their part in the fairer society, how far can they be used as a social service? The balance between state targets and employer goals is as tricky as the balance between wages and benefits. The key is for everybody to feel they're gaining.

This is the crunch with welfare. For maximum benefit to recipients and maximum acceptance by the taxpayer, welfare has to be less of a crutch and more of a conveyer belt, helping people move in a positive direction, i.e. back to independence through employment. I don't buy the easy argument that any kind of restriction or regulation on welfare provision constitutes a moral outrage.

At the moment, Scottish politicians send out extraordinarily mixed messages about the point of welfare. Well, in truth, the Scottish Tories send no message at all; Scottish Labour always take the idle 'anybody questioning welfare is evil' option; and the SNP's focus isn't on welfare, it's entirely on re-election. Yet, if we're looking to self-determination, even though welfare in Scotland is not a devolved issue, how we think about it is vital. Scotland may complain about the Coalition, but at least Westminster is grasping that difficult nettle and though there will be much gnashing of teeth, if we end up with a more beneficial welfare system, one that, as far as is possible through the blunt instrument of the state, actually becomes the hand-up and not just the hand-out, i.e. through preserving the motivation to work, I think, and hope you agree, that future generations will not curse us.

Yours,

Katie

Dear Katie,

The principles behind Iain Duncan Smith's welfare reforms have gained broad support. He has recognised the need to simplify the system for working age people. He has understood that taking a low-paid job is sometimes a risk – and even if people manage to move off benefits, there are other barriers to increasing hours of work. It's hard to disagree when he said getting on the bus is a way to get a job. That's exactly what a large number of people do, often at anti-social hours, to be just a little better off than on benefits. Let's forget the comparison with the Thatcher years. Since then, we've learned how neighbourhood cultures can restrict horizons and create powerful barriers that exclude people from opportunities only a couple of miles away. But he isn't starting from scratch and this isn't the whole story.

More than ten years of New Deal programmes under the last government have taught us some important lessons: it's possible to make progress when employment growth combines with active welfare policies; but progress was held back by a lack of ambition and the sheer complexity of the system under Labour. From where we are now, the big concern is sluggish recovery in the jobs market, even before the impact of spending cuts is felt. But I see two problems for the compulsory work element of the Coalition's Work Programme. First, conflict with low-paid workers who sweep the streets and cut the grass. At a time when their jobs are on the line, does it make sense to substitute them for benefit claimants? The second is a clash with the Community Payback options for offenders serving non-custodial sentences. Are we to have offenders competing with claimants for unpaid work? And what about other conflicting signals – like cutting support for childcare costs and increasing the number of hours worked before tax credits can be claimed. These make little sense and don't help the majority of jobseekers wanting to get back to work quickly.

Now, I'm not defending the status quo. We need a grown-up debate about long-term worklessness, family welfare and other issues that have stirred up concern. You're right – it is destructive to motivation, health and to the prospects of the next generation. And we need account for employer views – they want people who are reliable and ready to learn, not conscripts. So, I would rather see us develop training and work options for those with the poorest work

history. It's possible to distinguish those who have hardly ever worked from those who keep moving in and out of work. We could follow the Dutch approach of transferring benefits over to employment partnerships which are rewarded for getting people into work that lasts, with pre-employment training included for those who need it first.
The priority? Skills training for poorly qualified young people to increase their odds of moving up the ladder, not just getting onto it in the first place, followed by intensive work with households where no-one has had a job for years.

We agree on the need to reform welfare. If we're going to extend compulsion, let us have the imagination to offer quality experiences which are more likely to pay off longer-term than options that grab cheap headlines. And let's track the impact of the changes so that evidence of what works really does become our guide rather than 'Whitehall-knows-best.'

Yours,

Jim

Dear Jim,
There are always reasons for not doing things, and though your concerns about a conflict between the compulsory work element of Iain Duncan Smith's reforms and low-paid workers or offenders on Community Payback schemes are relevant, let's keep them in perspective. IDS's scheme has transformatory potential so let's give it a fair wind. We don't need a grown-up debate: we've had one. Isn't this why IDS is in office? Frank Field must be grinding his teeth ...

So, what does the next decade promise? At the opening of the Scottish Parliament in July 1999, the Queen declared that she had 'confidence in the future of Scotland'. I don't think her confidence misplaced. However, those who fought for the parliament fought as much for its supposed transformatory powers as its correction of a perceived democratic deficit. Nevertheless, Scotland has not been transformed. I don't mean that though smoking has been banned and myriad initiatives unveiled, we're still fat, unhealthy, violent and alcohol fuelled. That's true. But to continue generalising – we're also resilient, stalwart, witty, quirky and sometimes even good company.

What I mean is that far from transforming anything, even politics, Holyrood has turned out to be yet another stagnant pond, its presence welcomed in general by many Scots but its actual use to individual Scots questionable. Take the Scottish news. It's not Holyrood Watch, it's Crime Watch. On the business front, we're listed 18 out 20 in entrepreneurship for advanced economies. On the public services front, though spending in health, for example, is 12 per cent – 16 per cent higher than the UK average, our health service is not 12 per cent – 16 per cent better. In short, we're stuck.

In the next ten years, I'd like to see us unstuck, and I believe this needs a lurch out of the institutional conservatism (note the small c) which glues Scotland to failed models of governance – a bloated and inefficient public sector, the political old boys' network, the musical chair quangocrats making a good living from endless stifling committees – and into an era of institutional dynamism. If this dynamism, by which I mean an openness to ideas and courage to put some of them into practice, was linked to Scotland's much boasted community-mindedness, both communities and individuals might feel they had a vested interest in Scotland's future. Such a lurch doesn't require constitutional independence. In fact, constitutional independence is a red herring. What the lurch requires is the will to throw off of ideological shackles and embrace the revolutionary (for modern Scotland) idea that there's more than one way to do things.

True self-determination arrives when, whatever their birth circumstances, all Scots feel the same sense of hope and possibility. Since neither hope nor possibility cost anything, this can't be beyond us.

Yours,

Katie

Dear Katie,

Scotland has not been transformed by devolution. We agree that we're stuck and that conservatism is manifest, not just in our institutions, but in our narratives and worldview. Your indicators of Scotland's relative position provide a snapshot of where we are. They're certainly part of the story – but snapshots don't tell us how we've fared over time. Let me propose that the glass is half-full *and* half-empty at the same time. Half-full because there has been some progress in recent years: improvements to housing, the employment rate before recession, the NHS (unless you're over 70 and have a chronic condition) and health, if measured by fewer deaths from heart disease and people living longer. From the painstaking task of reducing violence by disrupting gang culture to the proven benefits of housing associations and development trusts, there are signs of brave innovation. But half-empty at the same time, since the rate of progress is slow and trends in alcohol misuse and obesity tell us that even these gains are under threat.

What matters next is how we frame our response. I suspect we'll agree that manifesto pledges and specific government policies seem like a rounding error set against the scale of these issues. We shouldn't give up on the role of government leadership – but we should, by now, recognise its limits. In the next ten years, we need to tackle the bed-fellows of conservatism: complacency (how about the scale of wasted potential before children even start school?) and conformity (taking comfort in what's familiar or similar).

Without action, neither hope nor a sense of possibility will appear where they are currently lacking. They usually emerge from love, consistency and security. When people have lacked these things as children or go on to experience chronic stress, debt, violence and addiction, families don't thrive. Addressing the needs of children before they learn to speak is an obvious test of social justice. There are other significant markers of self-determination as well – enabling frail older people to live well; developing advocacy networks to improve personal skills; supporting carers and volunteers; and making work pay so that it really offers a route to independence. But children's wellbeing in the face of neglect and consumerism? That's a more noble and just national purpose than economic growth.

What does our conversation reveal? Disappointment when we look at the divided social landscape of Scotland. Confusion over why the rivers of investment over ten years produced only modest streams of improvement. Frustration that there's been little serious assessment of why. So, where to next?

The insight of social democrats that structural barriers need to be removed (lack of jobs, poverty, discrimination) has always done battle with the view of conservatives that cultural barriers (attitudes, values, behaviour) matter as well. Looking ahead, we need to combine both. We won't make much progress to self-determination without cutting poverty, but let's do it in ways that build capability and aspiration where know-how, networks and practical support have diminished.

It seems that something important is stirring around the early years, about prevention and autonomy, about living well in older age. What matters is *how* we take these next steps, not just what we do. Maybe tougher times will be a pre-condition for a better kind of Scottish consensus: one that is self-critical and more ambitious. Perhaps then the desire to be in control of our lives will be the starting point for how we reshape public services.

All best,

Jim

Dear Jim,

I'm so glad we agree that positive attitudes, values and behaviour are just as significant as the removal of structural barriers for true self-determination. It's so disappointing – and for some, tragic – that manifest improvements in living conditions over the last 50 years have been overshadowed by a collapse in self-belief, self-motivation and aspiration in communities who could little afford such a collapse. To bicker about who's responsible, as Scottish politicians love to do, is ridiculous. We can't afford to hark backwards. However, the tougher times we're experiencing may finally do for this traditional self-indulgence as we're forced to forge a more restrained and less cripplingly ideological model of state service provision, and people begin to discover their own value once again.

I sense that you're hopeful for the future. I like that. If I'm less so it's because change requires brave imagination and steadfast desire, and our dear Scottish leaders, so far as I can see, show signs of neither. Still, they're quite old and some of them look pretty unhealthy. Perhaps the next lot will surprise me.

Yours,

Katie

The State of Scottish Housing and How We Change It

DOUGLAS ROBERTSON

How does Scottish housing compare?

INTERNATIONAL MEASURES of housing quality reveal Scotland to be a low league player. Mass produced housing, both private and public, built during a long period when energy was cheap, was always going to struggle when the social, cultural, financial and environmental expectations for homes altered some 30 years ago. Comparisons of building standards for Scotland, Denmark, Finland, Norway and Sweden for 2007 found that the 'model' house for Scotland 'does not meet the requirements in any of the other countries considered' (Sullivan, 2007). The reason given for these differences was put as climatic, and in particular the appreciably colder winters. That said, if Swedish standards were adopted here then heating requirements would drop by 23 per cent and CO_2 omissions would fall by 13 per cent, both of which would put Scotland on track to meeting the 'carbon omissions' targets recently set by the Scottish Parliament (which are to reduce carbon omissions by 42 per cent by 2020, over the 1990 level, and by 80 per cent by 2050 (WWF, 2009)). Housing, it is worth remembering, accounts for a third of all carbon omissions.

This is not merely an environmental issue, as important as that is. National survey evidence reveals that a third of Scottish households live in fuel poverty. Fuel poverty is defined where 10 per cent of household income is spent on all household fuel use (Scottish Government, 2010). Between 1991 and 2009, the percentage of dwellings with full central heating rose from 62 per cent to 95 per cent, partly assisted by a government-funded initiative to supply and install central heating to elderly and low-income households. Fuel poverty fell sharply between

1996 and 2002, mainly due to increased income and falling fuel prices. However, fuel poverty has been steadily rising since then, largely because current increases in fuel prices are only being partially offset by rising incomes and energy efficiency increases. So, by 2009 fuel poverty was almost back at 1996 levels. Through passing the Housing (Scotland) Act 2001, the Parliament committed itself to ending fuel poverty 'as far as is reasonably practicable' by 2016.

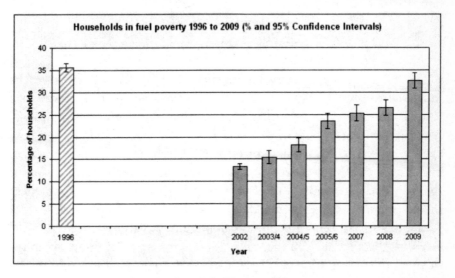

Source: Scottish Government, 2010

The UK generally fares poorly on fuel poverty indicators, compared to its northern latitude counterparts. Scotland, particularly rural areas such as the Highlands and Islands, compare poorly to other parts of the UK (Consumer Focus Scotland, 2010). The marked increased winter mortality in Scotland is linked to this, but we have long chosen to ignore the relationship between housing and health. Many people are simply living in property that fails to adequately protect them against the cold. Comparable small European regions such as the West German Lander, and countries such as Austria, Denmark, Finland, Holland, Norway and Sweden have each performed far better. Critical in this regard are building regulations, which despite recent reviews are still far less onerous in Scotland, when compared to these other nations. Triple glazing, for example, has been mandatory in Denmark for the last three decades; its thermal efficiency exceeds that of many dwelling walls, whether public or private. But what is so galling about this outcome is that it has been achieved despite substantial creative, financial and technical inputs by both the private and public sectors over the past century. Installing central heating systems in thermally inefficient housing ably illustrates this point. We know how to do housing well, but instead we continually opt for mediocrity. As a result over the last century Scotland has paid a far higher price for housing than its near neighbours and still, in relative terms, have the poorest housing conditions in Europe.

Limiting expectations

Arguably, given the outrageous housing conditions inherited from the industrial revolution, expectations were always going to be set extremely low; as a society we have delivered on that. The vast bulk of public housing was originally built to a very basic utilitarian standard, and now aged, is showing many signs of poor long-term maintenance practices and a high degree of obsolescence. As a result, a sizable proportion of this stock has succumbed to clearance over the last 20 years, nowhere more so than in Glasgow which is viewed by many as the epicentre of Scotland's social, economic, political and cultural woes.

With the advent from the mid-1960s of mass private housing, much of this limited ambition has been carried through into this tenure. It's not just that the build quality and design standards were equally poor, reflecting the fact that profit lies more with enhancing land values than producing a high quality housing product, but that cursory attention was paid to high energy usage and to external realm. Both gardens and public open space as well as local community facilities all failed to meet the grade. Scottish comedian Billy Connolly observed that Drumchapel was 'a desert wi windaes' (with windows), an observation which is as equally applicable to the mass of housing which has appeared over the last three decades. It is always odd that debates on housing across the UK, but particularly in Scotland, choose to focus entirely upon the actual built form, ignoring completely the wider environment in which the house is situated. It is here in particular that Scotland's housing miserablism scores so highly – soulless swathes of private 'ticky, tacky boxes' stuck in the middle of absolutely nowhere, contrast only slightly more favourably than the brutalised environments of poverty. For the poor and disposed there are the decrepit warehousing estates which still persist in unimaginable numbers encasing suburban Glasgow, and more generally the environs of west central Scotland, which combined constitute the country's old industrial core.

For 50 years our housing environs have been better planned for cars than for people. The design demands set by road engineers have long taken precedence over the needs of houses and people. This is one major contributor to the marked differences in the design and layout of Scottish and north European housing estates. Design will always be compromised if one objective, that of car movement, is allowed to be pre-eminent.

'Community' is a word often used in official circles to describe these resulting environs, both public and private, but many employing it fail to comprehend its meaning. Community demands far more than merely houses and roads. Despite (or perhaps because of) so much regulation, and thus the pursuit of the lowest common denominator, we continually get housing wrong. However, we continually reassure ourselves that it might not be right, but it's far better than what was there before. Yes, but it is never as good as it could or should be, and there are significant costs attached to pursuing this cheapskate approach.

And now into this long unchallenged mix we are being asked to throw in a new ingredient, that of sustainability. As noted earlier, challenging carbon reduction targets have just been set, and this forced a long awaited re-calibration of the building standards for all new housing. Although still nowhere near equivalent to northern European standards, private builders have reacted in traditional fashion. In their recently published Scottish Election Manifesto they demand their withdrawal, at a time of recession, and offer to compensate the Government through builders making direct financial contributions to carbon reduction funds (Homes for Scotland, 2010). Innovation and forward thinking is something that has long eluded the Luddite Scottish building industry. Contrast this with the building innovation in relation to sustainability and build quality witnessed in Austria, Germany, Holland and Scandinavia over the last 30 years.

Given the limited scale of new house construction taking place at present, the building standard changes will not be the main driver in ensuring improvements in housing quality. Replacement of the current built stock at present construction rates will take over 200 years.

Attention needs to focus on plans to promote the up-grading of existing stock, 90 per cent of which currently fails to comply with these revised building standards.

Partly as a consequence of the developing sustainability agenda, but more driven by a need to improve overall housing standards given the poor results emanating from the Scottish House Condition Survey, a new housing quality standard was introduced in 2004, the Scottish Housing Quality Standard. To meet this standard a house requires to be compliant with the Tolerable Standard, free from serious disrepair, energy efficient, be provided with modern facilities and services, and provide a healthy, safe and secure environment (Scottish Executive, 2004). At the same time, a target date of 2015 was set for all housing to comply with this standard. In 2003, some 500,000 social rented houses failed the standard, which amounted to 70 per cent of the entire social rented stock. The latest report on progress towards the 2015 target notes that by 2008/09 only 35 per cent of the stock now meets the target, with housing associations performing markedly better than local authorities in moving towards achieving that target (Scottish Housing Regulator, 2010). Energy efficiency it appears is proving a major challenge.

That is bad enough, but two other factors should be noted. Firstly, three times as many private houses, some 1.5 million, failed to meet the standard in 2004, yet local authorities were only asked to monitor the condition of private housing. Grant awarding powers to private owners were abandoned in 2006. Other bodies provide means tested grants for cavity wall and loft insulation, policies that have been around for over 40 years. The focus here is on home-owners and landlords getting their own houses in order, a tall order.

Secondly, this housing quality benchmark unfortunately still represents a very basic standard, one that is far less arduous than the equivalent English and Welsh target. Further, it in no way mirrors the revised building standards, which in turn fail to meet that expected in other northern European countries. It also says a great deal that the core element of the Scottish quality benchmark, the Tolerable Standard, dates back to the early 1960s and was explicitly designed to determine whether or not to demolish a slum property. Some 50 years on we thus still judge quality in terms of Victorian slum clearance policy. We set low benchmarks, then fail to achieve them.

For nearly two decades, real innovation in sustainability has been pursued as a cottage industry via one-off pilot projects by housing associations. Now, as a result of the swingeing public expenditure cuts, the capital subsidy to undertake this work will be withdrawn. While such projects did generate material for the never-ending stream of Ministerial press releases, it did 'hee haw' to change public attitudes and focus attention on the changes sustainability demanded.

Private house builders, for their part, still find solace in continually adopting a King Canute stance to sustainability and quality matters. Addressing sustainability through enhancing build quality is seen to be an affront to profit margins. Those picking up the baton were underfunded, and thus unable to mainstream their work. Now there is no funding. For their part Governments, or more accurately their civil servants, have continually resisted attempts to raise standards fearing the public expenditure consequentials and the resultant impact upon their budgets. This tradition has now become effectively institutionalised given the long dominant political mantra in the UK of not raising income tax.

So, while other countries pioneer new technologies and get them mainstreamed, we prefer to stick with what we already know – hiding under the weight of our familiar heavy blankets and quilts, while expressing deep scepticism at the light and airy 'continental quilt' approaches. No wonder Scotland has become a housing laboratory which attracts foreign housing and planning professionals to see how not to go about things.

So why has this been so?

The big problem with housing policy is that it has never just been about housing. At both the national and local levels other ambitions are always slipped into the mix and, on occasions, these have been so substantive that the original housing objective has been overwhelmed. Historically, when Lloyd George first introduced council housing in 1919, it was to be a concrete illustration of the irrelevance of Bolshevism. Later, Macmillan's mass council house construction programme of the 1950s, which threw up the fore mentioned notorious peripheral schemes, was as much about soaking up the post-war labour surplus and giving the private builders a financial fillip to help them get back on their feet, as it was to provide new homes for those suffering overcrowding. The private housing boom that emerged out of the 1960s was more about the development and marketing of new financial products than a response to pent up consumer demand. And now, as we pick our way through the fallout from yet another financial disaster brought about by a ballooning housing market, we fail to recognise it was all about institutional greed and manipulation, which feted home owners to view continually rising house prices as Mammon.

House price inflation harms the housing ambitions of the many and rewards the few – a perspective the media rarely acknowledges.

If these illustrate the macro contradictions inherent in housing policy the micro ones are equally substantive, but they have gone largely unseen and unchallenged. Council housing has for too long been as much about feeding the local councils corporate ambitions as their housing ones. Direct Labour Organisations (DLO), the council organisations originally created to build council housing, quickly transformed themselves into highly inefficient maintenance organisations when the money for construction dried up in the late 1970s. The DLOs, as large-scale employers, exercised their political clout through the trade union movement. This, in turn, had ensured the favourable attention of councilors who saw the political advantage of facilitating an ever more privileged working environment, which tenants paid for in full. Glasgow's housing department's survival in its new guise, as the Glasgow Housing Association (following the entire stock transfer and its £1 billion debt write off) was as much about preserving a DLO fiefdom, as improving the atrocious housing conditions suffered by their tenants.

In addition, long standing accounting practices adopted by all councils have ensured substantial sums have been filched from the 'ring fenced' Housing Revenue Account (HRA) to pay for the provision of a host of other council services, whether these be cleansing, parks and recreation, legal services or general administration. Block charges made to the HRA for 'services' occurs because it represents one of the few independent and unregulated income streams that flow into council coffers. But why are homeless services universally charged to housing and not to social work budgets? And why in West Lothian were the neighbourhood council offices charged solely to the HRA, and not the General Fund. As a result of such creative accounting, the poor were unknowingly forced to pay a high price for their mediocre housing, given that they were unwittingly subsidising other Council services. Why has this never need challenged? Surely Councils should not be adopting accounting practices that ensure the poorest subsidise the services provided to the many?

The most obvious explanation as to why this occurred was that tenants lost their political power. Nowadays very few tenants pay rent from their wages. Instead, rental income comes from Housing Benefit and is paid directly to tenants by the Department of Works and Pensions. In the eyes of officials, what's the harm? Its just Government money and those on benefit are not disadvantaged.

For a long time, improving housing conditions was a core political ambition of all Governments. From 1919 through to the late 1960s, this was largely achieved through the mass construction of new council housing for working class families, under a variety of differing subsidy arrangements. As a result, by the mid 1970s some two thirds of the Scottish population resided in some form of public housing, whether Council, New Town Corporations or the Scottish Special Housing Association. This was a large political and diverse constituency, but one that had few champions. When public money got tight, political commitment conveniently waned.

Substantial tracks of public investment were withdrawn from council housing capital budgets from the 1960s onwards. This was in response to both the Gold Standard Financial Crisis of 1967 and a decade later, the IMF crisis in 1977. From then on the focus was on promoting home ownership, and capital investment was switched away from clearance to the improvement and renovation of older private housing. Interestingly, the very last remnants of capital funding for housing have just been swept away in response to the latest financial crisis; percentage wise, cuts in the housing budget have been only second to those inflicted on higher education.

It was the earlier financial crises that heralded the introduction of the 'Right to Buy'. Given deep discounting, for anyone paying the full rent it made financial sense to either buy their council house or purchase on the open market. Again, council house sales were not all about housing, but rather a means to cut public expenditure and hopefully change individual political outlooks. The first of these objectives was delivered. The generated sales receipts were recycled by councils, and thus reduced their call on government funding. However, changing political allegiances through the overt promotion of a 'property owning democracy' was less successful, at least within a Scottish context (Williams et al, 1987). Tenants bought their houses, but increasingly voted anti-Tory.

But the 'Right to Buy' helped to accelerate already well-established social trends, which had occurred from the 1960s onwards. The rights of the individual increasingly took precedence over those of the collective. Hence, homelessness and matrimonial homes legislation, as well as statutorily defined needs based allocation systems, helped ensure poorer, marginalised people gained access to council housing. The advent of Housing Benefit helped them pay for it (Robertson and Smyth, 2009). So the 'good' housing, which had traditionally been allocated to the 'good' tenants, was taken out of the council house mix by the 'Right to Buy', just at the time as others were at last accessing it.

This has had profound social, financial and political repercussions. While financially the 'Right to Buy' was largely neutral for local authorities, it did result in its tenant base becoming almost wholly dependent upon benefits. Housing tenure now accurately mirrored what had become a far more socially polarised society. Reflecting this changed reality, council was re-badged as social housing so no one would miss its new welfare function. And this aptly illustrates the real political irony of the current devolution settlement; Westminster has far more say and impact upon Scottish social housing, and the third of the population housed by it (as the imminent Housing Benefit cuts will so aptly illustrate) than a Housing Minister with all his devolved powers but now no budget.

So what can we do about all this?

The poor live in poor quality houses, and these are expensive to heat. The wealthy live in better quality houses, but these can also be thermally poor. The difference here is that the rich can afford to heat them. Residents of social housing are seeing conditions slowly improve as the Scottish Housing Quality Standard (SHQS) 2015 target draws closer, but given its low ambition that is not saying that much. Evidence provided by the Housing Regulator reveals it is the thermal targets that are proving to be the big sticking point.

So how best to address this? The polluter pays is a widely accepted policy premise, but not yet in housing despite its major contribution to greenhouse gases. We could simply increase energy costs, via taxation, and thus force improvements in energy efficiency. We could operate a discount or premium charging arrangement for local property taxes depending on a properties energy efficiency rating, again promoting changed behaviours. Yet, while the rich could afford to respond to such stimuli, those on lower incomes could not. Social housing tenants would be dependent on the cash flow of their landlords, and they might only be able to respond by increasing rents and thus further intensifying the 'poverty trap' that currently afflicts this tenure. Given the evidence provided by the House Condition Survey, those who are tenants of private landlords, find themselves in the worst position, but the solution would have a similar impact financially. So, would the Government help fund the necessary investment in the housing stock? Given the social and environmental significance of such changes, and the fact they have set themselves clear targets both for fuel poverty and carbon reductions, this would seem an obvious yes. Given both the current public expenditure cut backs, and a pattern of reducing Scottish housing capital spend through expanding Westminster Housing Benefit revenue spend, this would represent a challenge.

It's also critical that we learn to invest in and value quality in all its various dimensions, in both new build and the existing housing stock. Equally, we should be willing and able to address poor housing quality and performance, given its major negative consequences for both individuals and society. Poor quality houses are today's slums, it's just we have chosen not to increase our benchmark of quality to reveal them as such. We also need to roll out successful innovation and that will demand the public support of creative and innovative work, while at the same time having mechanisms in place to properly mainstream successes. We require to increase our quality standards, reward and properly promote good innovative design while also educating ourselves that this embraces far more than house style. Functionality and simplicity in the design and use of space, both external and internal, and mode of operation are critical in this regard. Such an agenda will, in turn, demand that we address the woeful state of the building industry. For far too long, at all levels it has worked against creativity, quality and professionalism. Change here is critical. Overall, these are clear objectives; we have the talent. All that is lacking is the collective will to do this.

Taking forward this agenda in its various guises demands locally focused solutions and organisations. Both central and local government have failed to step up to the mark. Creating community assets, which can be used to reinvest in communities, is something the long under-utilised community-based housing associations has much experience off. As small locally accountable and focused organisations, they could facilitate other community initiatives such as district heating schemes within urban and clustered rural contexts. There is thus a strong case to expand community ownership, something that has been effectively mothballed since 1996. Critical to community ownership is access land; given the assets this helps to produce, and the income stream that can be derived from such assets.

In terms of funding these activities, we need to reinstate the link between property value and local taxation. Lloyd George understood the redistributive potential of property and thus proposed a land tax, for which a comprehensive register of land ownership was drawn up (Wightman, 2010). Yet such radicalism has not been on anyone's agenda for almost a century. While reforming local taxation is within the current powers of the Parliament, this has not been seriously considered. Other potential options, such as the Swedish house space tax, do exist. But this has less re-distributive potential than a land value tax, which should be the goal (Wightman, 2010). Other fiscal arrangements would demand a new constitutional settlement, and a society that demanded changes commensurate with challenges posed by our dramatically changing situation.

Conclusion

The case articulated here is that over time housing has become more and more detached from housing per se, but rather is a vehicle to support and fund a host of other ambitions. This has resulted in a decline of housing's overt political cache, in that it is the policy extras rather than housing itself that takes on prominence. What we need to do is re-establish housing as a core policy of Government, but one that is implemented and managed locally. Housing can and should be used to support other ambitions such as developing and re-designing communities and helping change the way we live. It also needs to link into a host of other facilities, and be viewed more collectively and communally - not just individually. It also demands to be conceptualised as a societal rather than merely a physical entity. Housing should be a critical building block in creating a fully functioning civil society, and that is something we desperately need to relearn.

The core aim of Scottish housing policy should be to achieve design, environmental and social 'excellence' rather than mere 'tolerability'. In seeking to achieve such a goal, if we do not quite succeed then at least the housing would be decent. There is a model of how to do this – we just need to learn from our northern European neighbours. What we can add is our understanding of community and some clear thinking as to how we can ensure local governance is truly local. And given the current financial and energy crises, what better time to do this?

References

Consumer Focus Scotland (2010), *Turning up the heat: Benchmarking fuel poverty in Scotland*. Glasgow: Consumer Focus Scotland.

Homes for Scotland (2010), *Homes for Scotland Election Manifesto*, Edinburgh: Homes for Scotland.

Robertson, D. and Smyth, J. (2009), 'Tackling squalor? Housing's contribution to the welfare state', *Social Policy Review*, 21, 87–108.

Robertson, D., Smyth, J. and McIntosh, I. (2010), 'Neighbourhood identity: The path dependency of class and place', *Housing, Theory and Society*, 27, 3, 258–273.

Scottish Executive (2004), 'Standards set for Scottish housing', http://www.scotland.gov.uk/News/Releases/2004/02/5000

Scottish Government (2010), *Quality–Fuel Poverty: High level summary of statistics trend*, http://www.scotland.gov.uk/Topics/Statistics/Browse/ Housing-Regeneration/TrendFuelPoverty

Scottish Housing Regulator (2010), *Scottish Housing Quality Standard–Progress Update 2008–09*, Glasgow: Scottish Housing Regulator.

Sullivan, L. (2007), *A Low Carbon Building Standards Strategy for Scotland: Report of a Panel Appointed by Scottish Ministers*, Edinburgh: Scottish Government.

Wightman, A. (2010), *The Poor Had No Lawyers: Who Owns Scotland (And How They Got It)*, Edinburgh: Birlinn Press.

Williams, N., Sewel, J. and Twine, F. (1987), 'Council house sales and the electorate: Voting behaviour and ideological implications', *Housing Studies*, 2, 4, 274–282.

World Wildlife Fund and Energy Agency (2010), *Achieving our potential: An analysis of area-based approaches to improving energy efficiency in Scotland's Homes*, Dunkeld: WWF and Energy Agency.

Environmental Self-Determination and Lifelong Education

EURIG SCANDRETT

Introduction

THIS CHAPTER WILL EXPLORE the opportunities for self-determination in Scotland's environment. At the heart of this lies the fundamental contradiction between the interests of economic growth, and those of social welfare and a healthy environment. One model for addressing this would be through a transformed planning system, in which economic interests are accountable to social and environmental interests. Drawing on the example of the 2006 Scottish Planning Act it is argued that, by seeking to compromise between these interests, it has inevitably favoured the former. However, to achieve the objective of self-determination also confronts a second contradiction which plagues ecological literature, that of local democracy against wider constraints of social justice and environmental limitations. It is a significant challenge for the participation of local and sectoral interests to reflect the context of a global environment and future generations.

The problems faced in achieving such ecological self-determination will be considered in the context of local communities and workers. Moreover, ecological self-determination should be regarded as a project of lifelong education, in which collective learning is a dialectical process of combining contradictory relations, rather than the linear or set-piece adversarial arrangements which pass as democratic public administration. Transforming our educational institutions could play a fundamental role in constructing such strong self determination.

Environmental planning and democracy in Scotland

In 1992, when world leaders met in Rio de Janeiro for the United Nations Conference on Environment and Development, there was a certain amount of euphoria as 'sustainable development' was presented as the winning formula for achieving the combined objectives of ending poverty and protecting the environment. The report of the Conference, 'Agenda 21', for a decade provided the framework for a wide range of policy, and especially in relation to governance and decision-making on the environment (UN 1992). Agenda 21 placed a great emphasis on the responsibility of states to involve diverse sectors of their populations in democratic processes to achieve a healthy and socially just environment, and especially sectors which were structurally excluded through unequal power relationships – women, children, indigenous people, workers.

Whilst the euphoria has long gone, and the formula 'sustainable development' has been effectively captured for use by the interests of big capital and neo-liberal policy, it is valuable to be reminded that, despite its flaws, Agenda 21 contained within it the potential for self-determination on the environment. Chapter 28 of Agenda 21 especially identified the local community as a particular location from which sustainable development can be built, from the bottom up. Local development planning, under the auspices of local authorities as the section of statutory government 'closest to the people', could be a means of involving these diverse interests in achieving a 'Local Agenda 21'. In 2006, some time after the influence of Agenda 21 had waned, Scotland's parliament passed an Act designed to 'bring in a much more inclusive and efficient planning system to improve community involvement, support the economy, and help it to grow in a sustainable way'.

The 2006 Planning Act was heralded as a major improvement in land use and development planning in Scotland (Scottish Government, 2006). It was sponsored by the Labour-Liberal Democrat coalition, and implemented in its entirety by the minority SNP administration from 2007. The Act was not inspired by the lofty principles of Agenda 21 but was a response to internal pressure from two directions. From developers came the accusation that planning law was slow and bureaucratic, a license for local nimbyism and too often creating an expensive barrier to development and therefore to economic growth: hence the objective of an 'efficient planning system to ... support the economy and help it to grow'. On the other hand, there was pressure from local communities, community councils and other representatives (as well as environmental organisations) that the planning system was stacked in favour of developers, that those affected had little control over decisions, and that too often unwanted and unsustainable developments were granted permission despite the environmental and social damage which they cause: hence the objective of the reforms for a 'more inclusive ... system to improve community involvement'.

These opposing objectives were to be achieved by separating developments into three kinds – Local, Major and National. Local developments are small and largely non-controversial, and require minimal public scrutiny. At the other end of the scale, National developments are those deemed to be of such national significance that decisions are made by government ministers, essentially bypassing local consultation. Major developments, require a higher level of public consultation by developers prior to seeking planning permission, to bring community views into the development and resolving as many objections as possible before the formal planning application.

At the time of writing, it is too early to say whether the Act was successful in its own terms. Already the National Developments are encountering problems. Selected and published in the National Planning Framework 2 in 2008 (Scottish Government 2008), the developments regarded as too important for local public consultation include such controversial and environmentally damaging proposals as the coal-fired power station at Hunterston, a gas-fired power station at Cockenzie and airport runway extensions at Glasgow, Edinburgh and Aberdeen. These have since been subject to judicial review (Hunterston), conflicts between SNP-led local authority and SNP national policy (Cockenzie) and campaigns of direct action (Aberdeen airport).

Contradictions of development planning and multi-criteria alternatives

Whatever the efficacy of the Act, it was a lost opportunity to introduce a strong, democratic planning system based on self-determination. Alternative, democratic resource planning mechanisms exist in the environmental literature, including such diverse approaches as contingent valuation (for example, assessing the value which local populations attach to environmental resources through surveying their 'willingness to pay' for its preservation, in comparison with the economic value of proposed development), citizens' juries, and stakeholder events such as 'future search' and multi-criteria analysis (O'Connor, 2000). Forms of this latter mechanism in particular hold the opportunity for a strong planning system because it addresses the fundamental conflict between economic and social interests, as described below. What the reformed and former planning systems had in common was a separation between the economic decision making of the developer and the social and environmental concerns of the local and wider populations. In a market economy, in which economic factors are generally privileged over social considerations, it is appropriate to separate these two forms of decision making to prevent the corruption of economic interference with social benefit. However, greater control over environmental decision making could be delivered by taking economic considerations relating to development out of market relations and making these accountable to social criteria.

In the current situation, economic cost-benefit analyses are considered by the developer prior to entering the planning system to make sure that the project is economically viable, and that they will get an adequate return on their investment, before considering seeking planning permission. For a developer, this economic imperative is paramount, whilst the planning process is a necessary hurdle to pass in order to realise the economic benefit. The projects that are considered for planning are only those which provide sufficiently high economic returns for the developer. Even where the developer is a public body and the project is designed for social benefit, economic viability remains paramount, the business case trumps the social case, and market conditions remain unquestioned. The economic criterion, or 'bottom line', supersedes any social or environmental criteria.

Multicriteria analysis (MCA) opens up the criteria for selection of development projects to democratic scrutiny (Martinez-Alier, 2002; O'Connor, 2000). Although not all forms of MCA include economic criteria, the mechanism makes it possible to treat economic considerations the same as criteria which may be generated by local, national or special interest groups, rather than privileging cost-benefit analysis above all others. Return on investment may be high on the agenda of developers and their investors, but the local community may prioritise the creation of decent local jobs, the provision of local services or entertainment, the resolution of local conflicts or the protection of locally valued environmental features.

Other stakeholders might add the protection of biodiversity, the provision of adequate housing, the generation of electricity, the promotion of public education etc. Multicriteria analysis allows these criteria to be placed alongside the economic imperative of developers and subjected to democratic scrutiny. Multiple types of development, including proposals from the local community or existing workforce, can be assessed for their fulfillment of this range of criteria.

Multicriteria analysis is one of a number of mechanisms which have been identified by ecological and socialist writers for bringing decision making, including economic decision making, under democratic control of stakeholders and away from the market (Devine, 1988; Pepper, 1993; Albert, 2003). That the 2006 Planning Act did not consider such radical transformations to planning is disappointing, although unsurprising given the adherence to neo-liberalism of all the major parties. However, the challenge for ecologists and those on the left who would advocate such economic democracy is whether such a radical transformation could deliver social justice within ecological limitations. Current experience suggests that it would not unless, alongside these structural changes, a stronger sense of self-determination is achieved.

Workers, trades unions and a just transition

One of Agenda 21's less known sections is Chapter 29, *Workers and their Trade Unions*, which promoted participation in sustainable development by the collective organisation of workers. Trade unions constitute a major historical force which contributed to the construction of democracy, and have successfully institutionalised significant features of working class interests and democratic forms of accountability (Williams, 1989). The historical zenith of the trade union movement and its parliamentary representation in the Labour party was the post-war settlement of welfare state and Keynesian social democracy, which was achieved in many parts of the industrialised capitalist world. However, despite the continuation of social democratic rhetoric, that settlement is in decline and being replaced with neo-liberal policies by parties of all political persuasions, including the major parties in Holyrood. Nonetheless, in the context of this weakened position, the trades union movement continues to make a significant contribution to democracy in society and economy, although not always in the environment, to protect some of the 150 jobs that would be lost with decommissioning.

A wide range of trades unions, including the STUC, have given support to the principles of just transition: that the transition to a sustainable society must occur in such a way that protects the workers who are currently employed in unsustainable industries. At its most radical, the just transition approach is a trade union led initiative in which workers themselves identify alternative, environmentally beneficial and socially useful employment opportunities drawing on their own skills and aspirations, leading to a worker-led (and presumably publicly funded) transition to sustainability. With its roots in the defence diversification movement back to the Lucas Aerospace Joint Shop Stewards' Alternative Plan in 1972 (Cooley, 1980), this approach continues to inspire radical social and environmental action amongst trade union activists and community workers. Its main problem is that it has never succeeded beyond producing alternative plans and marginal activities and its capacity for the effective redeployment of the thousands of workers employed in fossil fuel and petrochemical industries, let alone the diverse destructive and toxic industries throughout Scotland, remains untested. The vested interests of company owners, investors, executives, senior managers and political leaders are sufficiently threatened that a very strong countervailing force would be needed to force through a just transition.

However there is a deeper problem, which is the perceived interests of the workers themselves, not all of whom are convinced of the necessity to decommission unsustainable industries. Despite a position in favour of just transition, the STUC has publicly supported the development of the new coal-fired power station at Hunterston which, apart from its contribution to climate disruption, would be dependent on opencast coal developments which ravage working class communities across central Scotland, as well as imported coal from Columbian companies with a troubling human rights record in relation to their own trade unionists.

Community and industry

Another currently unused part of the 2006 Planning Act is the introduction into law of Good Neighbour Agreements. In its original form, this was the invention of the US environmental lawyer Sanford Lewis (Lewis and

Henkels, 2001) and was experimented with in Scotland with the energy-from-waste incinerator at Baldovie, Dundee (Friends of the Earth Scotland, 2004). In theory, Good Neighbour Agreements are contracts between the owners of polluting factories and their neighbouring communities, in which the company agrees to adhere to additional concessions set by the community, such as higher emission standards than the statutory minimum. Such agreements help to shift the balance of power towards the community and tend to work only when the community has some leverage or potential sanction against the company, whether legally sanctioned or through collective action. Although instrumental in introducing the Good Neighbour Agreement to the Dundee incinerator, I now believe it was not a success, partly due to the weakness of such a leverage, but also because of a weakness in self-determination.

The company which owns the incinerator, Dundee Energy Recycling Limited (DERL), is a joint venture including Dundee City Council, and the involvement of elected councillors in the Good Neighbour Agreement both facilitated the establishment of a liaison committee to address the demands of the community and also constrained what was legitimated as demands on the company. Moreover, the community representatives themselves were unambitious in their demands and the DERL management took the lead in what they regarded as community accountability – largely glossy newsletters with company editorial control. Essentially, there was no shift in power between the company and the community beyond what already existed through the involvement of elected councillors and the democratic mechanism of a publicly owned company. However, the community achieved concessions to prevent incinerator-related vehicle movements through housing estates whilst children were travelling to and from school, and to double the frequency of monitoring for dioxins (the agreement to make public monitoring data was never fully fulfilled). Despite the poor environmental record of the incinerator (three major fires occurred in the plant in the first two years of operation, the company reported exceeding its permitted emission levels 20 times and has received additional public funds to achieve its legal environmental standards) the community could exert no leverage to constrain its activities or have it shut down.

Good Neighbour Agreements, as Lewis and Henkel (2001) argue, are only as valuable as the sanctions which can be applied against the company, whether legal sanctions or from the mobilising strength of community action or the workers' trade union. The form in which they occur in the Planning Act, as voluntary agreements with statutory backing, has yet to be put to the test and the version included in the Act is unlikely to provide the legal sanction necessary (Comb, 2007). However, in order for this to be tested and to build a strong system of accountability of industry to their local communities, there needs also to be the capacity in the community for self-determination in a strong sense.

Community self-determination and subsidiarity

Ecological politics has consistently argued for greater subsidiarity of decision making, more community empowerment, organisation of social life on a decentralised and in some cases bioregional geographical basis. However, some writers have also pointed out the contradiction between local decision making and wider social interests of justice, equality, redistribution, environmental protection and ecological constraints. A certain leap of faith is required that all local communities will manage their resources sustainably or will voluntarily donate surplus – let alone essentials – to less resourced and needy communities, especially when these communities are in the future. That all communities will, when the burden of higher powers is lifted, start treating their own minorities with justice, refrain from exploiting workers and allocate labour in a gender-equal way, is also unlikely. Within the current planning system, communities and sectoral interests are often divided, self-interested, short-term and reluctant to accept reductions to their own privilege, let alone voluntarily opt for the lifestyle constraints which would be required for Scots to live within our fair share of the ecological limitations of the planet. This is what Mills has described as the contradiction between ecoauthoritarianism (demanding ecological constraint) and ecoradicalism (grassroots participatory democracy) in green political thought (Mills, 1996).

False consciousness has always been a problem for the left: the capacity of the powerful and privileged to portray their own interests as universal, and through their influence on the public discourse, to get the rest of us to incorporate their interests into the common sense of our own. For the green left, there is the additional problem that, when global ecological resources are taken into account, the basic lifestyle in the post-industrial, former colonial, 'developed' countries such as Scotland constitutes privilege which is hidden from consciousness. Even many of the basic necessities of the poor in Scotland which are, and should be, regarded as rights are produced at the expense of the majority of the world's poor and future generations. With such false consciousness, how is radical democratic participation able to produce environmental governance with social justice?

Moreover, local democratic participation which is constrained by political structures at a higher level leaves open the potential of distribution of environmental costs, and this is especially true when market forces remain intact, since this will always shift costs onto the cheapest and least resistant sink. This is the contradiction of participation and accountability, the fallacy of David Cameron's 'Big Society', and what, with reference to the weakness at the heart of the UN Conference on Environment and Development, was called the 'Hidden Agenda 21': what communities and excluded groups are being invited to participate in is what is left when the market has finished distributing the costs and benefits unequally. Attempts in the USA, following pressure from the environmental justice movement, of planned zones in order to distribute environmental damage 'fairly' have failed (Stevens, 2003) – so long as societies cause environmental damage, the rich and powerful will ensure that they do not have to live with it, and the poor and powerless will carry the burden.

Strong community self determination

'Community' has a tendency to be reified. It is not, however, a fixed geographical body or assemblage of people with representatives who can express its view, but rather a process of social construction. Martin (2003) has argued that the ambiguity of community contains within it the possibilities of a politics of freedom which is helpful in our consideration of environmental self-determination. He suggests that community 'is posed as a relational concept which articulates the shared experience of groups, or collectivities, of people … at an intermediate, or meso, level of social reality… It is in the dialectics of community, understood in this way, that people experience, collectively, the possibilities of agency within the pre-existing constraints of structure' (Martin, 2003, 61). Therefore, communities can be regarded as learning crucibles in which people test out, dispute and construct their collective views, their identities and interests in their environment with those who share a stake in this process. Only then can self-determination of the environment be constructed. Until we achieve this, opportunities for democratic participation in environmental and other resource based decision making will be constrained by the vested interests of power and how that divides the interests of the people. Moreover, communities engaged in such a process can connect with others to form meta-communities – or social movements – which engage in the processes of testing out, disputing and constructing collective views, identities and interests, most often in pursuit of common dissent against the powerful. Collective protest is a galvanising process of demanding answers to the flaws in society (Crowther, 2006).

A strong version of self-determination involves not only the structural transformation of decision making to ensure economic accountability and subsidiarity (where appropriate), but also a dynamic which ensures an ongoing process of dialogue. This dialogue aims to involve the collective interests of all stakeholders in communities, including where these interests cannot be expressed – those affected groups that cannot directly be represented, including future generations and the non-human environment. This is essentially an educational task. Gramsci's (1972) much-quoted phrase that 'every relationship of hegemony is necessarily an educational relationship' applies to the dialogical process of exposing power and privilege across continents and between generations as much as between classes. This is the project which Raymond Williams (1989) described as an 'educated and participating democracy'. However, it is considerably broader and more exhaustive than the current institutions of education, still less what passes for 'education for sustainable development' under the UN decade on this theme, 2005–2014. It is an altogether more dynamic and dialectical process, a political project.

Strong self-determination contains that educational task of holding together in dialectical tension the local and the global (or more specifically the global within the local, and at the same time the local in the global); the specific and the generic; the concrete and the abstract; the particular and the general; resistance and creativity. Freire in his *Pedagogy of the Oppressed* (1972) describes this process of connecting these dialectical opposites in a thematic universe:

It is as transforming and creative beings that *human beings* [men], in their permanent relations with *their environment* [reality], produce not only material goods ... but also social institutions, ideas, and concepts... These themes imply others which are opposing or even antithetical; they also indicate tasks to be carried out and fulfilled. Thus historical themes are never isolated, independent, disconnected, or static; they are always interacting dialectically with their opposites. Nor can these themes be found anywhere except in the *human-environment* [men-world] relationship. The complex of interacting themes of an epoch constitutes its 'thematic universe'. (Freire, 1972, 73–4. Italics indicate gender-neutral and environmentally appropriate alternatives to original terms, which are retained in square brackets.)

As Martin (2003) acknowledges, this project gives the appearance of Habermas' (1984) communicative rationality, in which the process of discerning clarity between diverse claims seeks to achieve a shared and rationally defensible, secular and normative space within the lifeworld in order to banish the colonising powers of economic and bureaucratic rationality. However, as Fraser (1987) has pointed out, Habermas underestimates the role of social power in the civic space in which such communicative rationality is supposed to be played out. The more dialectical approach of self-determination, incorporating Freire's pedagogical method, recognises the role of power and occurs rather in the space of resistance, in the posing of problems which are both political and environmental.

Scott and Gough (2003) have developed a comprehensive proposal for an educational approach to sustainable development. They argue that the interrelationships between environmental, social and economic problems lead to situations of such complexity and inherent uncertainty that solutions can only be found by addressing problems simultaneously from several different viewpoints. They argue for *meta-learning,* a collective social process which is able to harness diverse learning situations working with multiple epistemologies. Insights from multiple formal and informal processes of learning in concrete situations are systematically distilled at a higher organisational level. Thereby, whole societies are able to learn what is necessary for sustainable development to occur.

For Scott and Gough, real situations are too complex to usefully describe relations as socially or environmentally 'just' or 'unjust', or to identify groups as 'oppressed' or 'oppressor', or to identify a direction of social change which achieves greater social justice. They are therefore dismissive of the pedagogical approach of Freire and the associated radical education tradition on the grounds that it 'tends to be associated with a particular egalitarian project in which superior social knowledge – which dismisses contrary opinion as either selfishness or false consciousness – coupled with socialist managerial ingenuity, will create a collectivist utopia' (Scott and Gough, 2003, 49). On the contrary, they argue that complex problems can only be addressed through expansive and open ended social learning processes. However, they acknowledge the impact of inequality and power on these deliberations:

> the question of understanding sustainable development and related learning revolves not around *how* to sustain things, but about *whose* things it is proposed to sustain, *what* is to be developed in *whose* interests, and *who* is to be encouraged to learn *what*. (Scott and Gough, 2003, 26)

Such inequalities are not provided with structural explanations. It is hard to find answers to their rhetorical questions without resorting to the structural categories of class, gender, 'race', geographical location and generation to which they object. However, there is much in Scott and Gough's analysis that is commendable, not least for the importance they place on education in the achievement of social change towards a sustainable relationship between society and ecology. To their complex of particular education and metalearning can be added more dialectical approach, such as that proposed by Harvey (1996), which can provide a process closer to what might be regarded self-determination. Harvey points out that social change occurs through dialectical interactions between 'moments', which give the appearance of stability but always in the process of change through their own internal contradictions. The dialectical relationship between the various moments of social change mean that it is impossible to consider one moment without simultaneously considering the extent to which it contains the dynamics of other moments. Thus, if we are to understand self-determination of the environment as a process, it is essential to recognise the relationship between a community and its environment is dialectically related to its wider social relations, power relations, material practices, knowledge production, value systems and discourse construction.

So how might this educational project be conducted? Scotland has a range of institutional opportunities. Since its inception with the Alexander Report in 1975, community education has been a potent source of the methodologies for responding to the challenge of self-determination, although is now in significant retreat. Under New Labour, the profession found itself somewhat confined to its centre base through 'Community Learning and Development', restricted to fulfilling management targets and as a non-statutory section of the education departments of most local authority, being first in line for cuts. Despite constant institutional marginalisation, the practices of community education are being sustained in some areas of the profession, in the voluntary sector and in the university departments of community education (see, for example, Shaw and Wallace, 2008; Emejulu and Shaw, 2010).

Higher education policy has again been pushed further towards privatisation, although there have remained opportunities for dialectical engagement with environmental processes in support of groups engaged in struggles for justice (see Agents for Environmental Justice and Scandrett, 2003). Trades unions have successfully developed a network of union learning representatives who bring such interactions with the environment to the workplace, and communities engaged in resistance construct their own learning processes, drawing on sources of knowledge directly useful to their struggles (Scandrett et al, 2010). Environmental campaigners have experimented with educational work which has, for example, used popular education to build connections with communities facing similar forms of pollution in different parts of the world; construct dialogues between anti-airport expansion direct action environmentalists and fuel poverty campaigners; training workshops on the logistics of ecovillage construction on illegally occupied land during Camps for Climate Action (Scandrett, 2008).

A strategy for lifelong education can be built on the institutions and projects which exist in Scotland in order to support to this plethora of initiatives. What is needed is the flexibility and resources to be able to respond to social conflicts which expose contradictions. Resources need to follow social problems from which a curriculum of learning can emerge, rather than a market place of individual consumers. It is an institutional change in the provision of learning resources which is required if we are to respond to our relationship with the environment with self-determination.

References

Agents for Environmental Justice and Scandrett, E. (2003), *Voices from the Grassroots*, Edinburgh: Friends of the Earth Scotland.

Albert, M. (2003), *PARECON: Life after Capitalism*, London: Verso.

Comb, M. (2007), 'Good Neighbour Agreements: bad law?', *The Journal Online*, August, http://www.journalonline.co.uk/Magazine/52-8/1004430.aspx

Cooley, M. (1980), *Architect or Bee: the Human/Technology Relationship*, Slough: Langley Technical Services.

Crowther, J (2006), 'Knowledge and learning in social movements: issues and opportunities for adult community education', in Edwards, R., Gallacher, J. and Whittaker, S. (eds) *Learning Outside the Academy: International Research Perspectives*, Oxford: Routledge Falmer.

Devine, P. (1988), *Democracy and Economic Planning: The Political Economy of a Self-Governing Society*, Cambridge: Polity Press.

Emejulu, A. and Shaw, M. (2010), *Community Empowerment: Critical Perspectives from Scotland: The Glasgow Papers*, Edinburgh: Community Development Journal/ University of Edinburgh.

Fraser, N. (1987), 'What's Critical About Critical Theory? The Case of Habermas and Gender', in Benhabib, S. and Cornell, D. (eds), *Feminism as Critique: On the Politics of Gender*, Cambridge: Polity Press, 31–56.

Freire, P. (1972), *Pedagogy of the Oppressed*, London: Penguin.

Friends of the Earth Scotland. (2004), *Love Thy Neighbour: The Potential for Good Neighbour Agreements in Scotland* http://www.foe-scotland.org.uk/sites/files/gna_report.pdf

Gramsci, A. (1972), *Selections from the Prison Notebooks of Antonio Gramsci*, London: Lawrence and Wishart.

Habermas, J. (1984), *The Theory of Communicative Action, Vol. 1: Reason and the Rationalization of Society*, Boston, MA: Beacon Press.

Harvey, D. (1996), *Justice, Nature and the Geography of Difference*, Oxford: Blackwell.

Lewis, S. and Henkels, D. (2001), 'Good Neighbor Agreements: A Tool for Environmental and Social Justice' in Williams, C. (ed.), *Environmental Victims* London: Earthscan.

Martin, I. (2003), 'Inflections of 'community' in educational work and research', in *Experiential, Community and Work-based: Researching*

Learning outside the Academy, Conference Proceedings, Glasgow Caledonian University, Scotland, 27–29 June, Glasgow: Centre for Research in Lifelong Learning.

Martinez-Alier, J. (2002), *The environmentalism of the poor: a study of ecological conflicts and valuation*. Cheltenham: Edward Elgar.

Mills, M. (1996), 'Green Democracy: the search for an ethical solution', in *Doherty, B. and Geus, M. de (eds), Democracy and Green Political Thought: Sustainability, Rights and Citizenship*, London: Routledge, 97–114.

O'Connor, M. (2000),'Pathways for environmental evaluation: a walk in the (Hanging) Gardens of Babylon', *Ecological Economics*, 34 (2), 175–93.

Pepper, D. (1993), *Ecosocialism; From Deep Ecology to Social Justice*, London: Routledge.

Scandrett, E. (2008), *Lifelong learning for ecological sustainability and environmental justice: Contribution to national inquiry into lifelong learning*, http://www.niace.org.uk/lifelonglearninginquiry/docs/Eurig-Scandrett-ecological-sustainability.pdf

Scandrett, E., Crowther, J., Hemmi, A., Mukherjee, S., Shah, D. and Sen, T. (2010), 'Theorising Education and Learning in Social Movements: Environmental Justice Campaigns in Scotland and India', in *Studies in the Education of Adults*, 42 (2).

Scott, W. and Gough, S. (2003), *Sustainable Development: Framing the issues* London: Routledge Falmer.

Scottish Government (2006), *A Brief Guide to the 2006 Scottish Planning Act*, http://www.scotland.gov.uk/Publications/2007/03/07131521/0

Scottish Government (2008), *National Planning Framework for Scotland 2*, http://www.scotland.gov.uk/Resource/Doc/278232/0083591.pdf

Shaw, M. and Wallace, D. (2008), *Reclaiming Social Purpose in Community Education: The Edinburgh Papers*, Edinburgh: Community Development Journal/ University of Edinburgh.

Stephens, S. (2003), 'Reflections on Environmental Justice: Children as Victims and Actors', in Williams, C. (ed.), *Environmental Victims*, London: Earthscan.

UN (1992), *Agenda 21*, UN Department of Economic and Social Affairs, http://www.un.org/esa/dsd/agenda21/res_agenda21_00.shtml

Williams, R. (1989), *Resources of Hope*, London: Verso.

Land, politics and power: Elites and governance in Scotland

ANDY WIGHTMAN

LAND RELATIONS ARE CENTRAL to the development of any nation and Scotland is no exception, as the history of this country is infused with the power and politics of land. In the wake of the election of the Labour Government in 1997 and the commitment to establish a Scottish Parliament, a Land Reform Policy Group was established to consider proposals for land reform to be taken forward by the new Parliament. Those were heady days and, arguably, no other topic had the potential for demonstrating the importance of self-determination than a reappraisal of the laws governing property relations. Emblematic of this was that fact that it took until 2004 to abolish the last vestiges of feudalism.

From the start the project was faced with the thorny question of what constitutes land reform. Was it (as the dictionary defines it) the 'redistributing of large agricultural holdings among the landless' or was it (as the Land Reform Policy Group argued) about removing the 'land-related barriers' to the 'sustainable development of rural communities'? The genesis of some of the disappointment with land reform can be gauged from that rather opaque definition. Land reform was not to be about the redistribution of economic or political power but was a utilitarian project designed to promote sustainable development.

Land reform is about reform in power relations over land and in the economic, political and legal arrangements governing those relations. In this context, land includes the entire surface area of Scotland out to the territorial limits, the land beneath it and the atmosphere above. The rubric of land reform should thus encompass a wide range of land policy topics such as the affordability of housing, regulation of the marine environment, inheritance, land taxation, planning and land law.

The abolition of feudal tenure, the establishment of national parks, access legislation and the community right to buy were dramatic departures from the usual Scottish legislative fayre on offer at Westminster. Ten years on, it is worth reflecting on what this all meant and, in particular, whether we are closer to realising the potential of land reform than when this journey was embarked upon.

Arguably, only three politicians have properly understand land reform in Britain, namely David Lloyd George, Winston Churchill and Tom Johnston. Here's what the latter had to say 100 years ago:

> Show the people that our Old Nobility is not noble, that its lands are stolen lands – stolen either by force or fraud; show people that the title-deeds are rapine, murder, massacre, cheating, or Court harlotry; dissolve the halo of divinity that surrounds the hereditary title; let the people clearly understand that our present House of Lords is composed largely of descendants of successful pirates and rogues; do these things and you shatter the Romance that keeps the nation numb and spellbound while privilege picks its pocket. (Johnston, 1909, x)

What is fascinating about Johnston's observations is that one can substitute the role of bankers for that of the nobility and get some sense of how power, money and land may have shifted focus over the past century, but have continued their merry dance.

Ireland is probably a good place to start in understanding this. Close to bankruptcy and on the verge of serious civil disorder, Ireland's economic woes are rooted in the same land that played such a decisive role in the struggle for independence. Only now it is the greed and self-interest of the banks, financiers, property developers and homeowners that has driven the country to the brink. At the heart of the Irish crisis was a property boom, based on the unquestioned idea that land values could and would continue to rise and could be used as security forever, that increased levels of borrowing to fund such lavish lifestyles. The UK, though not on the verge of bankruptcy, is not immune. Gordon Brown, in his first budget in 1997, claimed that, 'I will not allow house prices to get out of control'. He finished by labelling his budget 'a people's budget' (House of Commons, 1997). Since then prices have more than doubled, tying up trillions in land as securities and loans and acting as a deadweight on the economy[1].

In December 2010, the total UK personal debt stood at £1.452 trillion, of which 85 per cent (£1.236 trillion) was debt on property (Credit Action,

2010). This compares with the total UK national debt that in October 2010 stood at £845 billion. The borrowing on houses is therefore over 70 per cent greater than the UK's national debt and represents 83 per cent of Gross Domestic Product (Office for National Statistics, 2010).

Land reform is thus about much more than community buyouts and feudal abolition. The economy of land is central to national and global wellbeing. Ask any number of politicians whether they would like to see house prices (which are a proxy for land values) going up or down over the next two years (and by how many percentage points) and you will be stunned by the silence. Ask why the average age of the first-time buyer is now 38 and you will be told of various measures being taken to assist them. However, none will involve the reduction of land values to elimi-nate the speculative profits of developers and volume house-builders that would make housing affordable for all.

Recently, a colleague working in the housing sector told me of a con-versation he had had with a leading figure in the house-building industry a few years back, when the boom was still booming and it seemed that house prices would rise forever. The house-builder was lamenting the figure quoted in the Barker Review of 2004, that only 46 per cent of new home purchasers would recommend their house-builder to others (Barker, 2004). This astonishingly low level of consumer satisfaction was, our house-builder argued, a direct result of the way the industry generated return. No money at all, he confided, was made on building homes. All of the profit came from buying and selling land. Hence, all the best talents in the industry were focused on dealing in the land market rather than on product development and innovation which explains why the house-building industry remains so conservative in relation to the product that consumers actually see.

Thus, vast amounts of wealth have been transferred into the hands of those sectors with interests in land, leading to quite gross inequalities in wealth. This in itself is a phenomenon worth exploring more closely since it reveals a neurosis at the heart of public policy. Beyond doubt, there is enough land, enough building materials and enough labour to build an adequate, affordable and decent home for all who need it. The problem is land. As one leading Scottish house-builder put it, 'Any fool can build houses. Any fool can sell them. Ninety per cent of our work is getting hold of the right land at the right price' (Reid, 2010).

In 1909, one of Britain's most radical reforming governments attempted to reform land relations in the UK fundamentally, and to put an end to the land speculation which, a century later, was to prove Ireland's undoing. David Lloyd George knew all about the inequities in landownership in the UK and he, along with any member of the public, could have walked into their public library to consult the 1874 Return of Owners of Lands and Heritages which documented the owners of every parcel of land over one acre in the whole of the UK[2].

Lloyd George was incensed by the immense wealth of the patrician landed class. As David Cannadine wrote:

> All his life, Lloyd George had believed in attacking landlords, and in breaking their monopoly of the soil as the necessary prelude to overthrowing their social privileges and political power. Quite simply, and quite sincerely, he hated the grandees and the gentry, and everything they represented... In his 1906 election campaign, he promised that 'the next great legislative ideal' was the emancipation of ordinary people from 'the oppression of the antiquated, sterilising and humiliating system of land tenure'. (Cannadine, 1990, 69)

Lloyd George's response was the land tax proposals in his famous People's Budget of 1909. The land tax was eventually repealed in 1920, but not before the Inland Revenue had begun the mammoth task of mapping the ownership of every corner of Great Britain and Ireland. Indeed, it has been suggested that for Lloyd George, the tax was of secondary importance to the fact that the proposal would involve finding out the ownership and value of all land in the country. The Inland Revenue maps are a monumental testament to Edwardian government and reveal the ownership, value and occupation of every bit of land from the centre of the cities to the landward estates of the aristocracy. Both in England and Scotland we still have nothing of comparable extent and quality.

Landed power eventually killed off the land tax which, had it been implemented, would have contributed possibly more than any other fiscal measure to eradicating the inequalities in wealth in the UK and ensuring that every family could afford a decent home. It was that radical[3]. The failure of Lloyd George's reforms was not surprising. In relation to the governance of land relations, Scotland has a miserable history. It is no simple accident that Scotland has one of the most concentrated pattern of private ownership anywhere in the world. It has been the task of landed power down the ages to design this arrangement and to sustain landed hegemony. Critical to this has been the role of the law.

For centuries, Scotland's nobility and landed class made the law. The bedrock of Scotland's property system is the Registration Act of 1617 (which established the Register of Sasines) and the Prescription Act of the same year (which legitimises titles after a prescribed period), both passed in the aftermath of the Reformation. Most of the nobility had been appropriating the extensive lands of the church from around 1520 and these two laws enabled them to assert lawful ownership. From then on, the Scots law of property increasingly favoured the powerful over the weak by securing legal reforms (such as the laws of entail) that perpetuated landed privilege.

Even when the franchise was expanded in the 19th century, landed interests conspired to pervert the reforms by creating fictitious voters through the manipulation of property rights[4]. But landed interests still had their own forum for debating matters – the House of Lords. Some insight into its affairs can be gleaned from the debates surrounding the 1964 succession bill. One of the principal reasons for the concentrated pattern of landownership in Scotland is that, unlike most other European countries, children have no legal rights to inherit property. Back in 1964, Lord Haddington responded to proposals to provide such rights in cases of intestacy by claiming that:

> By assimilating heritable property, which from time immemorial has passed under the law of primogeniture, with moveable property and dividing it equally among the intestate's next of kin, you are striking at the very roots of Scottish traditions and undermining the whole fabric of Scottish family life. (House of Lords, 1964)

Indeed.

So whither land reform now? Following some important new laws in the first session of the Scottish Parliament, the subject has slipped off the agenda and the 2007–11 SNP government did next to nothing to advance it. But the reforms of 1999–2003 were only a small step on the way to meaningful land reform and deep-seated problems remain. Perhaps one reason for the waning of interest is the perception that land issues are matters concerning only the remoter parts of the Highlands and Islands and downtrodden crofting communities. There are issues there aplenty, but the land question is about much more than that.

It is about why common land in the heart of Edinburgh has been let for a penny a year to a commercial property company who, if the Long Leases Bill proposed by the SNP Government is enacted, will give them outright ownership[5]. It is about why Scottish Ministers paid £2.295 million to buy land in Perthshire that is common land and should never have been sold in the first place[6]. It is about why, in this day and age, children still have no legal rights to inherit land. It is about why at a time of austerity and proposed caps on public benefits of £26,000 per family, it seems to be quite alright to hand out millions in agricultural subsidies to some of the richest families in the country[7]. It is about a housing bubble built on cheap credit that has denied young people the opportunity of securing an affordable home.

Above all, it is about how the whole edifice of Scots land law has been constructed to legitimise what is, in many cases, little more than theft – just what Tom Johnston was complaining of over a century ago.

A few years ago, for example, I bought some land. It cost me £12.95 and is located at Area F-4, Quadrant Charlie on the moon. I will probably never visit though I did see it the other night – it's in the Oceanus Procellarum. The deeds for the property are detailed and they appear to be, in every sense, legitimate and proper. My problem is that were I to try and defend my property rights I would have difficulty doing so since there is no legal jurisdiction for lunar property. At the end of the day I simply have a few bits of worthless paper.

By way of contrast, a few months ago I uncovered the title deeds of a 400 acre parcel of common land in Scotland and was intrigued to find out that in 1986 it had been split up among the three landowners whose land bounded it, irrespective of the fact that many more people potentially had an interest in it. Not only that, but these landowners only had rights of use in the commonty and no rights of property. Even the Keeper of the Registers of Scotland made a note in the Register of Sasines 'agent aware granters apparently only have title to rights in pasturage.' In other words, the conveyancing solicitor (who shall remain nameless for the moment) knew that the farmers had no property rights in the common, but nevertheless drafted and submitted the deed for recording. Despite all the blatant defects, this deed (unlike my moon deed) actually enjoys the full protection of the Scots law of property, thanks to those ancient 1617 statutes on registration and prescription[8].

In 1872, Cosmo Innes, the famous antiquarian, advocate, and law professor wrote:

> Looking over our country, the land held in common was of vast extent. In truth, the arable – the cultivated land of Scotland, the land early appropriated and held by charter – is a narrow strip on the river bank or beside the sea. The inland, the upland, the moor, the mountain were really not occupied at all for agricultural purposes, or served only to keep the poor and their cattle from starving. They were not thought of when charters were made and lands feudalised. Now as cultivation increased, the tendency in the agricultural mind was to occupy these wide commons, and our lawyers lent themselves to appropriate the poor man's grazing to the neighbouring baron. They pointed to his charter with its clause of parts and pertinents, with its general clause of mosses and moors – clauses taken from the style book, not with any reference to the territory conveyed in that charter; and although the charter was hundreds of years old, and the lord had never possessed any of the common, when it came to be divided, the lord got the whole that was allocated to the estate, and the poor cottar none. The poor had no lawyers. (Innes, 1872, 155)

Not only did the poor have no lawyers, they spoke no Latin and were not in the habit of travelling to Edinburgh to examine the title deeds of the nobility.

With so many vested interests in the law, construction, estate agency, finance and landownership, it is hard to avoid the conclusion that nothing of any consequence will happen to the Scots law of property and in economic relations with land. When we have MSPs who have played the property market and at least one MSP who owns seven houses, it looks unlikely that they are going to be sympathetic to the need for land prices and thus house prices to drop to affordable levels.

Land is power. How it is derived, defined, distributed and exercised affects numerous aspects of how we live our lives. It is at the root of growing inequality in Britain, at the heart of the financial mess we are in and at the heart of the fairness agenda being promoted by David Cameron and Nick Clegg. David Lloyd George and Winston Churchill served together in government as social reformers over 100 years ago. One of their shared causes was land reform. We need more of the kind of radical, progressive and determined thinking that they espoused if we are to build a truly fair and just society. The division of land and the iniquities of the Scots law of property stand in the way of this.

Scotland likes to think of itself as an egalitarian country, but it is hard to look at the state of the country's housing, patterns of landownership, inequalities in wealth and the role played by Scots law and not conclude that we are deluding ourselves. Central to the resolution of these issues is a more radical debate about the role of land in society. Is it there to underpin economic growth in the form of an asset class? Or is it there to provide essential services such as food, homes and biodiversity?

Central to any resolution is also the vexed question of governance. Whilst the Scottish Parliament has breathed new life into the land question, the role of local government has been ignored. Since the abolition of parish councils in 1929 and town councils in 1975, local government has, in fact become more and more distanced from the constituency it serves. Matters that had once been within the purview of genuinely local politicians are now dealt with in perfunctory council meetings in regional power centres. The local administration of local affairs has led to a diminution of civic awareness and influence of their local environment.

Scotland is governed in a highly centralised manner lacking the parish, kommune, and municipal government prevalent across the rest of Europe.

As Lesley Riddoch wrote recently:

> France has 22 regions, 96 départements and 36,000 communes with an average population of just 380. The Swiss have 7.6 million people in 23 cantons and 2,900 communes with an average population of 2,600. Norway – same population as Scotland – has 431 municipalities responsible for primary and secondary education, outpatient health, senior citizen and social services, unemployment, planning, economic development and roads. The average Norwegian municipality has 12,500 people – the average Scottish council serves 162,500. (Riddoch, 2010)

The consequences of this struck me a few years when I 'discovered' an 88 acre parcel of common land in Lanarkshire. It is registered in the Land Register and thus enjoys a state-guaranteed title. Since popular opinion holds that Scotland's commons have effectively all disappeared, this was a significant discovery. However, none of the civic organisations in the parish knew of its existence, which of itself is an indictment of our ability to keep track of community assets. What was even more significant was that the common was in the middle of what was (at that time) Europe's largest wind farm. Scottish Power had not built a turbine on the land because, as they told me, 'we did not know with whom we would negotiate a lease.' Had the residents of the parish known of the existence of their common, they would now be earning a valuable annual rent. They knew nothing because in the parish of Carluke there is no institutional memory; there is no governance; there is no body with any real power to whom Scottish Power could have spoken to.

From governance issues to legal reforms, and from land taxation to land registration, there remains much to do. But Scotland's politicians have fallen asleep at the controls. Most importantly, civic Scotland needs to move from the relative confines of the charitable and voluntary sector to a more active role in engaging with the powerful forces that shape society.

It is possible for everyone to have a decent and affordable house (there's no shortage of land and construction costs have barely risen in 30 years); it is possible to increase social mobility and equity by reforming the law of succession (a draft bill lies ready to do it); and it is possible to return governance of land to genuinely local government. Above all, it is possible to introduce far fairer and more equitable arrangements for raising public finance.

Its high time we paid more attention to such topics. The key question is, can we be bothered? And if we can, do our political institutions have the capacity to respond to such demands?

Notes

[1] See www.housepricecrash.co.uk/indices-nationwide-national-inflation.php Prices adjusted for inflation.

[2] Available at www.scotlandsplaces.gov.uk/digital_volumes/book.php? book_id=553

[3] For a contemporary analysis of the role of land value taxation in Scotland see Wightman, A., *A Land Value Tax for Scotland*. Report prepared for Green MSPs in the Scottish Parliament. Available www.andywightman.com/docs/LVTREPORT.pdf

[4] See Wightman, A. (2010), *The Poor Had No Lawyers* for further discussion pp.58–61 and 75–77.

[5] See www.andywightman.com/wordpress/?p=104

[6] See Wightman, A. (2010), pp.205–211 and www.andywightman.com/docs/alythlegalhistory.pdf

[7] See www.andywightman.com/wordpress/?p=91

[8] The 1617 statutes have been revised but their essential principles remain embodied in current legislation.

References

Barker, K. (2004), *Review of Housing Supply. Delivering Stability: Securing our Future Housing Needs*, Norwich: HMSO.

Cannadine, D. (1990), *The Decline and Fall of the British Aristocracy*: Yale University Press, New Haven and London.

Credit Action (2010), *Debt Statistics*, www.creditaction.org.uk/debt-statistics.html

House of Commons Deb, 2 July 1997, vol.297, col.313.

House of Lords Deb, 12 March 1964, vol.256, col.585.

Innes, C. (1872), *Lectures in Scotch Legal Antiquities*, Edmonston and Douglas: Edinburgh.

Johnston, T. (1909), *Our Scots Noble Families*, Glendaruel: Argyll Publishing.

Office for National Statistics (2010), *Public Sector Finances*, October.

Reid, H. (2010), 'Review of Wightman, A. The Poor Had No Lawyers', *The Herald*, 1 November.

Riddoch, L. (2010), 'Mini-councils will energise Scotland's communities', *The Scotsman*, 28th June, http://news.scotsman.com/politics/Lesley-Riddoch-Minicouncils-will-energise.6386812.jp

Wightman, A. (2010), *The Poor Had No Lawyers: Who Owns Scotland (And How They Got It)*, Birlinn: Edinburgh.

The Challenge of Scottish Cultural Self-Determination

NEIL MULHOLLAND

IF SCOTTISH CULTURE were compared with a state, which would it be? For me, it would have to be a city-state like Venice: a tiny medieval state whose wealth was based on maritime trade (in the case of Scotland, on the ill-gotten gains of the British Empire); its welfare endangered by the world's industrialising nation states (Chindia); a fiercely independent nation, punching well above its weight; a re-emerging state beguiled by its own historical reflection that fails to notice that it is slowly sinking. It's useful to extend this medieval metaphor when thinking about how the visual arts are reproduced in Scotland, to consider how this impacts upon artists and audiences and most importantly, to enable us to think specifically about the future of the visual arts and, by analogy, of culture more broadly.

Big Society, Little England

There is a peculiar mixture of ambition and frustration in the visual arts in Scotland. The idea that Scotland is reborn is tempered by the fear that it is always just on the brink of collapse. While this feeling has never been more amplified than now, this anxiety seems to have magnified in the last 10 years. The idea that cultural renascence in Scotland has (or will) coincide with its political devolution is tempered by the insinuation that devolution will be its undoing. Much of this anxiety stems from the feeling that art in Scotland still can't be considered separately from the British context; Scottish culture has a symbiotic relationship with British statecraft. The British imaginary mediates how culture is reproduced at home (in Scotland *and* in Britain) and abroad.

A good example of the phantasmagorical Britain that haunts modern Scots is the Conservative Party's 'Big Society' – an idea loosely drawn from Phillip Blond's 'Red Tory' (Blond, 2010). Blond proffers a vague model of mutualism – something most Britons would associate with the left's attempt to empower workers and generate solidarity – as a justification for cutting back the state. In economic terms, 'Red Tory' ideology is neatly wedded to the neo-liberal annihilation of public ownership, a project unchallenged since the end of the 1970s. As the public sector is in danger of extinction, democratically elected state authority is replaced by something shadowy and unaccountable, a plutocratic distribution of power reminiscent of a time before modern nation-states. Culturally speaking, this ideology impacts more upon Scotland and the north of England since both rely far more upon the public sector than other parts of the UK. So, culturally, this version of 'Britishness' conflicts with the solidarism that makes 'public life' in Scotland so public.

The distributive state proposed in the 'Big Society' has profound implications for culture in the UK. As Scotland increasingly resembles the nation state it once was, England becomes progressively aware that it is the UK's sole remaining stateless nation. Thus, it falls victim to the democratic deficit, Red Tory style, 'awe nation, nae state'. On the one hand, people north of the border do not need to pay too much attention to 'British' statecraft; Westminster's ideas about 'British culture' no longer apply to 'Scottish culture'. On the other hand, since England's governance is a reserved matter, it is up to all British Citizens (wherever they live) to campaign for better English political accountability. Devolution in Scotland, Wales and Northern Ireland could not have occurred without UK Parliament backing (and can be withdrawn by Westminster just as easily). Doing our democratic duty to ensure that the UK is adequately federalised or broken up will at least finally clarify *who is in charge*, and enshrine Scottish self-determination.

Neo-medieval Britain

The worrying lack of political accountability in England is due to Labour's bungling of regional English devolution. With the exception of London, this was largely rejected and abandoned. The Tories plan to fill the void by selling off England's public riches – not the kind of devolution that Labour had in mind. Regional devolution does exist in England in the Arts Council of England's regional agencies established in 1994, long pre-empting the dissolution of a unified 'British' national imaginary in the UK. There is no 'UK' as far as the administration of culture is concerned – cultural policy is devolved from Westminster to Belfast, Edinburgh, Cardiff and the English Regions. This has been the case in Northern Ireland, Scotland and Wales since the 1960s – pre-empting political devolution by over three decades. The national Arts Councils have helped create the economic conditions in which independent artistic microclimates have grown. There is a quasi-federal system in play here. England, for example, not only has its own Arts Council, but has devolved bodies relating, more or less, to its Regions and their population density. Thus, the Keynesian bureaucracy designed to promote the imaginaries of 'British Culture' has been gradually dismantled, replaced by new European, national, regional and trans-urban cultural technocracies. This has generated shifting relationships between the local, national and international, and corresponds with what Hedley Bull prophesised as a New Medievalism: a 'system of overlapping authority and multiple loyalty' (Bull, 1977). The devolved UK state is one with competing legitimate organising principles for the cultural arena, where individuals are legal members of a transnational community while also having responsibilities to the local territory where they reside.

'Big Society' is an emerging example of such a competing organising cultural principle – an idea that *might* cross the UK's national and international borders and so is the legitimate concern of people of all nations and cultures. Blond's model of 'community' is a territorialisation of space and time that is overtly *cultural*. Although it appears apolitical, it harbours an overtly partisan agenda of de-politicising the social realm and justifying plutocracy by softening its image as philanthropic but its weakness lies in its provincialism. It is the Village Green Preservation Society, a mythologisation of heterogeneous Anglicism that is exclusively English. In neo-medieval terms, Red Tory is an archetypal conservative anti-modern whitewash, one that reduces the complexity and diversity of the past to justify a self-interested vision of the future.

Cultural devolution of the visual arts in Scotland has an untold history that pre-dates political devolution, radical spectres that, if exorcised, might provide a better blueprint for the nation's governance than Anglophone theories of 'cultural economy' or 'social entrepreneurism'. Let's now turn to an analysis of the infrastructure to consider how it might enable or prohibit self-determination.

Atlas Novus

There are many ways to map Scotland's cultural ecology. I will provide a key to institutions based on their terrain. By 'terrain' I suggest that some organisations relate to constituencies that are geographical (in relation to time and space) and political (they have agendas, they empower particular groups of people). So we can think of them in relation to how 'close' we can get to them in terms of democratic accountability, of their proximity to our bodies politic. The degree to which people are involved with them in order to perpetuate their existence, and the degree to which they are sustained and modified by this interaction, is central to this taxonomy:

Micro			Macro
TERTIARY	**PROVISIONAL**	**CIVIC**	**NATIONAL**
Education for *artists, administrators and audiences.*	*Organisations that are directly run* by *professional artists and/or members of the community.*	*Organisations run by local authorities* on behalf of *the electorate.*	*Organisations run by national bodies* on behalf of *the electorate.*
Schools; Local Authority Art Classes; FE Colleges; HE Art Schools; Universities; All Provisional, Civic and National organisations.	Student-initiatives; Artists' Studios; Workshops and Galleries (e.g. Generator, Dundee); Artist-Run Initiatives (e.g. Project Slogan, Aberdeen); Community Arts	City-run Galleries; Arts and Community Centres, Local Museums; Town Planning	National Galleries, Scottish Higher Education Funding Council; National Grants, Awards and Loans (e.g. Creative Scotland); Public National Representation (e.g. SNGMA, British Council Scotland, New Media Scotland)

'Tertiary' relates to organisations that support, nurture or train artists and audiences to engage with visual art. To different degrees all public organisations are obliged to do this, but some do more than others. 'Provisional' organisations are established and run by artists/community groups. They require the full participation of their members to exist, tend to be charities, run on a voluntary basis and are 'provisional' in the sense that they change in response to emerging conditions. While they exist in the public sector, their survival is equally dependent upon the gift economy. Thirdly there are 'Civic' institutions, established by local authorities to manage cultural 'provision' within their administration. While 'Civic' organisations are democratically accountable at elections, they have no members and thus are not patronised. Since they have responsibility for education, however, most local authorities find themselves aligned with the educational agendas of Tertiary arts organisations. Lastly, there are national organisations funded directly or indirectly by Government that broker Civic, Provisional and Tertiary organisations. Key instruments of statecraft, they are generally 'arm's-length' quangos and therefore not democratically accountable. Let's now think about this system from the point of view of aspiring artists, arts administrators and their audiences.

The New Vassalage

As in the High Medieval period, many artisans in post-devolution Scotland have been participating in a reinvigorated 'pre-industrial' economy wherein objects are valued more highly than experiences. From an entrepreneurial perspective, this 'cradle-to-grave' system offers the arriviste a path of least resistance to international market. It implies a rite of passage towards greater mobility, esteem and higher financial returns. At the macro end of the scale (National) artists are often patronised by the private sector, while directors of successful 'Provisional' organisations learn how to survive as private businesses. Some of the more established artists based in Scotland now have dealers and patrons in different fiefs (states, or, more accurately 'fields of cultural production') – in neo-medieval terms they are serfs and must, wittingly or not, serve the different lords simultaneously. Dealers and curators act as mercenaries who vie for trade and power at art fairs, events and biennials held around the globe. Dealers and curators are vassals who lord over their temporarily bestowed fiefs. International collectors and the public grant awarding bodies are the overlords.

Much of this is the product of a seismic appropriation of public property by private hands, of operating blithely in an exploitation economy. From such a perspective, the audience doesn't really figure. They are simply there to applaud achievements decided somewhere else by someone else (and to help pay for their developmental phase). Some Scotland-based artists have enjoyed 'independent' participation in biennials such as Venice, where Scotland is represented separately from *and* in addition to the UK. Who does this 'independent' participation serve? In many ways, Venice is a trade fair, but it's not one that trades fairly, despite being presented as *the* celebration of multiculturalism. In fact, the curatorial celebrations of cultural supranationalism found at Biennials such as Venice not only serve to mask such centrifugal forces of vassalage that have dominated the art world in the 'Noughties; *they are a product of vassalage.*

Artists are encouraged to take part in this supranational system, since it raises their profile and of other artists in their milieu. This might be fair enough if it was based on genuine international co-operation; however, with only 46 per cent of the world's nations represented at the Venice Biennale, it is not a legitimate barometer of internationalism (as opposed to transnationalism) and conversely represents art's neo-feudal hierarchy. In participating, Scotland must take full advantage of the wealth it has 'acquired' as part of the UK. This makes it the recipient of a gangsterism uncritically accepted in the artworld. A small nation of five million people is represented *twice*, and given more global visibility than many African nation-states. The exploitation economy that gave birth to the Union and was, for a very long time, the basis of an Empire and a territoriality that excluded external actors from British domestic authority, remains Scotland's route to the international cultural market. Just how long can this go on?

From the late '60s to the late '90s, Scottish cultural self-determination was principally an attempt to emerge from this culture of Empire. It was possible to talk about 'Scottish Art' only insofar as many artists and writers were united by the common cause of Scottish Internationalism. The fact that there were fewer artists and institutions in Scotland also helped construct this constituency of unity in diversity. The results are evident in the richness and inclusive ambition of much of the infrastructure Scotland enjoys now. This has generated confidence and (allegedly) capital. It is oft cited as a reason for Scotland's accolades in the international artworld, Turner Prizes, Becks Futures, and ubiquitous 'excellence'. But are these decorations really what Scotland deserves? Are they the reason why artists have contributed towards such a rich culture? The sense that this mythologised history of self-determination has achieved a degree of 'success' has to be held in check.

To return to my Venetian analogy, the gangsterism, feudalism and idolatry found in the 'successful' brand of Scottish art internationally is built on foundations that harbour very different principles; values that equate more readily to another medieval analogy – that of the commons. The mercantile economy of art fairs and international biennales finds its stock and skilled labour in a prosumer economy that *isn't* inspired by the logic of growth. The visual arts ecology in Scotland is formed and structured around a unity of social interests. The true value of objects in the mercantile art market is linked to the cultural capital they accrue through participation in culture, rather than something that is posthumously bestowed upon them in an act of canonisation. This cultural capital is generated in the long tail, in the grassroots wherein experiences and community are valued rather than 'objects'. Objects are meaningful here mainly as nodes in a socially oriented gift economy. Without this ritualisation of cultural practice, there is no property to exploit.

Rather than work their way up a greasy career pole, artists operate in ways that involve 'interpretive flexibility'. Scotland's artworld sometimes resembles a village – artists occupy multiple interdependent roles. They might show in an international biennale one week and at a friend's home the next, give a lecture one day and do a part-time job the next. Artists do not have autonomy, but equally they do not answer to a single employer. Their careers and relationships with organisations in Scotland aren't linear. The education of artists is reliant on the health of each layer of this infrastructure. An artist might go through the art school system, but they might only find themselves there thanks to what they learn at School, in a gallery, in a community.

Scotland is very lucky to have many types of art institutions. In its biggest cities this means considerable overlap of 'provision'. For example, at the 'Civic' level, Edinburgh has the City Art Centre, the Fruitmarket, Stills and Collective (among other venues). Organisations often overlap and compete healthily with one another for the attentions of tourists, locals and artists. In this market they are joined by 'National' organisations such as the Scottish National Gallery of Modern Art, the Dean Gallery, the Royal Scottish Academy (RSA), New Media Scotland and the only UK arts body destined for Scotland (V&A Dundee). National organisations are often explicitly concerned with an export economy based around brand identity. With the possible exception of the RSA, these organisations could exist easily without the presence of any home grown artistic talent – they lack interdependence and so find it harder to attract the 'investment' of the public. In stark contrast, 'Provisional' organisations – such as artists' studios, workshops, galleries and community arts – simply would not exist were they not established and patronised by eager participants. They are one of the few regions of public space where engagement is voluntary. Beyond its main urban centres there are few 'Provisional' organisations, Pier Arts in Orkney and Scottish Sculpture Workshop in Lumsden among others. There are national public galleries in the countryside such as Duff House, and some private organisations such Glenfiddich Distillery's artist-in-residence programme. But, even in the countryside, the provision is often there to serve a peripatetic audience of tourists and visiting artists (the community-based and 'Provisional' Deveron Arts in Huntly and Highland Institute for Contemporary Art near Inverness are notable exceptions).

The relationship between these institutions and their audiences is like that of a narrator to their readers – it controls the level or degree of knowledge imparted and enables degrees of participation accordingly. Organisations that specifically operate at the civic and national level are like public service broadcasters; they have an informative relationship to audiences. There is a supposition that their role is to bring 'the best' to a constituency and therefore improve the public good (taste). They are burdened by Victorian assumptions of authority in matters of national unity and public mores, with the regulation of 'suitable behaviour'. Their problem, in this sense, is that they are out of time. They don't fit comfortably in a world in which culture is (allegedly) ordinary, in which people are their own representatives and must be enabled to construct their own public spheres. Are they fit for the state we're in? Recession or not, we need to start asking tough questions about this legacy and the aristocratic culture of inheritance that it supports. Do we want another *Three Graces*? What are the alternatives to a plutocratic culture and the paternalism of state culture? Let's look at two related models of cultural self-determination in action, one led by artists, one by an audience.

Scottish Interdependents

Generator, Mid-Wynd Industrial Estate, Dundee. As we have seen, art produced in Scotland is part of a global system that provides alternative supplies of sovereignty to players in the artworld. This manifests itself in two ways. Firstly, there is a grassroots, the 'Provisionals', in which much of the value is generated. In this economy, artists act as producers, distributors and audience, often at a local level, to generate cultural capital needed to participate in the international art world. The arts in Scotland are therefore often self-governed in ways that enable this capital to be based on a democracy of creative endeavour (Mulholland, 2008). This involves enabling or playing a part in Bull's 'system of overlapping authority and multiple loyalty'. For example, the loyalty of many of Scotland's artist–run or collective arts organisations is to their members, many of whom are city-specific but also many of whom are not. Since their origins lie in the drive towards the more self-determined arts infrastructure that emerged at the end of the 1960s, many of these organisations share similar political and constitutional platforms. For example, a number of collective arts organisations in Scotland and Ireland (Transmission, Collective, Generator, Embassy in Scotland and Catalyst and 126 in Ireland) share a network that is global but which has, in these cases, been established using a constitution based on the New 57, founded in Edinburgh in the mid 1960s.

The collaboration has to negotiate two nations and three arts councils – but is driven more by the shared sensibilities of the collectives than by statecraft. This means that ideas developed locally are understood and nurtured globally. People have fostered a confident and sustainable art ecology *in Scotland* from which to connect with the world. Rather than flatten difference or erase complexity, the way in which artists have become transnational is due to an imaginative process of exposure to otherness; it has meant *getting out*, choosing and participating in a number of networks that transcend linear and closed communities informed by nationhood, statehood and ethnicity. One of the positive cultural implications of the 'Balkanisation of Britain' for Scotland, then, is that since the 1960s, collective organisations and creative independents have been started with the explicit aim of foregrounding a *neo-medieval* self-reflexiveness as the basis of a post-British alterity.

Big Things on the Beach, Portobello, Edinburgh. The renewed interest in 'public art' in Scotland signified by organisations such as PAR+RS
(www.publicartscotland.com) is part of a transnational return to the
commons. Big Things on the Beach, Portobello, is one model of a radical
neo-medievalism that reintroduces the principle of subsidiary that the art
world sorely lacks. Based in Edinburgh's Portobello, Big Things is run by a
community group united by a shared interest in art. They are also motivated by an enthusiasm for their home and a desire to make it more interesting. From this they have developed a confidence in where they live and
want to connect to the world, to bring artists and visitors to their borough.
Big Things have embarked upon a process of self-education, enabling themselves to figure out the process of commissioning public art projects, of
negotiating the complexities of the funding process, of talking to artists.
In this, they are good examples of the *Ignorant Schoolmaster* (Rancière,
1991) – autodidacts who teach what they don't know. In doing this, they
are emancipated from the Victorian educational inheritance of many arts
organisations. Crucially, in their production of a process of reflexive feed-
back they have not become independent. Big Things could not happen
in its current form without the support of public funders and working
artists who operate in a gift-based economy – they are interdependent.
They are managing their own culture, taking greater control of representations of their neighbourhood, and with it changing the rules about who
patronises art. They are involved in a social production of space, something that is important to grasp if we are to understand the value of what
artists have achieved across Scotland.

Big Things reminds us that it's not enough for artists to form their
own community, they have to find ways of integrating with their wider
environment if they want to build a sustainable base. Organised communities have the power to mobilise their political representatives, to
balance the security that 'community' represents with the responsibility
for protecting the freedom to 'not-belong' that is the more politicised
objective of collective action.

Internationally, Scotland's most feted arts organisations are not its
National Galleries and Museums (as good as they are). It is artist and
community-led activity that attracts the attention of the world. Artists
establish their organisations locally, create activity and give new life to
places. They are, geographically at least, at the heart of many communities.

By being more involved in politics at the community level, artists might find a new route to gaining wider public knowledge, trust and vital support for their activities. If policy has to respond to the common good, artists need to organise themselves accordingly. The proliferation of arts centres under New Labour, the attempts to colonise artists by herding them into arts ghettoes actively prevents this integrated approach to cultural vitality. Even if Scotland wanted to follow Le Corbusier's conservative dictum of *Architecture or Revolution* – we just can't afford more new arts centres. Will this cast new light on Scotland's inimitable competence, the unique cultural contribution to 'reflexive' or 'liquid' modernity that is peculiar to its recent history in its provisional cultural initiatives?

Towards a Creative Commons

How might Scotland capitalise on the current crisis in zombie capitalism (Harman, 2009), to pursue a more distinctive policy in the visual arts? Scotland needs to engage with its cultural and political pasts in a way that sets international standards. The legislative powers that Scotland has regained can be abused under the pressure to follow rather than lead. The SNP have not proven themselves any more competent in this regard than their predecessors and have, largely, failed to capitalise on how Scottish cultural self-determination can be aided and abetted by informed governance at Holyrood. For example, the kind of spaces that have a good track record of nurturing the arts in Scotland are frequently incapacitated by a predictable model of globalisation, followed unthinkingly by the SNP who seem unable to differentiate cultural capital from culture *as* capital (Hassan, 2009). So, while Scotland has gained autonomy in Balkanisation, it's also suffered greatly from not using this power to its best advantage.

The SNP's culturalism is arguably less inviting than the Tory 'Big Society' fantasy in as much as it offers nothing to people who live in Scotland, it's pitched solely at the export market (who else would have it?) The pitiable, slapdash spectacle of *Homecoming Scotland* is testament that culture is not a theme restaurant or festival – culture is a changing response to changing conditions. It's a lazy device to equate a complex series of cultural practices with a blunt instrument like nationhood. The SNP have not grasped that, in relation to the cultural economy, the nation state, be it British or post-British, is not the dominant site of reproduction. The discourses of national culture are always subordinated to the pursuit of a more localised, more independent, cultural capital. The SNP can't see beyond Walter Scotticisms – whisky, golf, clans, absentee lairds (Donald Trump) – a neo-medievalism fit only for the mid 19th century. This sits alongside a cultural enterprise Scotland which is the equivalent of modern Brigadoon: pre-crash Ireland, post-crash Norway. Scotland desperately needs to *invent* a post-industrial 21st century neo-medievalism. This is a challenge to be met by artists and their audiences, not government. The SNP's unimaginative response to globalisation is at a local level – it's what we find reproduced across Britain, as the UK state is Balkanised into fiefs, city-states and overlapping territories. Scotland doesn't have to follow British examples of how to mismanage culture.

The Scottish Government must invite artists to generate cultural policy that is informed by the landscape we have in Scotland now, rather than a Narnia based on the ideas of Charles Leadbeater or Phillip Blond. It needs to develop a distinctive cultural policy that is uniquely adapted to the shape shifting of neo-medieval international relations today. It needs to be based around the resources Scotland have at the 'Provisional' level and the best means to exploit them. This would mean taking the following into consideration as part of a Cultural Covenant. The first task at hand involves radically reassessing the 'Civic' level of cultural governance. This often overlaps with the 'Provisional' and has much to learn from it. To what extent might local government increasingly find itself challenged by community activists in the climate of cuts that Scotland is faced with? The 'Civic' has to be *democratically* devolved to enable communities to determine how culture is produced and reproduced – it has to be structured from the bottom up. This means that civic funding should follow activity, that it should be tactical rather than strategic.

Secondly, we need to reconsider what the Scottish peoples need from national organisations. They should be responsive and facilitate a cultural commons rather than promulgate a canon of proprietorial high culture. Specific programming niches and expertise must be devolved from Creative Scotland to 'Provisional' bodies composed of lay members that understand, participate, generate and advocate what's happening in their field (e.g. to New Media Scotland, Sunbear, H-I-C-A, Public Art Scotland, etc.) National organisations should enable the 'Provisional' to access and develop in a mixed economy. Rather than force 'Provisional' organisations to go private in order to wean them off state funding, the Scottish

Government should recognise that, in the arts, Scotland are dealing with a unique gift based economy. Providing cheap accommodation to arts organisations is a loss leader. Giving them the means to operate as mutual cooperatives, collectives and charities within a credit union or local economic trading scheme (LETS) makes more sense than sending them packing into the private sector with free grants, research and development courtesy of the taxpayer. Scotland can lead a different form of mutuality in the arts. Since it is our most valuable cultural (and economic) asset, we need to connect and disseminate 'Tertiary' knowledge internationally. Lots of arts organisations embody knowledge, something to be archived and made freely accessible as an open source. We can go much further still, removing copyright legislation from Scots Law – knowledge that is universally owned cannot be stolen by private capital.

This democratisation of the intellect is our inheritance (not least since we have already paid for it), our creative commons; it is what enables us to innovate and to engage transnationally. This is an invaluable and ambitious international role for national organisations such as Creative Scotland, the National Galleries, Museums, and National Library. It is also the best reason for nationalising higher education into a federal and open source University of Scotland. Of course, even the most basic level of cultural provision is threatened by cuts imposed by Westminster thanks to its failure to regulate the London stockmarket. Scotland has an answer to this: the journey to Scottish cultural self-determination is linked and made stronger by that of making real the promise of political self-determination.

References

Blond, P. (2010), *Red Tory: How Left and Right Have Broken Britain*, London: Faber and Faber.

Bull, B. (1977), *The Anarchical Society: A Study of Order in World Politics*, New York: Columbia University Press.

Harman, C. (2009), *Zombie Capitalism: Global Crisis and the Relevance of Marx*, London, Bookmarks.

Hassan, G. (ed.) (2009), *The Modern SNP: From Protest to Power*, Edinburgh: Edinburgh University Press.

Mulholland, N. (2008), 'The Creative Economy', *Renewal: A Journal of Social Democracy*, Vol.16 No.2.

Rancière, J. (1991), *The Ignorant Schoolmaster: Five Lessons in Intellectual Emancipation*, Palo Alta, Stanford University Press.

Between a Creative Scotland and a Cultural Scotland

PAT KANE

THERE IS MUCH ACADEMIC dispute about what the term 'creative industries' actually means – and by implication, how that meaning shapes policy-making. Galloway and Dunlop make it clear that there has to be a distinction between 'cultural industries' and 'creative industries' (Dunlop and Galloway, 2007). For them, culture implies 'the production and circulation of symbolic ideas', and has a direct relationship to the right of self-expression, and by association the health of a democracy as defined by various articles of the UN Declaration of Human Rights (and further refinements by UNESCO).

The question of 'cultural industry' is about the extent to which public policy supports 'the space for different types of cultural expression, including local, regional and national cultural identities, which may not play to a global market, and may never make big bucks'. A cultural perspective has to consider how communities need 'structural possibilities of continuity and reference', and 'a shared vocabulary of tradition and convention' (Dworkin, 1985), in order to get the most out of culture. Those structures and vocabularies can be built through public goods like museums, libraries and particular subsidies of artists and scenes, aiming to secure the widest possible access to cultural meaning.

The problem with subsuming 'cultural industries' under 'creative industries', for Dunlop and Galloway, is that it blurs and fuzzes this linkage between culture, self-expression, democracy, and non-market values. They make the obvious point that 'creativity' – the application of new ideas to conventional conditions – exists in almost every 'industry', and that the term is so capacious as to be effectively meaningless.

But they also identify that the term has salience in very political contexts: in particular, the post New-Labour era of promoting the idea of a 'knowledge economy' – where all ideas and sensibilities are regarded as inputs into a commercial environment; where the outputs are most evidently in those cultural forms that combine technology and 'symbolic ideas' (film, TV, publishing, internet, computer games); and where revenue comes from the accumulative sale of objects/services and the exploitation of intellectual rights.

Dunlop and Galloway have fears about a 'creative industries' paradigm – centrally concerned with the commercial rent to be derived from symbolic and semiotic expression – and how it might come to dominate how public bodies think about the support and development of culture. Might it be part of 'a longer term strategy to undermine the ideological basis for state cultural support? When the distinctive attributes of culture are being so purposely ignored, we may ask whether we are slowly heading for a US approach to culture, as in healthcare and education?' These writers powerfully alert us to the implications of the use of the term 'creative' in any debates about cultural policy.

So does a 'Creative' Scotland anticipate the kind of creeping marketisation of cultural provision that Dunlop and Galloway fear? The consistent formulation used on the department's new website – as the 'new national leader for Scotland's arts, screen and creative industries' – implies (at least syntactically) a distinct understanding of something called an 'arts industry', which in its policies might reflect those 'distinctive attributes of culture' – around democracy, common resources and rights of self-expression – that the writers adamantly defend. One should also remember the parting statement from the outgoing chairman of the Scottish Arts Council (Creative Scotland's predecessor), Richard Holloway:

> Creative Scotland is going to have to pull off the difficult feat of trying to forward the Government's agenda for growing the economy by unleashing Scotland's creativity, without taming the anarchic energy that lies at the heart of the creative act ... Living with this tension without trying to resolve it will give us edge and keep us on our intellectual toes. But Government, too, will have to recognise that we cannot always be a comfortable ally for them as they pursue their different but legitimate purposes. We will be vigilant in protecting the spiritual integrity of Scotland's makers, including their ancient right to bite the hands that feed them. And we will never forget Graham Greene's admonition that disloyalty is the primary virtue of the artist. If we can all learn to live within that tension without trying to resolve it, then Scotland will have become a truly creative nation. (Holloway, 2009)

Is this a tension that can be 'lived with... without trying to resolve it'? The early indications from the new leadership of Creative Scotland are fascinating. A story in the *Scottish Review* revealed correspondence from Creative Scotland's head, Andrew Dixon, regarding a grant application, in which Dixon wrote that 'we will not be a funding body in the old sense of the Arts Council but a strategic body'. A minor public dispute resulted, where Dixon answered the *Scottish Review's* charge that the secret agenda of the new Creative Scotland is 'the privatisation of the arts'. Dixon said:

> We intend to promote cultural exchanges between this country and the rest of the world and to ensure that the country's creative professionals can profit from their talent. That is not 'privatisation'; it is about valuing the skills and ideas of talented people and protecting their intellectual property. (Roy, 2010)

From a commercial arts and media perspective, the underlying meaning of this is familiar. Creative Scotland begins to sound more like a record company, book publisher or maybe even venture capitalist. 'Ensuring that creative professionals can profit from their talent' doesn't imply the old idea of giving a grant to an artist so they can clear the time in their lives to be creative, with outcomes expected but not prescribed, and with the ownership of the object staying with the artist to deploy as they wish – Dunlop and Galloway's vision of arts practice as a public good connected to democratic self-expression. Those of us who have dealt with managers, investors and svengalis of the music business, have heard for years talk about 'valuing the skills and ideas of your talent' and 'protecting your intellectual property'. And in the course of protecting their 'investment' – another code word in Dixon's discourses – they demand a cut of the overall royalty of the intellectual property of the artworks you produce.

What might be haunting the new Creative Scotland is the J.K. Rowling scenario: a few thousand pounds from the Scottish Arts Council is granted to a struggling writer to help her complete her children's novel, the book becomes one of the biggest multimedia cultural franchises of the last 20 years – and no scrap of royalty returns to the organisation that played a foundational role in making it possible.

But there are many subtle dimensions to the relationship between markets, property, subsidy and the autonomy of the artist. Until recently,

I've never taken a penny from public arts subsidy and then was given a few thousands pounds to be a judge, in 2009 and 2010, for the Scottish Books of the Year. This provided an overview of just how widely, and sensitively, the old Scottish Arts Council supported the continuing dynamism of Scottish literature.

The novel category winner in 2010, John Aberdein's *Strip the Willow*, bore its SAC-funded symbol proudly and was published by a successful Scottish commercial publisher (Polygon, enjoying the fruits of Alexander McCall Smith's success, but long the recipient of SAC grants and funds), with Aberdein receiving a £5,000 prize from the sponsors Scottish Mortgage Investment Trust.

But there is no inevitable happy spot to be found between artistic autonomy and more commercially aware public arts bodies – and there shouldn't be. One look at the SAC-funded arts journal *Variant*, which devotes large stretches of its editorial to detailed critiques of arts-funding policy, demonstrates that this tendency won't be going away any time soon.

Do we go to see contemporary art, for example, hoping that it's going to be 'customer-sensitive'? – or do we want it to be customer-insensitive, to rattle and shock us into the new? The right of pure artists to maintain a creative distance from their funders (or as Holloway would put it, a 'creative disobedience') must be maintained. In the overall balance of arts, even commercial artists want to be able to turn up to a space that hasn't been squeezed through the sausage grinder of formats and markets. However much Creative Scotland wants to develop its role as a rights-sharing venture capitalist, they must still recognise their ultimate function: as the organisation that allows imaginations to lift free from the usual pressure of consumer or investor expectations.

Culture as a 'public good' is about providing intense visions in our lives, available generally and at no or low cost. And that's about an 'intellectual commons', not intellectual property – not just a competitive market, but an ecology of creativity. Talk of an 'intellectual commons' or an 'ecology of creativity' should prompt us again to look at what we mean by creativity, beyond Galloway and Dunlop's account of it as a terminological stalking-horse for commercialisation of the arts. Could there be a understanding of Scottish 'creativity' that evades both its assumed conjunction with the 'industrial', and the implication that commercial relations and property rights are necessarily involved?

In an aside, Galloway and Dunlop note that 'individual creativity could equally well include developing scientific innovations, yet industries that develop these are not typically included in definitions of the creative sector'. They seem to have overlooked one of the most notable institutional innovations of the New Labour era – the National Endowment for Science, Technology and the Arts (NESTA). Though its current incarnation is the promotion of innovation in the public sector, its original ambit in 1997 was to encourage collaboration between the arts and sciences, in cross-disciplinary endeavours and projects.

Yet with the increasing spread of information and communication technologies (ICT) into every area of social existence in the developed West, it would be easy to say that such a collaboration between arts and sciences has been going on entirely by itself, without much need for public policy of any kind at all. And where do the productions of the internet sit in a debate that counterposes 'cultural industry' to 'creative industry'? Where do phenomena like Google, YouTube, Facebook and Flickr sit between the poles of symbolic communication as an expression of freedom and human rights (at one end), and functional systems, instrumental technology and marketed products (at the other)? Surely the latter facilitates and enriches the former, equally as much as it subjects it to the law of the market?

Cyberculture – an old term, but still useful – has a complex relationship to debates around culture, creativity and the relationship between public and private. We are living through an era, comparable to that of the introduction of movable type in the 14th century, where the transformation in the production of cultural representations and expressions is causing a shift in several regimes of power – political, organisational, economic, even familial and emotional. Beyond debates about public or private subsidy of the arts, or policies aimed at exploiting new ideas, the operations of the Net reveal some fundamental strata of the human condition – among them a 'creativity', or openness to change and transformation, which is far more elementally subversive than any particular cultural or business initiative.

The distinct neoteny of our species – that is, the extension of youthful characteristics far into our maturity, by comparison even with other simians – keeps us always, as the Italian thinker Paulo Virno says, in a state of 'permanent formation' (Virno, 2009). We have kept this endemic and anxiety-inducing openness to the world under control, says Virno, by means of what he calls 'cultural and social devices' – religions, castes, class identities, civic values, educational systems, regional and national cultural traditions. Virno warns that the regime of flexible production and informationalised management that typifies contemporary Western capitalism is now uniquely exploiting our neoteny. Post-Fordism (should we bite the bullet and call it Googlism?) deliberately accelerates this indeterminacy – the faculties that open us up to endemic flexiblity and openness – to make it the very fuel of the social and economic order: 'The death of specialised instincts and the lack of a definite environment, which have been the same from the Cro-Magnons onwards, today appear as noteworthy economic resources'. Virno moves through our natural faculties of potentiality, and lashes them methodically to the flexible personality required by informational capitalism.

Our biological non-specialisation? The grounding for the 'universal flexibility' of labour services: 'The only professional talent that really counts in post-Fordist production is the habit not to acquire lasting habits, that is the capacity to react promptly to the unusual'. Our neotenic forever-youngness, always ready to learn and adapt? We are now subject to 'permanent formation... what matters is not what is progressively learning (roles, techniques, etc) but the display of the pure power to learn'. That fact that we are not determined by our environment, but make and construct our worlds? This is mirrored by the 'permanent precarity of jobs', where we wander nomadically from one cloud in the nebulous world of labour markets to another.

With a sardonic gloominess worthy of Theodor Adorno, Virno denies that this intrinsically unstable system necessarily leads to unruliness – 'far from it'. In traditional societies with less pervasive markets (which one presumes includes Fordism), our deep ontological anxiety could be contained by 'protective cultural niches'. The 'omnilateral potentiality' of flexible capitalism shakes those niches to fragments. Yet even though this disembeddedness allows for an 'unlimited variability of rules', when those rules are applied, they are much more 'tremendously rigid' than the Fordist workplace. Each productive instance is like the tight rules of a competitive game, easily entered into but severely binding when the play begins.

When commanded by our managements to respond to today's adhoc list of tasks and projects, in a world of frazzling openness and potentiality, we display 'a compulsive reliance on stereotyped formulae'. It is via these formulae that we 'contain and dilute' the pervasive indeterminacy of the human condition. Virno characterises them as:

> reaction-halting behaviours, obsessive tics, the drastic impoverishments of the ars combinatoria, the inflation of transient but harsh norms... Though on the one hand, permanent formation and the precarity of employments guarantee the full exposure to the world, on the other they instigate the latter's reduction to a spectral or mawkish dollhouse. (Virno, 2009)

To return to our theme: if being 'creatively Scottish', according to our public bodies and their optimistic political managers, is about maintaining our potentiating flexibility, about fuelling the plural energies of the playful self, this may not be – according to Virno – as progressive as it thinks. To describe some products of our cultural industries as a 'spectral or mawkish dollhouse' – in a UK regularly gripped by reality and talent shows that repeat some of the most enduring passivities of commercial culture – doesn't seem too far from the mark. And what might it profit a generation of media studies, liberal arts or cultural studies graduates to gain a full facility in the 'ars combinatoria', yet deploy them in the 'drastic impoverishments' of the reality TV show or the taste-marketing analytics consultancy?

Virno claims that the playfulness which has been a touchstone for artistic practice from has now become the Achilles Heel of productive subjectivity – the point of susceptible engagement with processes of miasmic exploitation (or at least expropriation) of human creativity. How do we question the baroque mechanisms of psychological capture that Virno so mordantly describes, all their fine-grained capitalisation of our playful natures? Is there any escape from a vision of our post-Fordist cultural existence as 'bigger cages, longer chains'?

Certainly, Virno's is not the only social-scientific reading of our wide-open, neotenic natures which is available. The educational psychologist Brian Sutton-Smith identifies one evolutionary function of play as the continuation of 'neonatal optimism' throughout the life-span (Sutton-Smith, 2009). The 'unrealistic optimism, egocentricity and reactivity' of the growing child, all of them 'guarantors of persistence in the face of adversity', characterise many of our adult play behaviours. Play brings a sense of joyful indefatigability and energetic resilience, which – like the pleasure of sex for procreation – is evolution's 'salute' to the human animal for maintaining a 'general liveliness' in the face of the challenges of existence.

Sutton-Smith sees play forms as an expression of reflective 'secondary' emotion, as ways to deal constructively with the 'primary' emotions located in the more reactive parts of the human brain. The amygdala that generates shock, anger, fear, disgust and sadness is mediated by a frontal-lobe that trades in pride, empathy, envy, embarrassment, guilt, and shame, with happiness as the emotion that operates across both brain areas. The 'secondary' emotions are much more 'rule-based' or 'situation-based' – our play, games and simulations operate as the medium whereby our basic emotions can be translated into manageable interpersonal and social phenomena.

Compared to Virno's 'potential human', fated to indecision in its very constitution, Sutton-Smith's 'adaptive potentiator' has a healthy dynamic in its use of play. For the latter, play is

> a fortification against the disabilities of life. It transcends life's distresses and boredoms and, in general, allows the individual or the group to substitute their own enjoyable, fun-filled, theatrics for other representations of reality in a tacit attempt to feel that life is worth living. (Sutton-Smith, 2009)

In the Sutton-Smith vision, play is not the soft spot whereby we are made into controllable 'dividuals' by hyper-capitalism, but the resilient optimism out of which the very possibilities of societal difference are generated. Cultural policy, founded in this socio-biological vision, becomes a constructive exercise in building forms of simulation, combination, virtuosity and performance which exercise that deeply-rooted 'neonatal optimism'.

Yet, isn't such a constitutive 'optimism' just what the desiring-machines of Virno's info-capitalism most wishes to exploit? The answer returns power to the cultural policy-maker – but not via institutions which take their dominant character from an 'industrial' age. Cultural institutions have to build those rich, public 'grounds of play' in which the optimism of our species can flourish, in a way which outflanks and surpasses any dominion that a powerfully calibrating control-society might assert.

In this, Dunlop and Galloway's distinction between 'cultural' and 'creative' becomes relevant again. How can distinctively *cultural* plat-forms enable, through artistic production, the kind of joyful, exhilarated freedom that surpasses the behaviour-calibration of the creative indus-tries? For organisational inspiration, they could do worse that to attend to the peculiarly persistent linking of commons and dynamism that char-acterises the internet.

Neoteny's generation of play and playforms throughout the human life-span is one of the deeply constitutive processes shaping the design, functionality and culture of the internet. One epochal answer that the internet could represent to our potentiating faculties is that of an extension of the 'ground of play'. We see this across the higher complex mammals – that open but distantly monitored developmental zone of time, space and resource, where potentiating risks are taken by explorative, energetic organisms, in conditions where scarcity is held at bay.

Lion-cubs or chimps compelled to diversively play, risking injury and predation, but in a delimited zone with ultimate defences; children in their local playground, enjoying their rough-and-tumble with solid equip-ment and open space, under some kind of municipal governance; all of us on the internet, improvising our sociality and extending our conviviality with powerful communication tools, resting on a complex but (so far) resilient infrastructure. All of these can be cast as complex-mammalian 'grounds of play', sharing three conditions – they are 1) loosely but robustly governed; 2) a surplus of time, space and materials is ensured; 3) failure, risk and mess is treated as necessary for development.

So the 'constitutive' power of play in humanity – that neoteny-driven potentiation that excites both autonomists and socio-biologists – seems to also require a 'constitutional' dimension: a protocol of governance securing certain material and emotional conditions, to enable a rich plu-rality of playforms. When Lessig speaks of the Net as an 'innovation commons', the resonance with a socio-biological vision of the ground of play is clear. His idea that the internet represents an 'architecture of value' is also homologous with these conditions for play: both are discernable zones of rough-and-tumble activity in which our social-ethical identities are forged; a cultural ecology where security and risk are in dynamic, mutually fruitful balance.

Of course, in the Scottish political context, the constitutional question is always a live issue. A constitutional approach to the support of Scottish arts and culture, inspired organisationally by the Net, might begin to look beyond the very confines of cultural debate itself, and attend to those 'material' and socio-economic conditions that would support a rich plurality of free expression. Perhaps the best cultural policy for this doesn't lie at all with an arts body – but with housing, welfare, labour-market regulation and taxation. Cheap living rents, a creative enterprise allowance, a general nationwide policy of working hours reduction, and tax breaks for artists would generate the right balance of security and risk that supports healthy culture. Vibrant artistic scenes don't necessarily want a grant for their art – but they do want freedom to dispose of their time, talents and energies as they choose.

Those three conditions of a 'ground of play' – loose but robust governance, an surplus of resources in time, space and materials, and an expectation that process is more important than outcome – maybe be more lastingly secured by a move towards a 21-hour week, as the New Economics Foundation proposes, than whatever a dedicated 'arts, screen and creative industry' body could ever do (Coote, 2010). Helping to raise the floor of that basic social autonomy – not just for the creatives, but for their possible audiences and co-creators – may be the most effective measure to support the continuing development of Scottish culture.

References

Coote, A. (2010), *21 Hours: Why a shorter working week can help us all to flourish in the 21st century*, London: New Economics Foundation, http://www.neweconomics.org/publications/21-hours

Damasio, A. (1994), *Descartes' Error: Emotion, Reason, and the Human Brain*, New York: G.P. Putman and Sons.

Dworkin, R.M. (1985), *A Matter of Principle*, Cambridge, MA: Harvard University Press.

Galloway, S. and Dunlop, S. (2007), 'A Critique of Definitions of the Cultural and Creative Industries in Public Policy', *International Journal of Cultural Policy*, Vol.13, No.1.

Holloway, R. (2009), 'Creative Disobedience', Scottish Arts Council Position Paper, Edinburgh: Scottish Arts Council.

Roy, K. (2010), 'A public body and SR', *Scottish Review*, September 13th, http://www.scottishreview.net/KRoyspecial19.shtml

Sutton-Smith, B. (2008), 'Play Theory: A Personal Journey and New Thoughts', *American Journal of Play*, Vol.1, No.1, 80–123.

Virno, P. (2009), 'Natural-Historical Diagrams: the 'New Global' Movement and the Biological Invariant', in Chiesa, L. and Toscano, A., (eds), *The Italian Difference Between Nihilism and Biopolitics*, Re-Press, http://3.ly/virno.

When did the media lose its Scottish accent of the mind?

JOAN MCALPINE

IN HIS OBITUARY of the great Scottish journalist Arnold Kemp, the writer Neal Ascherson evoked scenes from days when the two worked together in Edinburgh in the 1970s. He describes Kemp as a 'champion of Scotland,' with ambition for his country as well as his newspapers. Ascherson wrote:

> I met him properly when he was deputy editor of *The Scotsman* under Eric Mackay. Between them, the silent, patient Eric and the ebullient Arnold had turned the paper round and put it on a winning course. The old *Scotsman* had been boring and respectable, leavened with *belles-lettres* fine writing for the Edinburgh literati. Now it became a strong but not uncritical supporter of Scottish devolution, craftily steered by Mackay against the deep suspicions of the England-based management, while Arnold made it into an arena for talented, lively feature-writing and reviewing. At lunchtime he would lead his writers in a session of impassioned intellectual argument in the Halfway House, followed by a heavy lunch at the Doric Tavern ending, dangerously, in several rounds of Calvados. Scotland, past and future, was always the topic. (Ascherson, 2002a)

Kemp's boozy lunches were legendary (even in 2001) when I arrived at *The Herald*, a paper he had edited until 1994. There was a certain romanticism about his period in the editor's chair, though some felt that this management style had, latterly, allowed a certain drift, a lack of sharpness in the news operations, a tolerance of heavy drinking, indolence and sexism among certain sections of the mainly male workforce.

Yet, these observations are of little consequence when judging the impact and influence of *The Herald* and *The Scotsman* from the 1970s to the 1990s. In terms of Scottish politics, and the Scottish public realm more generally, the two broadsheets led the debate about the country's future. They were nationalist in the small 'n' sense of the word. The sober news pages – in those days these were very much papers of record – gave committed and comprehensive coverage to public policy. The campaign to get a Scottish Assembly, as it was then called, was at the crusading heart of the journalism. The proviso was how to achieve it – both papers preferring patience and negotiation to the 'one big push' approach of the SNP at the time. Commentators, and there were dozens of them, explored the conflicting demands of socialism, nationalism and unionism which caused upheaval inside Labour, the Conservatives and the SNP at the time.

The post-1979 demolition of Scottish industry, and the country's increasing frustration at its powerlessness, the talk of 'Doomsday scenarios' and how few Tory MPs you had to have in Scotland to render the government's mandate null and void, took up endless column inches. The steady progress of the Constitutional Convention, the *Claim of Right for Scotland*, the fall out from progressive by-elections, the march of the SNP, the wrangles over how best to oppose the poll tax and the rise of the non-payment campaign from a base in the housing schemes of Glasgow – you could rely on the papers' army of reporters to have it covered and analysed.

Sometimes the coverage, like the campaign for devolution, was repetitive, perhaps even a bit dry. But thank goodness for it. There was never any doubt that the media was, in the broadest sense of the word, 'on Scotland's side'. This was illustrated during the Herald editorship of Harry Reid, formerly Kemp's deputy, in the wake of the death of Diana, Princess of Wales. The paper held out against the national hysteria that gripped the country in the run up to the 1997 referendum on a Scottish Parliament.

As well as the editors Mackay, Kemp and Reid – and later Magnus Linklater at *The Scotsman* – we should remember that by the late 1990s we also had two new quality Sunday newspapers, *Scotland on Sunday* and *The Sunday Herald,* that campaigned for constitutional change. They also added to the breadth and depth of commentary on Scottish affairs, and brought a younger readership into the topic through coverage of contemporary Scottish culture. Even the tabloids played their part. *The Sun,* for a time in the 1990s, threw its weight behind the SNP and ran columns by the Govan by-election victor Jim Sillars and Jimmy Reid.

The Daily Record was always staunchly Labour but probably had more space in those days to cover the national political dimension, and certainly stirred-up the anti-Tory feeling that built popular support for a Scottish parliament during the Thatcher/Major years. Its sister paper *The Sunday Mail* did likewise and, for a time, employed Angus Macleod, one of Scotland's finest political journalists, who focused on investigations.

From the 1970s to the 1990s, many Scottish newspapers all had erudite and/or politically committed young people staffing their politics desks. Ascherson, despite a glittering career in Fleet Street, returned to Edinburgh as *The Scotsman's* political editor in 1975, leaving only after the failure of the 1979 referendum. By that time he had joined the Scottish Labour Party, mainly made up of breakaway Labour activists who wanted socialist home rule. Ascherson is an expert on Eastern Europe and viewed Scotland's predicament from a broader global perspective. In his book *Stone Voices* he commented that the number of Scots who backed full independence was one in three: 'In any normal country the fact that a third of its citizens rejected the constitutional order would be a terrifying alarm signal' (Ascherson, 2002b).

Another *Scotsman* political editor, Andrew Marr, was equally engaged with the cause, though not politically aligned. His book *The Battle for Scotland* (Marr, 1992) remains one of the most entertaining volumes on the struggle to achieve a Scottish Parliament. Another well-known BBC man, James Naughtie was also on the *Scotsman's* political desk at the time, going on to win a Laurence Stern fellowship at *The Washington Post*. Murray Ritchie, the political editor of *The Herald* for many years, was a founding member of the cross-party Scottish Independence Convention after he retired.

The saltire flew, metaphorically, above the broadcast media HQ in the pre-devolution years, despite tougher rules on impartiality. The period 1975 to 1982 saw BBC Scotland lead by Alastair Hetherington, the brilliant journalist who had transformed *The Guardian* newspaper during his editorship from 1956–75. Hetherington set about his own internal devolution campaign – more autonomy for the Scottish operation – but he was eventually defeated by London. Still, the 1980s and 1990s saw Scottish politics receive a higher profile under the controller John McCormick. Kirsty Wark's interview with Margaret Thatcher, in which the then PM made the famous 'We in Scotland' gaffe, stood out as a significant cultural event. Scottish current affairs was shown at prime time. There was, at one point, a monthly Scottish opt-out from the popular *Question Time. Reporting Scotland*, the flagship news programme, was still a serious bulletin – though in the mid 1990s it was dumbed down. 'If it bleeds it leads' was the approach, with less politics and more emphasis on car crashes, crime and sport. With the approach of the parliament in the late 1990s, both McCormick and Wark threw their weight behind an internal campaign for a 'Scottish Six', which would replace the bulletin from London with a merged programme of Scottish, UK and international news. As well as having the backing of Scottish broadcasters it was supported by a wide variety of opinion across the political spectrum and by Donald Dewar (who at the time was Secretary of State for Scotland). They were defeated in 1998, like Hetherington before them, when the board of governors declared they were 'not minded' to make the change. Vice-chairwoman of the governors, Baroness Barbara Young, flew to Scotland to announce the decision: 'We felt we had to take the best decision, not just for Scotland, but for the reporting of news in the rest of the UK,' she said (BBC News, 1998).

The 1980s and early 1990s also saw positive changes at Scottish Television, which embarked on a blossoming of Scottish programming such as *Reid about Scotland* with Jimmy Reid and *Scottish Assembly*. As at the BBC, politics and current affairs were shown at peak viewing time. The journalist George Rosie wrote challenging documentaries such as *The Englishing of Scotland* in 1989 and *Independence Day* in 2006.

Robert Louis Stevenson spoke of a 'Scottish accent of the mind'. This phrase seems appropriate when applied to the Scottish media up until the opening of the parliament in 1999. Writing in *Scottish Affairs* after the successful 1997 referendum, Peter Jones, then Scotland correspondent of *The Economist*, noted:

> The national Scottish media, with the single exception of *The Scottish Daily Mail*, were overt 'yes-yes' supporters, and backed devolution to a far greater degree than in 1979. Had the media been evenly divided, or mostly hostile, the result might have been very different. There is every sign the newspapers relished their partisan role even to the extent of encouraging or allowing reporters to editorise heavily in news stories rather than sticking to impartial reporting and an editorial comment. This partisanship is likely to continue as Scottish politics moves towards elections to the Scottish parliament. (Jones, 1997)

As things turned out, the media was partisan, but not in the direction that Jones predicted. The patriotic, left-of-centre, 'Scotland First' tone of pre-devolution days had, by 2010, disappeared almost completely. Critics of the media would accuse it of – at best – indifference to the Scottish cause, ranging through cynicism to outright hostility. There is none of the 'Caledonian Dreaming' of previous decades. The media's default position is often indifference. Most Scots consistently say they want more power devolved to their parliament. In the Scottish Social Attitudes Survey of 2010, 69 per cent of respondents wanted significantly more powers for the Scottish Parliament. 59 per cent for tax and 60 per cent for welfare benefits, which shows a majority want the Scottish Parliament to make the decisions for Scotland (Scottish Government, 2010).

But this strength of feeling is not reflected in media coverage. Arguments do appear in favour of full economic power from time to time, and the newspapers have even supported such measures in their leader columns, but much news coverage of the subject in these same outlets remains lacklustre, contradictory, ill-informed and often negative. When it does gather support, it often tends to be couched in language that suggests Scots are wasteful and must be made responsible for the money they spend. There is no sense, for example, of entitlement to the resources from, say, North Sea oil and gas. No mainstream Scottish media outlet supports independence, despite its solid base among a section of the public – a section more inclined to use Scottish media.

This is even more the case in broadcasting, and the BBC in particular. The landscape has changed markedly. In the days of four channel television, BBC1 Scotland was fairly central to most viewers lives and they were familiar with the opt out programmes aimed at them. Now, with multiple channels and rolling news from London, Scotland is squeezed out of the big picture. Even the BBC's successes have been to Scotland's detriment. Considerable effort has been made to make politics and current affairs accessible to a more diverse audience. We have breakfast television, three major news bulletins with different tones (*Newsnight* for the hard analysis, *The Daily Politics* for more fun, *The Parliament Channel* for anoraks), weekly programmes such as *The Politics Show* and Andrew Marr (who combines friendly political interviews with celebrities on the sofa). Add to that Radios 4 and 5 offering very different approaches to serious news, and even Radio One's excellent *Newsbeat* taking relevant issues to young people. Add on Sky, News 24, ITN and the UK is extremely well catered for regarding quality news and current affairs. But it is a UK of the English majority. Scotland occupies a tiny ghetto which simply does not compete with the high quality network offerings. When Scotland is covered it is in a simplistic, explanatory way – as with a foreign country. This would be just fine if we had our own excellent current affairs coverage at home, but we don't. Our only outlets for intelligent coverage are *Newsnight Scotland*, which broadcasts at 11pm for four nights only, and *Newsweek Scotland* on Radio Scotland at 8.30am on Saturday. Neither is primetime, both are under resourced and rely heavily on the strengths of their presenters. The political radio show *Brian's Big Debate* can also be informative, but at lunchtime on Friday it is not reaching a wide audience either. The main bulletin, *Reporting Scotland*, continues to focus on crime and football.

Alex Salmond attempted to tackle this imbalance by setting up the independent Scottish Broadcasting Commission. It was widely welcomed and, in the inclusive spirit of the time, the new minority SNP Government resisted stuffing it with people who would deliver their own preferred outcome. Instead, they went for respected establishment and industry names, most of whom were not nationalists. The final report, assembled by Blair Jenkins the former head of news and current affairs at BBC Scotland, received the backing of all political parties in Holyrood (Scottish Broadcasting Commission, 2008). It recommended a Scottish Digital Network, but did not accept that control of broadcasting be passed to the Scottish Parliament from Westminster. This was a fatal mistake as it meant that the BBC in Scotland continued to look to London and not Edinburgh for a lead. Another mistake of the commission was emphasis on the desirability of Scottish television producers winning more network commissions. This is something the BBC has strived to deliver, with some success. It may be good for producers who get more work. In some cases it has merely resulted in the nominal transfer of a non-Scottish show, such as *Question Time*, to Glasgow. It does nothing to enhance the coverage of Scottish culture and politics specifically tailored to viewers in Scotland. In fact, it may have harmed it. A programme aimed at audiences across the UK will handle a Scottish subject very differently from that aimed at a home audience. The shift also means that Scottish producers think first of the 'network', as it is a more prestigious commission. Less is now made by and for Scotland.

The former BBC journalist Kenneth Roy, who now edits the *Scottish Review*, is one of his previous employer's harshest critics. In a December 2010 article, he uncovered research that shows far less money is now being spent on 'Scotland only' programmes (Roy, 2010). He found that, in 2004, BBC Scotland and STV had between them spent £72m on English-language programmes made for viewers in Scotland, but in 2005, the budget for this core programming suddenly dropped to £65m – an unexplained fall of 10 per cent in one year. He continued:

> After smaller reductions in expenditure in the following two years, there was another precipitous drop in the first full year of the SNP administration, 2008, when BBC Scotland and STV's combined spend on English-language television for Scottish viewers fell from £61m to £49m – a decline of 20 per cent in a single year. Last year, (2009) it nosed marginally upwards to £50m.

It is likely that the rise was due to STV, which recently made a commitment to produce more Scottish content.

Roy summarises that the spend on Scottish programmes has fallen 30 per cent in five years and wonders why it has been so little commented upon:

> It has coincided with a period of fundamental reform in Scotland: the early years of the Scottish Parliament, a perceptible mood of national self-assertion and renewal, growing dissatisfaction with the Labour establishment, the historic coming to power of the SNP. Yet, just as the Scottish people stirred from their prolonged slumber, our national broadcasters were being deprived of the budget to hold a mirror to our new society. How ironic is that?

This general unhappiness about quality and quantity of the BBC's Scottish coverage is compounded by specific unhappiness among pro-independence viewers, who feel their point of view is not reflected or acknowledged. They constitute at least a third of the license payers – more than half if you count those who want substantially more devolution inside the UK. There is a view that, on occasions, the corporation is actively trying to undermine the SNP administration at Holyrood. This is compounded by the fact that its political unit is run by a former Labour Party activist who has recruited other Labour Party activists as journalists – one of whom went on to work as a spin-doctor for Iain Gray.

Even if bias was proven, there could be a number of reasons. Perhaps a weak leadership at the BBC Scotland HQ in Pacific Quay tolerates sloppiness and the sort of tabloid television that would be unacceptable in London because 'it's only Scotland'. There may be a tendency to look to London for the purposes of career advancement and so tailor editorial judgements to suit a UK agenda. Or it may simply be a case of lazy journalists who are fed stories by the opposition parties and do not bother to check or scrutinise then.

The emergence of the BBC website as first stop for Scottish news makes its attitude particularly concerning. Much of the site is made up of Press Association stories from the courts and police – lots of crime and councils. It gave little attention to the resignation of Glasgow Labour council leader Stephen Purcell and the linked stories about criminal contacts, corruption and drug taking. The Scottish arm of the website occasionally makes judgments that suggest its editor answers to a BBC Online manager in England (attempts by this writer to have this confirmed by BBC Scotland have been ignored). If this is the case however, the Scottish editor will always be judging his stories on how they might be viewed by his UK boss. The success of those stories, if web etiquette is applied, will be judged on the number of hits they receive. This means Scotland's online editors will strive to have their stories picked up by the UK site – but that will only happen if they have a UK appeal. This is uncontroversial in a story about, say, a scientific breakthrough. In the case of political stories, it can mean the angle is changed to one that is hostile to Scotland.

In early 2011, the Scotland section of BBC online news coverage reported the launch of the SNP Government's Green Paper on the future funding of higher education in Scotland. The Scottish press took a number of angles on it, some outlining the options, others complaining that a decision must be reached soon. However, the Scotland section of the BBC website approached the subject from the perspective of English domiciled students who faced charges. This appeared designed to attract more 'hits' from elsewhere in the UK. Interestingly, comments were allowed on this story, something that doesn't normally happen with Scottish news stories. Many of the comments were anti-Scottish. Moderation of

comments on the BBC website is done in England, and Scottish contributors complain they are regularly censored for innocuous material.
However, anti-Scottish comments are deemed acceptable. The appearance
of the 'anti-English' story on the website then allowed the BBC to pick
up on it elsewhere. *The Daily Politics* devoted a discussion to the alleged
discrimination of Scottish decision – which was designed to prevent a
flood of 'fee refugees' applying to universities. The SNP contributor, Kenny
Gibson MSP, had to fend off assumptions about Scotland's higher levels
of public spending. At one point a guest, Rachel Johnson, editor of *The
Lady*, suggested she would be bashed with haggis next time she visited
her Scottish holiday home. This was a programme the BBC claims meets
its requirements to serve the whole of the UK. There has been a rise in
the amount of 'jock-baiting' permitted by the national broadcaster – a
broadcast of *Any Questions* on Radio Four featuring Baroness Deech
and Douglas Murray drew hundreds of complaints when they accused
Scots of living off benefits and said Scottish ministers should 'crawl back
under their stones'. It is difficult to imagine similar comments about ethnic
or religious minorities being dismissed so easily (McAlpine, 2010).

Newsnet Scotland has devoted considerable space to analysis of BBC
coverage of the SNP. It has exposed a case of misleading editing, when
the SNP First Minister Alex Salmond was depicted as mocking his own
finance minister John Swinney in a debate about the loss of the Standard
Variable Rate of income tax or 'Tartan Tax'. The First Minister's ges-
tures were in response to remarks by the Liberal Democrat Tavish Scott,
but the subsequent film had been cut to give a different impression
(Newsnet Scotland, 2011).

BBC Scotland seems to have given up on itself. When the BBC's former
Director General came to Scotland in 2010 to advocate a Scottish Digital
Channel as recommended by the Scottish Broadcasting Commission, he
was interviewed on *Good Morning Scotland* by Aileen Clark. The presenter spent most of the slot telling him the country could not afford such
a thing. It was left to the Director General, bizarrely, to suggest that the
campaign for Scotland to have control of its own tax revenue might make
the channel a reality.

There was concern about bias in the BBC in 2010, with the exclusion of
the SNP from the televised 'Leaders Debates' during the UK general election.
There was a widespread perception of BBC senior staff incomprehension

about Scottish politics and the UK post-devolution. The most notorious example of the BBC's failure was the edition of *Question Time* from Glasgow when the Deputy First Minister, Nicola Sturgeon MSP, was a guest. The audience was not allowed to ask questions specific to Scotland, although that is not the case when *Question Time* comes from Northern Ireland and was not the case for Scottish *Question Time* in the past. When the panelists were asked about the economy, Sturgeon started to explain the SNP's policy of fiscal autonomy or full economic power for Scotland, but the presenter David Dimbleby silenced her by saying that only UK wide issues could be discussed. The guests had, however, spent 10 minutes discussing housing costs in London. Later Dimbleby, of his own accord, raised the issue of the Scottish government's release of the man convicted of the Lockerbie bombing. He asked each of the panelists to comment – except Nicola Sturgeon, who was then forced to interrupt to get her point across. My understanding from BBC insiders is that there has been considerable concern about the *Question Time* programme. However, the BBC's official response to a barrage of complaints was defensive and conceded nothing (Hassan, 2010).

The print media in Scotland has also changed beyond recognition since the heyday of Arnold Kemp and Harry Reid. The Parliament was officially opened by the Queen in 1999, in a day remembered for its relaxed sense of occasion and optimism. But no sooner was Sheena Wellington's last verse of 'A Man's A Man for A' That' complete, and the goodwill evaporated. The year was dominated by negative headlines about MSPs expenses, holidays and their decision to award themselves commemorative medals. Things got so bad the presiding officer David Steel condemned 'bitch journalism' and cruel personal attacks. The following year, even Tony Blair was forced to come to the Parliament's defence. Addressing MSPs from their first building on the Mound he said, 'Scepticism is healthy. Cynicism is corrosive. And there is no cause for it' (Rosie, 2000).

Writing about the relationship between the new Parliament and the press in 2000, journalist George Rosie said:

> Holyrood has been dubbed the 'pretendy parliament', the 'jimmy parliament' and the 'wee parliament'; the First Minister, Donald Dewar, has been labelled 'Dismal Donald' and 'Donald the Ditherer'; our lady parliamentarians have been unkindly described as 'a bunch of fat councillors';

MSPs of all parties are a bunch of 'numpties' who are not delivering; and so on.

There was a clear difference between attacks on Holyrood and Westminster, as Douglas Fraser, then *The Sunday Herald's* Political Editor, now of the BBC, told Rosie:

> No newspaper thinks to question the validity of the House of Commons or its MPs, whereas some newspapers are continually challenging the existence of the Scottish Parliament.

Politicians, along with their civil servants in both Westminster and Holyrood, must shoulder some blame. The rising costs of the new parliament building that Dewar had insisted on commissioning were due to a faulty contract being signed. Early on, the MSPs were warned it could be twice the estimated £50m. It ended up costing £414m and was completed three years later than scheduled. The deaths of its Catalan architect Enric Miralles and its champion Donald Dewar added tragedy to the farce. But over the piece, the building saga overshadowed – and poisoned – the Parliament's early years.

There was also a series of expenses scandals, with the highest profile casualty being Henry McLeish, who became First Minister after the death of Donald Dewar. In 2005 the leader of the Conservative group, David McLetchie, was forced to resign after a *Sunday Herald* investigation into his taxi receipts. Though he insisted that he had done nothing wrong, the evidence that he took taxis to Conservative fund-raisers at public expense meant he had little option but to go (Hutcheon, 2005). An investigation by the same *Sunday Herald* journalist also led to the resignation of a second Labour group leader, Wendy Alexander. She had accepted an illegal donation from an overseas donor, and attempts had been made to cover this up. Alexander resigned on the 28 June 2008.

Yet, the press hostility was not simply provoked by misbehaviour on the part of the politicians. The arrival of the Parliament coincided with a period of expansion in the print media – a sense that Scotland could offer established UK titles room for growth. *The Sun* and *The Sunday Times* already had Glasgow based operations which were considerably beefed up. They were joined by new 'kilted' English titles, such as *The Daily Mail* and *The Mail on Sunday*. *The Telegraph* and *The Times* hired high profile journalists and columnists for Scotland. *The Scotsman* titles were bought by the elusive Barclay twins, who brought investment. However, they appointed the right-of-centre Scot Andrew Neil as publisher, and this former *Sunday Times* editor had strong views about the faults of his native land. Eventually he left and the papers ended up in the hands of the regional newspaper group Johnston Press. There is far less money today. *The Herald* experienced a management buy-out, then became part of The Scottish Media Group along with STV. Sadly, this attempt to build a media conglomerate with its HQ in Glasgow was short-lived and the titles were sold to Newsquest, the UK division of the American group Gannett. Again, the budget was slashed and journalism has suffered.

The new legislature was under the close glare of 40 or 50 journalists, all competing for stories, and the arrival of *The Daily Mail* changed journalism in Scotland. As in England, the middle-market defied downward circulation trends seen in 'the broadsheets', so the latter began to mimic what they saw as *The Mail's* winning formula – constant exposes, sharply angled, opinion lead news and an accusatory approach to all politicians left of Norman Tebbit, (which was just about everyone in Scotland). The impact of the Mail's arrival is illustrated in the career of Martin Clark, the young Englishman who set up its Scottish edition. So successful was he judged to be, Clark was quickly head-hunted by Andrew Neil as editor of *The Scotsman*, then poached again to become Editor-in-Chief of the *Daily Record*. Clark was one of a number of high profile *Daily Mail* trained executives whose influence was felt across the industry in Scotland. They were a different breed from the editors of old.

The new editors also promoted softer features, human interest, entertainment and more visuals – all trends well established in London titles. Another affect of this change was papers that were less distinctively Scottish. If the kilted London titles had more Scottish content, the indigenous titles increased their non-Scottish material to compete with what readers might consider more sophisticated products. You couldn't be *too* Scottish, in other words. It was similar to the trend triggered in television by the emphasis on creating content for the network.

The greater variety of stories on offer to editors, and the increased use of pictures and graphics, meant that all those political journalists had to fight to make the paper. Policy development, parliamentary powers or social justice did not interest editors. They wanted scandal, impropriety, duplicity, dishonesty and – most of all – revelation. The genuine scandals that hit Westminster – 'cash for questions' for example – didn't happen in Scotland, but the highly competitive press did its best to replicate them. In one great irony, the Freedom of Information legislation passed by the Scottish Parliament, more radical than in England, became the journalists' favourite tool. MSPs were scrutinised in a way they could not have imagined.

Such an atmosphere attracts a different sort of reporter. The political commitment and scholarship of a Neal Ascherson, or even the ebullient intelligence of an Andrew Marr, would be trampled underfoot in today's Holyrood bearpit. Where are their modern incarnations? Could they be found within the political system itself – as MSPs, researchers, lobbyists, analysts and special advisers now attracts the brightest and best? Many parliamentary journalists in Holyrood today have no specific interest in Scottish politics, culture, or history – and certainly no loyalty to, or respect for, *the idea* of a Scottish Parliament. Some are talented investigative journalists, like Hutcheon. Others are former sports reporters, which is significant. Sports journalism is traditionally notorious for hyperbole, speculation, unreasonableness and a tendency to pursue the 'kill' until he surrenders. Gender too is important. In Holyrood, the parliamentary press pack is mainly male, leading to a more aggressive approach. A herd instinct can sometimes grip the entire corps. It is not unusual to see the same distortion of an issue across all newspapers and television outlets, whether they are red top, middle market, quality or broadcasting. The volume is constantly set to loud, meaning you never really hear anything. This is not an exclusively Scottish problem, but in England and America where over-amplification also exists, there are many other spaces for intelligent, thoughtful analysis of politics. Scotland is less fortunate – because of the financial squeeze on quality print journalism, the lack of a news magazine sector, and the failures of BBC Scotland.

The changes in the newspaper sector since 1999 have also brought a strain of neo-conservative commentary that was quite alien. There was a determination to attack pillars of Scottish society such as teachers, or the public sector more generally. Certainly, Scotland can be complacent and give vested interests too much room, but some commentary was vicious and counter-productive. *The Scotsman's* virulent campaign against teachers under Neil is believed to have lost it thousands of readers. Commentators such as Alan Cochrane in the *Telegraph*, John McTernan in *The Scotsman*, Jenny Hjul in *The Scotsman* and *Sunday Times*, Katie Grant in *The Daily Mail* and Tim Luckhurst in most of these papers, questioned the very spirit of devolution. A recurring theme of this type of commentary is anger at the Scottish Parliament straying on to Westminster territory or 'getting above itself'. Henry McLeish was denounced for taking decisions in defiance of London, such as introducing free personal care for the elderly, and attempting to re-name the Scottish executive the Scottish Government. Jack McConnell was mocked for his laudable initiative to use Scottish money to address poverty in Africa, particularly the nation of Malawi. Alex Salmond was vilified for attending the Summit on Climate Change in Copenhagen. Climate change was not reserved under the Scotland Act, because it was not then on Westminster's radar, so it falls under Holyrood's remit – but only sovereign governments were invited to Copenhagen. When Salmond attended a fringe meeting at the summit, Alan Cochrane wrote:

> Like the small boy who is not invited to the birthday party but turns up anyway and presses his nose to the window pane, Mr Salmond has always refused to accept that Scotland is represented, as it always is at these international gatherings, by the United Kingdom government. (Cochrane, 2009)

The SNP Government has survived despite the media – and indeed had quite a long honeymoon period after 2007. It is generally seen as competent; the financial scandals that dogged previous administrations are absent; so too is the kind of plotting and internal tension that affected the Labour-Lib Dem coalitions – the SNP group is extremely loyal. However, the SNP is a minority government that now confronts a united unionist opposition determined to trip it up. One of the most respected political commentators in Scotland, Iain Macwhirter of *The Herald* and *Sunday Herald*, calls the recent rows in the Parliament 'scandalettes' which are ratcheted up beyond their natural level. He was particularly scathing of the hysteria that followed a story alleging that the SNP government have lost the ability to use the parliament's tax-raising power, the Standard Variable Rate of three pence in the pound. (It has since emerged that the fault lay with HMRC).

Writing after the parliamentary debate Macwhirter observed:

> The world held its breath as conflict erupted between North and South
> Korea; Ireland braced itself for civil unrest as its government imposed
> a crushing austerity budget; British students and school six formers took
> to streets and occupied universities over tuition fees. And Holyrood
> spent the afternoon rowing over the unspent cost of collecting a tax, the
> SVR, that no one intends to raise and is about to be abolished. Cover
> up? Abuse of power? Grow up. There is a strand of infantilism in the
> Scottish Parliament which occasionally causes MSPs to get things out of
> proportion. (Macwhirter, 2010)

Macwhirter was too polite to point out that many of his newspaper and
broadcasting colleagues are as infantile as the politicians. Does it matter
and will it change? The issue of broadcasting matters greatly as it has
increased in influence as newspapers have declined. The failure to have
broadcasting devolved, however, means leadership in BBC Scotland seldom
challenges London. A detailed academic analysis of its coverage of the SNP,
and Scottish affairs more generally, is required to examine allegations of
bias. Sloppy journalism may be easier to prove. STV is generally considered more balanced in its political coverage, but commercial restrictions
mean it has nothing like the resources of the publicly funded BBC. The
press has its own problems. Circulation figures for December 2010
showed an average fall of 6-7 per cent for the main Scottish titles. This
is a trend everywhere because of internet use, and some observers have
asked why no newspaper has thrown itself behind the Scottish cause, as
Kemp did in the past. Might that not have attracted many more Scottish
readers? Recent attempts to develop the commentary section of *The
Scotsman*, which once again gives space to opposing views on the constitutional question, is encouraging. But is it too late? The indigenous
newspaper websites remain poor compared to the large free sites, such
as *The Guardian* or *The Telegraph*, which cover little Scottish material.
The BBC website is dominated by crime stories and appears to follow a
London agenda. The danger is that Scottish readers, particular the young,
will become detached from issues affecting their country, seeing themselves instead as citizens of the web.

However, post-devolution Scotland has, however, seen a surge of online journalism and social networking. The success of the site Newsnet

Scotland, offering news and views from a pro-independence viewpoint, is rapid and impressive. Local news operations such as For Argyll (which cover politics seriously alongside local issues) have built loyal followings. Scores of pro-independence bloggers offer the commentary that is missing from the diminishing mainstream. There are many sites offering entertaining and specialised coverage of culture, history and business, such as 38 minutes for the creative industries. Going directly to sites for political parties or cultural institutions (such as The National Theatre of Scotland or the National Library) is also an attractive option as the content is professionally produced and displayed. BBC Scotland's online non-news content – education for example – is also of a high standard, but difficult to find. STV is posting its rich back-catalogue. Scotland is alive and sparkling on the internet, but is spread somewhat thinly. With television and newspapers likely to be entirely online in ten years time, the challenge for Scotland is to create its own media space there. Hopefully it will be less restrictive and more ambitious than the old one.

References

Ascherson, N. (2002a), 'A true champion of Scotland and a much-loved friend', *The Observer*, 15 September, http://www.guardian.co.uk/uk/2002/ sep/15/2

Ascherson, N. (2002b), *Stone Voices: The Search for Scotland*, London: Granta Books.

BBC News (1998), 'BBC rejects Scottish Six', 11 December, http://news.bbc.co.uk/ 1/hi/uk/232121.stm

Cochrane, A. (2009), 'Alex Salmond pretends to play with the big boys in Copenhagen as patients go untreated at home', *Daily Telegraph*, 15 December, http://www.telegraph.co.uk/comment/columnists/alancochrane/ 6814782/Alex-Salmond-pretends-to-play-with-the-big-boys-in-Copenhagen-as-patients-go-untreated-at-home.html

Hassan, G. (2010), 'Nation to Nation: The Problem of Speaking for Britain', 29 October, http://www.gerryhassan.com/?p=1399

Hutcheon, P. (2005), 'McLetchie: More Questions in Taxi Driver Controversy', *Sunday Herald*, 15 October, http://www.govanlc.com/ sundayherald151005.htm

Jones, P. (1997), 'A Start to a New Song: The 1997 Devolution Referendum Campaign', *Scottish Affairs*, No. 21.

McAlpine, J. (2010), 'BBC failing Scots by allowing prejudice on the air', *The

Scotsman, 1 September, http://heritage.scotsman.com/thebbc/Joan-McAlpine-BBC-failing-Scots.6505370.jp

Macwhirter, I. (2010), 'Swinney didn't lie about Tartan Tax', *Now and Then*, 26 November, http://iainmacwhirter2.blogspot.com/2010/11/swinney-didnt-lie-about-tartan-tax.html

Marr, A. (1992), *The Battle for Scotland*, London: Penguin.

Newsnet Scotland (2011), 'Scottish News From the BBC and a Question of Diplomacy', 4 January, http://newsnetscotland.com/speakers-corner/1354-scottish-news-from-the-bbc-and-a-question-of-diplomacy

Rosie, G. (2000), 'Coming adrift on the Mound', *New Statesman*, 20 March, http://www.newstatesman.com/200003200026

Roy, K. (2010), 'The Hidden History of Scottish Television Part One', *Newsnet Scotland*, 2 December, http://newsnetscotland.com/speakers-corner/1124-the-hidden-story-of-scottish-television-scotlands-broadcasting-malaise-part-i)

Scottish Broadcasting Commission (2008), Platform for Success: Final Report of the Scottish Broadcasting Commission, Edinburgh: Scottish Government, http://www.scottishbroadcastingcommission.gov.uk/news/finalreportnews.html

Scottish Government (2010), 'Scottish bill published at Westminster', *News Release*, 30 November, http://www.scotland.gov.uk/News/Releases/2010/11/30124218

Global Capitalism and the British State

ANTHONY BARNETT IN CONVERSATION WITH WILL HUTTON

AB: We start with a simple question: tens of billions have been 'lost' and even more lent to save the banks, so where did the money go?

WH: Into extravagant personal lifestyles, bankers' bonuses and an extraordinary stock of financial instruments backed by assets worth a fraction of what people thought. Something like ten trillion dollars worth of collateralised debt instruments – world GDP is 60 trillion dollars – sits in the Cayman Islands, Bahamas, Jersey, Hong Kong, Singapore, in London, New York, Paris and Berlin, Frankfurt – backed by assets which have proved to be ephemeral. These are pieces of paper allegedly backed by assets.

Bank A made an issue and sold it to Bank B who sold it, perhaps chopped up, to Bank C who sold it to Bank D. And sometimes Bank A will find itself owning part of what it originally sold. Nobody knows. In terms of the current uncertainty, the banks are not confident who owns what, or what the character of the assets are that are supposedly underpinning their lending. This was the origin of the recent crisis, but at each step everybody is taking a commission or the transaction permits a bonus to be paid.

AB: If you look at what happened as a whole, surely they're skimming capital off society ?

WH: Making money out of money, which is what the banks were doing up to 2007, ends up being a tax on the rest of society. Bankers would contest that, but that is my view. There is a profound risk of another crisis and no one knows which way this will fall. If, in the first six months of 2011, Spain is forced to restructure its debts and there's a run on the Spanish banking system which would include Santander, that would come straight into the London system. There is a very high chance that we'd be forced to recapitalise our banks again and extend into backed guarantees as in 2008. If that happens, the economic consequences for Europe of a second banking crisis will affect the single market, European integration and the European financial system. The political fallout will be phenomenal. I don't know how British citizens and taxpayers would react to a second recapitalisation of the banks, but I think there would be rioting in the streets – the student tuition demonstrations would look tame by comparison.

AB: While in America, cities across the country have been issuing municipal bonds that apparently can't be covered.

WH: Essentially the world has got too many debt contracts. You've just named American local government or state and city debt, you've then got sub-prime mortgage debt which is still too burdensome for the American residential property market. In the UK the hotspot is commercial real estate debt – there's too many debt contracts, and the ability of the real economy to provide the revenue to commit organisations and individuals to have the profits to service the debt doesn't exist.

At the same time, financial transactions are 30 to 40 times world GDP. The stock of private debt in the G20 is more than double the G20's GDP. Some countries (like Japan, the UK and United States) have debt three times, or approaching three times, GDP. These are stunning sums. Historically what's been required is either inflation to get rid of the debt, or debt default. One of those two things is going to happen.

AB: Which is better?

WH: Default means slump, trade protection, breaking neighbours' policies and potentially war. The better option is inflation, but controlled inflation – hyperinflation leads to the same consequences as default. The transition from state A (a banking system which has suddenly taken enormous write offs) to state B (a recapitalised banking system able to carry on lending as it did in the past) isn't one that happens seamlessly and without cost. The transition has always been associated in history with slumps, because people can't carry on financing themselves. Or you start having the same situation as the Irish have where bank debt morphs into sovereign debt and then the credit worthiness of the whole state becomes in doubt. The IMF and European Central bank can support Ireland, but couldn't support the UK or USA if they get into the same problem.

AB: So, how did the British state get into this situation?

WH: The rise of finance was a global phenomena. But one necessary condition was the fact that the American and UK governments permitted the New York and London money markets to fuse and make the running in creating a world financial system. Beyond doubt, the world financial system is run out of New York and London – and in both countries the financial community captured their respective states.

AB: So Thatcher's Big Bang, backed by North Sea oil, was the crucial moment in creating a transatlantic financial system?

WH: The combination of removing exchange and capital controls in Britain between 1979 and 1981, followed by the Big Bang of 1986, permitted American banks to do in Britain what they could not do in America. They could evade the Glass Steagall legislation in Britain, which prevented commercial banks, from engaging in investment banking. This can be very profitable but is much more risky and prone to bubbles; hence the Act. But in London they could become market makers and issue securities, which they had been banned from doing in the United States. Merrill Lynch, Bear Stearns and Lehman could all come to London, and because they could do it in London after the Big Bang, they argued that Glass Steagall should be dismantled in America. No one in London wants to accept this, but it's obvious: Big Bang happened in summer 1986 and, by the end of 1986, the SEC and the Fed committed for the first time since 1933 that five per cent of US commercial bank assets could be held in securities. The Glass Steagall Act had hitherto prohibited this, it had not been done since 1933, and was a direct that was a direct consequence of what happened in London.

Slowly, some British banks followed. Barclays with Barcap came in late in the mid 1990s; Lloyds didn't get involved at all; Royal Bank of Scotland came in after Barcap (and screwed up as we now know), and HSBC ran their investment banking division from both London and New York. British banks were actually slightly later; the big five American investment banks in London led the process.

AB: I'm trying to understand to what happened to the British state. The city rarely speaks with an openly political voice; it was always behind the scenes, powerful and influential, making money. Historically, they represented the interests of the Empire. Today, you feel that Frankfurt is run by Germans who have a sense of what German interests are; you feel that while American banks may screw up, Wall Street has some sense of American interests. But the financiers in London just appeared to have given up the ghost in terms of British national interests they simply serve the world.

WH: They didn't give up the ghost. They were delighted by what they called 'the Wimbledon Effect' – no British tennis players win Wimbledon but it's the greatest tournament in the world: it may be that no British bank was in the top ten, but at least the action was in London. And if core activity wasn't provided by British based banks, round the edges it was. The top four accountancy firms became the world accountancy firms – Ernst and Young, KPMG, Price Waterhouse and Deloitte; the top law firms – Allen and Overy, Linklaters, Freshfields – became the worlds top law firms. All this was happening in London. British law has become the gold standard, with British legal contracts and accountancy standards being used worldwide. All this means that Britain has developed a service infrastructure, and an incredible lobby with successive governments to go with it, to protect it, saying this is something that we are good at: the Germans have manufacturing, the French luxury goods, the Americans have defence, the Japanese semiconductors and consumer electronics, and we British have financial services.

AB: But doesn't this mean they gained an upper hand over a state that, instead of being an imperial state that looked after British imperial or world interests, became a neo-liberal state that sees its interests as part of servicing a global economy?

WH: Yes. There was a ready made economic system of ideas – neo-liberalism (market fundamentalism) – that seemed to justify the kind of policy needed to allow this to happen. There's a slight tendency of liberal onlookers to see it wholly in conspiratorial terms, but the men and women who ran these banks really did believe in it. Whatever anyone may think of him, Fred Goodwin at RBS genuinely believed in it and as a result lost his reputation and a small fortune.

The thing was, the regulators bought the bloody ideology. This was an absolutely collective intellectual first order mistake. But it was not a mistake done self-consciously – it was not, 'lets have this ideology because it very happily justifies what we're doing that we know to be wrong'. It was the other way around – they thought what they were doing was right. That's one of the reasons why the FSA and others find it so hard to bring these people to book, because to nab a criminal you have to have someone who knows he's doing wrong. From their point of view there wasn't wrongdoing. They were openly able to sell this mess of potage to high officials and the political establishment – see Gordon Brown, see Ed Balls, see George Osborn; all of them bought it. I was a great sceptic about the whole thing and then got browbeaten into being a more subdued sceptic, but I always thought the whole thing was doomed.

AB: They bought market fundamentalism. It made them rich, which is convenient, but in that process they kind of suborned what is supposed to be a democratic state. It became captured by the financial, neo-liberal 'narrative'.

WH: The state got rebuilt on the most rickety of foundations on every level. Firstly, the problem about the British state in 2009 was that tax revenue just disappeared. Corporation tax and stamp duty evaporated, the property market went south so there were no capital gains, meaning the state had constructed expenditure plans on a completely false perspective. Secondly, the state had actually decided it would connive in the kind of economic structures that were delivering endless fiscal growth. It assumed that credit could grow – and that property prices could grow at two or three times normal GDP – never endingly. Half the growth between 1997 and 2007 came from property financial services and construction, and it was assumed that this would go on for the next ten years. You watched the diminution, not just of manufacturing but of anything that added value.

The British state also bought the notion that private was necessarily better than public: there was the invention of a £60 billion industry under PFI (Private Finance Initiative) because it was 'obviously' better for the private sector to be given assets to build on the state's behalf than for the state to do it itself; there was an 80 billion pound contracted- out services industry – Serco and others – who would *obviously* provide services better than the public sector; there was the erosion of the very notion of public-ness and the state felt it couldn't do anything, couldn't initiate anything. All it could do was 'enable'.

And as for your choices as an elected politician, you could do nothing about the private sector. It was a force of nature, driving forward, you had to observe it and collude in it, couldn't change or reconstruct it. The only area you could have a purchase on, as a politician, was the public sector. You could reform the public sector, but you couldn't reform the private sector – that was now off agenda for elected democratic repre-sentatives.

This was even more true in the United States (less true of Germany and France but they have moved in this direction too). It was a collective error across the West and makes putting it right so difficult. The banks have to accept the losses and run themselves with a great deal more cap-ital. All the assets that they created need to be traded in organised exchanges that are transparent and can be monitored so that the assets underpinning the things that are trading actually exist and aren't ephemeral. The banking sector needs to be forced to recognise that which it doesn't want to admit, but the political and official classes don't have the conviction to do this. There are individuals in regulatory struc-tures around the West, in our own system, with this view but they're outnumbered. That's the trouble.

AB: And there's no democratic or liberal Keynesian ideology that is arguing for this in an organised fashion?

WH: No. There are only individual people around because the financial crisis morphed into a physical crisis, and because the language 'getting debt down' more naturally comes to the right than the left, and because the left has wanted to respond by fiscal activism, which is logical but seems illogical in popular parlance – 'why would you solve a debt crisis with more debt?'

AB: It's not beyond the realms of popularism to make a counterargu-ment, right?

WH: I say this in my columns whenever I can; I say this privately and publicly to politicians! Others do too – Martin Wolf who writes for the *Financial Times*, Robert Skidelsky, Anatole Kaletsky, and Adam Posen on the Monetary Policy on the Bank of England says it. There are people saying it, but we are a minority.

AB: What are the collective interests of those who are against it?

WH: Well, they think that there is a public debt problem. Investors want to see debts under control, and that governments understand that we cannot stuff the international investment community's bellies with bonds in a never ending and increasing supply, or at worse print them and get inflation. To retain people's confidence you have to take tough measures. Of course, the trouble is that the investment community want the impossible – to know that the money they're lending is going to be solid and that the country borrowing it will be in a better position to repay it in three, four, five years time. But this means they need to grow. One of the problems that investors have with Ireland and Portugal and Spain is not just that they're in a fiscal crisis, it's that they're really concerned they can't grow. And then you can't go forward or backward – the only thing to do is inflate or restructure the debt.

There's bound to be another cycle of crisis and everyone knows it. I said earlier that there is a 10 per cent chance, rising to possibly 20 per cent, that in the next year a big country like Spain could find itself in the corner that Greece and Ireland found themselves in. As the size gets harder to handle, and the corner gets bigger, the bigger the risk that there'll be a debt restructuring and financial spillover. There's a 10 per cent chance of that happening in 2011 (and by 2020 more than 50 per cent), particularly if the bankers don't accept the reforms that are being argued for.

AB: I'm very struck by the fact that it has to end up in a national sovereign debt crisis.

WH: Lehman was allowed to go, but then the Federal Reserve stepped in. Goldmans, who held credit gold stocks on Lehman insured them with AIG the world's biggest insurance company, but AIG said they couldn't pay them. What happened then was extraordinary. The Fed gave insurance companies the wherewithal to settle bogus insurance contracts, it permitted banks worldwide to exchange money, to take second-class assets to the Federal Reserve and get cash dollars in exchange. It won't be so easy a second time around because taxpayers, particularly in the States, will be much more hawk-eyed about what the Fed is doing. If things go terribly, the taxpayer ends up holding the valueless assets that the banks held; that's the risk.

An asset says it is worth 100 and the taxpayer buys it for 85, but the thing is only worth 30! In ten years time it may be worth 100 again. But in the meantime the money wrapped up could be doing other things. So opportunity cost is one thing which is a measurable cost, and sometimes there's an actual cash loss that taxpayers are taking.

AB: To what extent will growth in China, India and Brazil compensate?

WH: The entire consumer demand in Asia – China plus India plus Indonesia plus Japan – is not five trillion dollars. This idea, that Asia can somehow be a counterweight to America or Europe, does not add. At the moment, the world needs consumer demand from the European Union and the USA. And if it doesn't have it, it's in trouble. That's if you assume that Asia's both dynamic and never endingly growing, by the way. I challenge that. There's been a Chinese bubble staring us in the face for some years and, you can never quite tell when these bubbles are going to be pricked, but the Chinese one will undoubtedly be pricked (and with political consequences) when Hu Jintao steps down as President in 2012. It's not a question of Asia bailing out the Western banking system's mistakes.

The real driver of Western capitalist economy is technical and scientific innovation – that's where the drive will come from. And the capacity of the Indians and Chinese to be the authors of this is limited – whether it's health, informatics, whatever. They are the people who make the kit that's developed in the West. This has been the model for the last 20 years and, although it will fray, it will still be the model for the next 20 years.

AB: Now, what about the role of the British state in this? You are saying it has been captured by a global financial narrative, not just in a cynical way – the people in the state have bought into it, the civil servants, the administrators.

WH: They're disillusioned. There is much more readiness... there's much more fluidity and change now, and the banking system is working much harder than it ever did to justify its position.

AB: You're involved with the Fair Pay commission on public sector pay, but it exists within a much larger corporate framework where there are completely different sets of values.

WH: I haven't put it in these terms, but there's been a dramatic increase in CEO remuneration in the last 23, 24 years, which is part of the financial narrative. What's driven this rise has been the fact that company chief executives are paid in shares and share packages, to the point where half their compensation comes from that (in America it's four fifths). This is an enormous rise in remuneration to incentivise them to do their job better. Actually, they probably do do their job a bit better and the companies they run are more complicated and challenging than 24 years ago. But they're not seven, eight times more complicated and challenging, nor has the performance of the companies gone up that much.

AB: Are they also skimming the capital?

WH: Except that the degree they're skimming is trivial. For a ten billion pound corporation, the fact that you're paying the man at the top five million rather than three million is trivial. But it's not trivial in terms of income distribution. It's not trivial when you think of the cascade effects on pay dispersion within the company, because the more you pay at the top, inevitably all salaries get dragged up.

In the Fair Pay review we show that when the public sector has to go outside for a mid-level professional who might be paid £75,000 a year, but in the private sector they would be paid £95,000. That's £20,000 more for a senior accountant, senior HR professional, whoever. The pay differential between public and private is widening which means it becomes harder for the public sector to attract a private sector person.

The public sector gets into a very dangerous vortex. The fact that the person who runs the Home Office, (a ten billion pound department) gets £200,000 and the person who runs a ten billion pound corporation gets paid two and a half to three million, is astonishing. And when people make career choices they're saying, 'I want to work in public service' but if you get paid £200,000 and want to buy a house in central London then you can't. People in the public sector are living in outer suburbs or cheaper towns. The whole London housing market is driven by the very prosperous and well-paid private sector. This is not necessarily a bad thing, but it means problems if you want people to live there who work in your public sector.

I'm attracted to your notion of the state being captured by the financial narrative because that's a more subtle and accurate way of describing what's happened. I mean, the heart of fairness is due dessert for discretionary effort. If great people do great things they should be proportionally rewarded. I'm not a flat out egalitarian, but I am for stakeholder capitalism and believe that if people do great things you should get paid more.

AB: But there's a difference in believing in the market (with its freedom, democracy, differentiation, reward of effort and ability to initiate), and believing in huge centres of financial capital, which are controlling the market and creating absurd financial instruments – basically a sophisticated form of robbery, whether or not they think it's right or wrong. It doesn't mean they've got to have masks on and think of themselves in those terms, but there is a process of a transfer of wealth that is not being earned, gained through their control of the system.

WH: What they're doing is creating what economists call 'economic rent' – a kind of tax on the rest of us – which is giving them disproportionate reward. I'm not going to be tempted into calling it robbery, which I think occupies another set of propositions. But I object violently to what is happening and I think that the state's job is to ensure due desserts. The job of the state is to ensure impartiality of process, and to ensure a properly competitive market and genuine acts of wealth generation. If it finds itself overwhelmed by what you describe as the 'financial narrative' it necessarily finds itself reducing both, and is unable to permit democratic outcomes that checkmate or obstruct the financial narrative. That is where we have been. The interests of finance are critical.

AB: And in Scotland?

WH: Interestingly, when you look at the map of British economic activity, the private sector knowledge economy is very strong in London and Oxford and Cambridge and Milton Keynes (as you'd expect), strongish in Leeds, Bristol and Manchester, but weak everywhere else. In some of the small industrial towns – Wigan, Burnley, Blackburn, Hull, Bradford, Barnsley – the private sector and the knowledge economy part is tiny, there's nothing happening, and you worry about their economic future. But look at Glasgow and Edinburgh, where the last ten years have seen some quite interesting developments in the private sector knowledge economy, and they're right up there. I think the Scots have used devolution quite effectively – either that or something has happened which I don't fully understand. I think that there's the germ of an economic turnaround in Scotland. It may be early days, but they may have begun to use Scottish Government in an intelligent way. I do some work in Scotland and I really want to understand and build on it.

Politics, power and the shape of things to come

GERRY HASSAN IN CONVERSATION WITH ZYGMUNT BAUMAN

Dear Zygmunt,

This is a time of multiple paradoxes, widespread uncertainties, dislocation and a festering, growing unrest in certain communities in the UK
and even more markedly across the Western world if I can use that
term. There is a sense of shifting, myriad movements, and of many of
the certainties and assumptions we have grown up with being
questioned. Maybe a good place to start is to ask and identify where
on earth are we? For unless we know where we currently sit there is
little chance of making sense of the world, or working out if we have
any kind of route map or alternative.

All of this seems to point to a very strange state of affairs. The
crisis of the neo-liberal model has become a crisis of the left. A second
neo-liberal revolution could be upon us. I wonder if it is even useful to
use the term 'left' anymore. The main parties of the left in the UK and
US, under Blair and Clinton, became embodiments of the 'near-left'
and advocates for the neo-liberal project. There once was long ago a
powerful left story, noble, potent, far-reaching and with a sense of
mission, history and agency. Yet even at its peak it was always, despite
its rhetoric and claims of universalism, a partial story of humanity,
and a partial story of potential liberation.

The left used to believe that 'the future' was its property: that
tomorrow belonged to 'us'. Well, no more. Neo-liberalism has become
the last modernist utopia standing, believing it can endlessly re-engineer
human souls with its individualist answers to our human wants. It believes
the future, 'the official future', is their exclusive property: a narrow,
economic determinist world where we all have to rush to the bottom of
the competition ladder, where every individual is sovereign and an
autonomous SME, and the social fabric of society deemed worthless.

Where do we go after the left? How can we take the best from the left but transcend it? How do we begin to resist the onslaught of neo-liberalism? And crucially, how do we re-open the debate – fundamental to being human – about the future?

Regards, Gerry

Dear Gerry,

You say (and rightly so!) that the left 'used to believe that 'the future' was its property'. The snag is that what hides behind that melancholy is not the feeling of being robbed by someone (like neo-liberalism Mark One or Two, or 'populism' here at home, or 'neo-conservatism' in the case of our American cousins) whom we, the left, can confront and fight back with a chance of winning, but a much more awkward sentiment of the future itself having vanished, fallen apart or crashed into smithereens, liquefied or pulverised: no way to touch it, let alone handle. The very possibility to believe in 'the future', being on the left or on the right or anywhere else, is hard to conceive. And this new, disabling feeling is nowadays not just the left's idiosyncrasy, but a sentiment fully and truly 'beyond left and right' (except some lunatic 'fundamentalist' fringes). Its effect is the paralysing, hope-and-imagination-murdering loss of self-confidence: the impression of teetering at the brink of impotence, if not having already tilted into its bottomless hole.

In other words: if half a century ago the enigma and the bone of contention was what is to be done, today's enigma, though not the bone of contention, is who is going (capable of, willing) to do it. There is an awareness (though seldom betrayed to the electorate...) that no one – no force, no extant institution or political body - meets that bill. Neither the Left nor the Right bothered with the question 'who will do it' because of the obviousness of the answer: the State! The State is where the power (ability to get things done) and politics (ability to decide what things are to be done) are.

What has happened? Having been robbed by the globalisation of finances, capitals and trade of much of its power, the State has little choice but (whether by design or by default) to 'de-politicise' many of its previously assumed and jealously guarded prerogatives (by 'contracting them out' to the markets off political bounds or 'subsidiarising' them to yet more powerless local 'authorities' or down-right to individual cunning – regardless of what partisan brand occupies the governmental offices. The blatant inadequacy of extant instruments of political action, and the jarring dearth of new ones able to do the job better, is a non-partisan or supra-party ailment.

This is, I repeat, the weakness shared by the whole political spectre. Having said that, though, we must also admit that the changes on the political scene, particularly when considered together with the profound social transformations, render left-defining objectives, particularly in our, the 'developed' part of the globe, especially difficult to implement.

Z

Zygmunt,

On one level, neo-liberalism and social democracy may be sworn enemies and opposites of left and right, but on another level are natural bed-fellows. Both are modernist utopian projects about grandiose schemes and visions, both view human nature as endlessly pliable and focus on a very narrow notion of human need, are economically determinist seeing growth as the solution, and see planet earth's resources and eco-system as a support mechanism for our endless material desires.

Therefore, it is completely unsurprising that this crisis is as much one of the exhaustion of the centre-left as it is of neo-liberalism. What is surprising is the ease with which neo-liberalism has turned the tables on the centre-left, and made the focal point of the crisis the unsustain-ability of the Western social model. Instead, the only solution on offer is a second wave neo-liberal revolution which extends the commercial-isation of public life, goods and services into previously protected, mostly non-market areas.

A major contribution to why this has occurred and looks likely to be the continued state of affairs for the foreseeable future can be found in the way globalisation has articulated, imagined and captured the future; and given the left's previous history on this you think the left might understand this. Globalisation has presented a version of the world as 'the official future', the summary of the official narrative of government, policy makers, business and other key institutional opinion.

Since the fall of the Berlin Wall, 'the official future' has become an increasingly belligerent, doctrinaire, intolerant worldview, lecturing, prodding and evangelicising for its mission. That is an economically determinist world where prized and prioritised relationships are market driven, social and non-market values are always secondary, wealth and privilege are celebrated, inequality tolerated or championed, and bonds which hold societies together slowly and inexorably weakened.

Globalisation and 'the official future' will in time go the way of the left's modernist dream, and will be destroyed by its own hubris and over-reach: the last modernist utopian project left standing. For this to happen, the beginnings of a counter-story and vision has to emerge. That has to challenge the view that the future has already been decided, which can never be the case, and dare to find the confidence, energy and resources of hope to begin imagining a very different future. At the moment, we seem to be as far away from this point as it is possible to conceive. Do you agree with this? Are there any signs of a viable counter-story emerging and if so where? And if the above is the case, where do we draw resources of hope and imagination from to challenge the closed 'official future'?

G

Gerry,

Your passionate statement is full to the brim with issues, each one con-tentious, each one yet more grave, important, and urgent than the one before. I'll limit myself to three on which, I believe, the fate of all the rest hangs. The first: do social democrats hold a utopia of their own? I doubt it. Not in the world we inhabit, at any rate. For at least 30–40 years, the policy of social-democratic parties has been articulated, one year of neo-liberalism rule after another, by the principle 'whatever you (the centre-right) do, we (the centre-left) can do better'. This state of affairs has its reason: social democracy has lost its own separate constituency – its social fortresses and ramparts, the enclosures inhabited by people at the receiving end of political/ economic actions, waiting/yearning to be recast or lift themselves from the collection of victims into an integrated collective subject of the interests, political agenda and political agency all of its own.

The second: You are fully right in suspecting that 'social state' is nowadays un-sustainable. But for the reason of having nothing to do with the specificity of the 'sociality' of the state, but with the generalised weakening of the state as an 'agency'. I need to repeat what I said before – this is, after all, the hub of all other problems the remnant of the 'welfare state' need to face up to. Our ancestors worried and quarrelled about 'what is to be done'; we are worried, though hardly ever quarrel about 'who is going to do it'; our ancestors on that point never quarrelled, being in complete agreement: 'of course, the State'! The State, that union of power (that is, the ability to have things done) and politics (that is, the ability to decide which things need to be done) is all we need to make the word flesh, whatever the word we may choose. But the self-evidence of such an answer is no longer the case. Politicians leave us in doubt, monotonously repeating after Margaret Thatcher: 'TINA' (There Is No Alternative). Meaning: we make our choice under conditions of not our choice. On this point at least I am inclined to agree, though for different reasons.

The third: globalisation or not, can we go on indefinitely measuring the rise of happiness by the rise of GDP, let alone spreading that habit to the rest of the globe and raise the levels of consumptions to the heights viewed indispensable in the richest countries? There its the impact of consumerism on the sustainability of our shared home, the planet Earth, to consider. We know now all too well that its resources have limits and cannot be infinitely stretched. We know that its resources are too modest to accommodate the levels of consumption rising everywhere to the standards currently reached in the richest parts of the planet – the very standards by which dreams and prospects, ambitions and postulates of the rest of the planet tend to be measured in the information-highways era (according to some calculation, such feat would require multiplying the resources of our planet by the factor of five; five planets instead of the one would be needed). And yet the invasion and annexation of the realm of morality by consumer markets has burdened consumption with functions it can perform only by pushing the levels of consumption ever higher. This is the principal reason for viewing the 'zero growth' as measured by GDP (the statistics of the quantity of money changing hands in buying-selling transactions) as not just economic, but social and political catastrophe.

The moment of truth may be nearer than the overflowing shelves of supermarkets, the websites strewed with commercial pop-ups and choruses of self-improvement experts and how-to-make-friends-and-influence-people counsellors would make us believe. The point is how to precede/forestall its coming with the moment of self-awakening. Not an easy task, to be sure: it would take nothing less than embracing the whole of humanity complete with its dignity and well-being, as well as the survival of the planet, its shared home, by the universe of moral obligations.

Z

Zygmunt,

Thank you for your thoughtful and insightful comments. I am going to respond directly to your three areas and then explore the terrain and possibilities of an alternative politics to the orthodoxies of the age.

First, on the end of the social democratic utopia I agree with your comments: we have witnessed the drift of social democracy until it has become in part 'neo-liberalism with a human face'. There was once a powerful utopian impulse in social democracy and socialism; some of those who still support it cite the success of the Nordic model – the quality of life, public services and economic competitiveness – as proof it still exists, yet even here there is a palpable sense of anxiety, erosion, doubt about the future, and concerns about sustainability in the face of neo-liberalism.

Second, on the social state there has been a profound shift from the question 'our ancestors' worried about, namely 'who is to be done?' to today's 'who is going to do it?'. As you write, 'our ancestors' never quarrelled or doubted that the answer to the first question at the height of managed capitalism was the state.

Third, the official version of globalisation – the forward march of markets, free trade and capital, a vision of linear optimism – of a world of boundless possibilities, opportunities and a better future, is actually one of deep depowering pessimism, of claiming that history is at an end. There is a recognisable argument about the limits to growth and GDP which has been made for the last 40 years, and the lack of a clear relationship between increased GDP and life satisfaction.

However, there are limits to the happiness and well-being industry and critique; the case put by Richard Layard in the UK, and Martin Seligman in the US, is one that leaves untouched the economy, ideology and power. Even the more sophisticated arguments of Wilkinson and Pickett in 'The Spirit Level' exclude the role of ideology and in particular, neo-liberalism, advocating for 'the good society' while saying next to nothing on the economy.

This leads us to wider ground for a feasible alternative and the emerging agenda of self-determination which can combine politics, psychology and power at individual, collective and societal levels. At the individual level, there is a growing academic literature about the requirements for self-determination, namely autonomy, resilience and capacity. This points to the development of a different kind of self: one connected and interconnected, deeply social and thoughtful.

Self-determination could be the progressive answer to neo-liberalism and globalisation, offering an economic, social, cultural and futures politics, of which the last is perhaps the most crucial. We have to defeat the idea of the closed 'official future' and dare to believe that we can make a politics and ideology which takes on and defeats the orthodoxies and deceits of our age: of neo-liberalism and the lies it tells about Britain and the world. All of this raises many questions about visions, ideas, will power, hard and soft power and prospective constituencies, yet these need to be urgently explored.

G

Gerry,

I need to restate that point at the risk of repeating myself, since in your latest statement you've shifted our conversation from 'here and now' and 'within the reach and sight' to an (indefinite) 'out there', 'somewhere in the future'; in short, to 'points of (undated) arrival'. With my incurable sociological bias I feel more at home speaking of the 'points of departure'; and having no prophetic skills, while being aware of the stubbornly self-guided, only retrospectively graspable nature of historical change, I find it terribly difficult to follow you to the ground where you invite me now. We need to know what exactly keeps us where we are stuck, and what hindrances stop us from moving elsewhere? I am not saying that the hindrances, however powerful, can't be overcome by collective concerted effort – the point is that it is the degree of correspondence between the call to move and the popular wisdom derived from daily experience that decides how likely (or unlikely) such a collective/concerted effort is. How probable, or improbable, is it that the call will be heard, listened to, accepted and followed?

You are right when you insist that a 'change to the better' would not arise if reform is diminished and that any programme of improvement needs to be multi-faceted. You unpack that general principle saying that such a programme must combine political, social, psychological and power change. It is the social (the way in which we are 'placed in' and 'incorporated into' the society, having thereby our existential condition and the set of our options shaped) that divides life strategies into realistic and unrealistic and effective and ineffective, and therefore raises or lowers the probability that we, rational beings as seeking the best means to our ends, will rather select some strategies and dismiss some other.

The point I wish to emphasise strongly is that *the time needed by present-day society to rise up to the challenge may be long, as the necessity and the task it needs to confront, point blank, are profuse and daunting.* So maybe the meta-postulate, the condition of sensibility of all and any postulate, is to drop the habit of allowing elections to set the time-frame for thinking, and reorient ourselves to the long term. And I *mean* long. This in itself would be a major breakthrough, if we only manage to do it. Timescale is the socially produced, mind-imprisoning carapace's most vulnerable point: the one point in which that carapace may, conceivably, be broken by what you call 'psychology'. All the same, this feat would need time, determination and patience to be accomplished (among the obstacles, do not count a view that 'future is already determined', but stripping the thought of future dimension, the conditioned reflex which I call 'pointilist' or 'episodic' perception of time; future must first re-enter thought to recover its capacity of guiding human choices).

Let's not be fooled by the amazing speed and facility with which neo-liberal troops dismantled and disabled the web of social institutions sustaining human solidarity: what has been destroyed in a moment of madness or fury, takes years to be rebuild. Destruction is fast and easy – building takes a lot of time and hard work.

Z

Dear Zygmunt,

Thank you for your thoughts which stopped me in my tracks – which can be no bad thing. Lets start with your comment that *the time needed by present-day society to rise up to the challenge may be long, as the necessity and the task it needs to confront, point blank, are profuse and daunting.* This means that we need to start from where we are and say this is our world, this is the state it is in, and this is the dynamic and direction of the unsustainable market fundamentalist vision. And that the current explanations and strategies that are on offer at a British and global level – which call themselves centre-left or progressive – are barely adequate.

This is a good starting place, but is not enough. We need to start thinking of a politics of timescales: of short, medium and long-term approaches, in which the short-term is focused on the above, and the medium to longer-term poses more strategic questions. However, a politics and philosophy which focuses on just getting through the present – and only that – does not seem to be aiming very high, or to be able to mobilise, capture the imagination or succeed. This would be a politics of the negative and opposition; the sort of approach conducive to the last 40 years of the left's backward march, the retreat from socialism to social democracy, and then an even more amorphous 'progressive politics'.

How do we imagine a project of humanity and hope after socialism (if that doesn't sound too much like the way the Kremlin Popular Fronts used to talk at the height of the Cold War)? Firstly, even this opening question reveals the limits of where we are: a project without a name, aims and agency. Secondly, our confusion about language illustrates the wider issue about what the remnants of the left are for: resisting the neo-liberal onslaught, or something else? And then there is the issue of what kind of political and social change we want to imagine and nurture, both in the here and now and more distant future?

There is a long journey to this – 'the century of the self' and the rise of the meritocracy. Michael Young's 'The Rise of the Meritocracy' published in 1958, tells us much that is relevant. Young wrote this as a satire of the Britain of 2033, looking back on a century and half of mass education and selection for the civil service. He found a world where intelligence had been redefined by constant, narrow testing which led to a remaking of terms such as 'ability', 'talent' and 'merit'. This resulted in winners in society thinking that this was because of their personal qualities and virtues, while the non-winners thought that individual weakness and shortcomings had left them where they are. This produced a society where the notion of a social contract, and connection and empathy for one's fellow citizens, began to weaken, then dissolve. Power, finance and politics congregated around 'the new class' of winners, while the excluded minority were left leaderless, unloved and with no political force representing them. Young saw in this dystopian world a quasi-prophecy of the politics of New Labour, whereby Labour broke from its anchoring and mooring and became a technocratic party of 'the new class', with the resultant consequences for politics and society.

Of course, we don't quite live in Michael Young's Britain, but there are some ominous signs. Young invented 'meritocracy' as a warning, but the political class and institutional opinion continually misuse and misunderstand it, believing it a positive virtue and opening, rather than a closing, and evolution of an elite. I don't think that's an accident. Similarly, the massive extension of supposedly open systems of selection based on intelligence testing hasn't led to a new age of egalitarianism, but narrow notions of 'ability' and 'talent' and new elites.

Where this takes us has to be to a politics which goes beyond current definitions and categories, and does not remain shaped by the tribal politics of left and right. After the fall of the Berlin Wall, I stopped calling myself a socialist, and I have never felt comfortable invoking social democracy, still less progressive politics. Yet we face a powerful political project based on the false premise of liberation, freedom, choice and individualism which believes that it goes with the grain of human behaviour and historical trends.

G

Gerry,

Fernand Braudel, the great French historian, made us aware that short-term, middle-term and long-term views uncover and reveal different processes and factors guiding them – each visible solely within, as you put it, 'timescale'. But he addressed his suggestions to historians, hardly to the politicians, let alone to forecasters – since the conclusion drawn from his suggestions was that the game of forecasting is doomed. Historians, professionals of *retrospection*, could discover what the objects of their study could not – precisely because they had no way to divine how their own short-term intentions and deeds may inadvertently coagulate in 'middle-term' trends and then into 'long-term' departures. Only looking back, only with the benefit of hindsight, historians could do it. They already knew, or at least could know, that such-and-such short-term occurrences dovetailed with such-and-such middle term developments, and that ultimately such-and-such transformations took place.

Braudel's recommendations were, even if implicitly rather than explicitly, a manifesto against 'historical determination': nothing can be determined unless it's already happened. This is why I believe that the transplantation of 'timescale thinking' from historiography to political programming is ill-advised and misleading. In opposition to historians, who investigate what-has-already-happened, politicians try to design the non-existing state of affairs called 'future'.

The values we struggle to keep alive are, so to speak, thorns in the body politic that deprive it of the luxury of self-satisfaction and self-complacency. As I keep repeating, socialism is, to borrow the phrase from Santayana, 'a knife with its edge pressed against the future'. What we need do, and what we CAN do, is to prevent that edge from being blunted. Socialism's mission is to force societies to measure themselves against principles of justice, freedom, equality and solidarity, and to admit that it falls well short of either and there remains a lot to be done to come anywhere close.

You ask: 'what the demands of the present are, while looking to the future? And are there any forces emerging which begin to point in the most hesitant way towards what this may look like?' Let me offer you just a few recent examples.

There are growing material proofs, though somewhat lesser number of declarations of faith, that testify that this truly watershed shift in high-level thinking is indeed taking place. The International Labour Organisation's idea to include social security in the list of fundamental human rights is still widely decried as utopia. But in international political practice that idea steers closer and closer to the present and any foreseeable reality. In July 2010 the UN, in a step almost unrecorded in the world press or reaching public awareness, took a bold step of appointing Michelle Bachelet, the former President of Chile, to promote the cause (indeed, a crusade) of spreading the social-welfare practices to the parts of the world that heretofore lacked them. This has been done with the wholehearted support of the World Monetary Fund and the World Bank – the two institutions on record as fighting tooth and nail for merciless cuts in state expenditure and against state-guaranteed social protection in developing countries. A formidable change of heart indeed, if true. The big question is whether the new mood (steadily turning into the new mantra) will survive the reverberations of the current credit/financial instability.

These are all heart-warming sights. Though, I repeat again, we cannot look into the future (the only thing likely to be found there is our own imagination, and we have no way of deciding is this imagination sober or fanciful). Human history has few 'iron rules', but here is one hardest of them all: all beginnings of great transformations are too inconspicuous to be noted.

Z

Dear Zygmunt,

I would like to start with some brief thoughts on the future of the left and the future per se, and the search for alternatives. First, earlier in our discussion you mentioned that the social democratic utopia no longer existed, and that 'social democracy had lost its social fortresses and ramparts'. Yet, in your last contribution you talked of socialism as a current relevance which we could use to assess our societies in relation to justice, freedom, equality and solidarity. If social democracy is in the state you say, surely socialism as a living project is over and instead we have to imagine new forms of social solidarity.

Second, the perils of predicting the future are well documented.

However, thinking about and imagining the future has been fundamental to being human since the evolution of human consciousness. What I want to emphasise is two fold – that we are living in a multi-dimensional crisis of 'progress', and related to this a crisis of how we imagine the future; and that irrespective of the flaws, limits and pitfalls of how we have conceived of the terms 'progress' and 'the future' we are now, in relation to these terms, in a new kind of era.

I would like to conclude by returning to themes closer to home, and then expanding to a global level. Scotland's political experiment has seen the exploration of self-government through the establishment of a political project focused narrowly on the Parliament and politicians. This has been an important phase in many respects, beginning the slow democratisation of parts of Scottish public life, but woefully inadequate and unambitious. I think that there is the political appetite and constituency in Scotland for an agenda of self-determination, of shifting power economically, socially and culturally to individuals, communities and society, developing a politics which is appropriate to the age of 'liquid democracy' and 'liquid modernity'. A genuine politics of self-determination has the prospect of informing a different politics of self-government: of a politics which isn't about the age old constitutional question – of Scotland in the union or independent – but fleshing out an economic and social agenda, and making the connection between political power in the UK and people's lives.

Such a politics has the potential of drawing from the best of the Labour and Scottish Nationalist perspectives, articulating the idealism and hopes of their early radical traditions, while developing a politics which is relevant today: post-socialist and post-nationalist. There is a prospective constituency for this north of the border: in our search for a radical, egalitarian politics and society which is profoundly different from the neo-liberal heartland of the UK political system. This would fit with the search in the Nordic nations for a sustainable politics of social solidarity. Rather than see these societies as the future (as some in Britain do) we should join them in assessing how we can preserve what is best in the social democratic vision, but start from an understanding that dealing with the neo-liberal leviathan will not be served by a politics of appeasement and market creep in our societies.

I would like to conclude this fascinating discussion with a set of questions. How do we challenge the dystopian vision of the future which is integral to enlightenment globalisation? Do you think there is any prospect of the British left realising that the British state they invest their hopes in is at the heart of the problem and one which not only has repercussions at a UK level but a global one, given the neo-liberal advocacy of the British state across the world? And could the beginnings of part of the solution, or more accurately, a different politics come from the smaller nations of northern Europe: those who have a social democratic mentality and who could develop a post-neo-liberal politics?

G

Dear Gerry,

In a most recently published (*Indigo* journal) essay, as before in his study *The Idea of Justice* (Harvard UP, 2009), Amartya Sen does not beat about the bush when analysing the lessons to be drawn from the 2008 global economic slump. Whereas some very rich persons saw their fortunes somewhat diminished, it was the poorest people, local or global, that have been affected most badly - 'families who were already worst placed to face any further adversity have often suffered from still greater deprivation, in the form of lasting joblessness, loss of housing and shelter, loss of medical care, and other deprivations that have plagued the lives of hundreds of millions people'. The conclusion, Sen avers, is all too obvious. If you want to correctly evaluate the severity of the current global crisis, examine 'what is happening to the lives of human beings, especially the less privileged people – their well-being and their freedom to lead decent human lives'.

But wouldn't we rather begin with defining the standard of justice, so that we would be better armed to spot and isolate the cases of injustice whenever and wherever they appear (or rather hide)? Easier said than done. Amartya Sen would not advise to take this line. Asking what the perfect justice would look like is 'a question in the answer to which there could be substantial differences even among very reasonable people'. Obviously, we may add, as reasonable people seasoned in the art of argumentation and rhetoric are to be found in every one of the camps determined, in a bizarre reversal of Kant's categorical imperative, to flex the proposed universal standards so they may fit their anything but universal interests; in other words, to summon the idea of justice to the defence of a particular injustice that rebounds as their privilege. There is little hope, then, that a debate about universal standards of justice will ever bear fruits palatable to, let alone welcome by, everyone involved and acquire genuine universality.

In somewhat different and perhaps simpler terms, a society up in arms to promote the *well-being of the underdog*; 'well-being' including the capacity of making real the formal human right to decent life – recasting 'freedom de jure' into 'freedom de facto'. I believe that it is social democracy (or at any rate it is social democracy that has been called) to be *the conscience of such a society – its spur and moving engine* – because 'being an underdog' and 'suffering most blatant of injustices' are for all practical intents and purposes synonyms. And that necessitates what Richard Rorty has called a 'politics of campaigns'.

But at what level of multi-tier, human self-organisation do such 'politics of campaigns' need to aim? You are right in complaining that the problem, at least on the British Isles, lies with the Westminster state. But I doubt whether much can be done to change it. For reasons discussed before and others, the Westminster state – like all other nominally 'sovereign' territorial states – seems nowadays to be the least hope-inspiring of targets. Power to do things evaporates from the states into the extraterritorial global 'politics free' space, together with the states' ability and desire to define the uses to which that power ought to be put; what is left to the incumbents of Westminster is to confess to their haplessness by repeating that 'there is no alternative' to the game dominated/dictated by 'global forces'. Hopes for more state-level justice are, it seems, least prudently invested. I suppose that the more promising targets for the kind of political strategy suggested here lie both *above* and *below* that level. Below? What you rightly point out when you bring in the issue of local self-government (in my view playing, potentially, a double role: of the agency able to bring more justice to our neighbourly, face-to-face cohabitation, and a laboratory in which the ways of mutually beneficial coexistence on *all* levels are designed, experimented with and put to test). Above? Let's start with social democracy making up its mind about Europe, our nearest, immediate 'above'.

The truth is that *we cannot effectively defend our freedoms here at home while fencing ourselves off the rest of the world and attending solely to our affairs here at home...* Fellow socialists, time to raise our eyes, above the nearest fences!

The present momentum seems to be shaped by two different (perhaps complementary, perhaps incompatible) logics – and it is impossible to decide in advance which logic will ultimately prevail. One is the *logic of local retrenchment:* the other is the *logic of global responsibility and global aspiration.*

The first logic is that of the quantitative expansion of the territory-and-resource basis for the *Standsortkonkurrenz* strategy – 'competition between localities', 'locally grounded competition'; more precisely, competition between territorial states. Even if no attempts were ever made by the founders of the European Common Market and their successors to emancipate economy from their relatively incapacitating confinement in the *Nationalökonomie* frames, the 'war of liberation' currently conducted by the global capital, finances and trade against 'local constraints', a war triggered and intensified not by local interests but by the global diffusion of opportunities, would have been waged anyway and went on unabated. The role of European institutions *does not* consist in eroding the member-states' sovereignty and in exempting economic activity from their controlling (and constraining) inter-ference; in short, it *does not* consist in facilitating, let alone initiating, the divorce procedure between power and politics. For such purpose the services of European institutions are hardly required.

The logic of global responsibility, on the other hand (and once that responsibility is acknowledged and acted upon, also the logic of global aspiration), is in principle aimed at confronting the globally generated problems point-blank – at their own level. It stems from the assumption that a lasting and truly effective solution to the planet-wide problems can be only found and work through the *re-negotiation and reform of the web of global interdependencies and interactions.* Instead of aiming at the least local damage and most local benefits derived from the capricious and haphazard drifts of global economic forces, it would rather pursue a new kind of global setting, such in which the itineraries of economic initiatives anywhere on the planet won't be any longer whimsical and guided haphazardly by momentary gains alone, with no attention paid to the side-effects and 'collateral casualties', and no importance attached to the social dimensions of the cost-and-effects balances. To quote Habermas, that logic is aimed at the development of 'politics that can catch up with global markets'.

Like our ancestors, we move at present on the rising slope toward a mountain pass which we have never climbed before and have no inkling about the view that will open once we reach it. One thing we can be sure of is that where we are now, at some point of a steeply rising slope, we cannot rest for long, let alone settle. And so we go on moving; we move not so much 'in order to', as 'because of' – we move because we can't stop nor stand still. Only when (if) we reach the pass and survey the landscape on its other side, time will come to move 'in order to'; pulled ahead by the sight of a visible destination, by the goal within our reach, rather than pushed to move by current discomforts. The choice we confront is between our cities turning into places of terror 'where the stranger is to be feared and distrusted', or sustaining the legacy of mutual civility of citizens and 'solidarity of strangers', solidarity strengthened by the ever harder tests to which it is subjected and which it survives – now and in the future. The choice is between 'left future' and no future.

What lies ahead has been prophetically put in writing by Franz Kafka – as a premonition, a warning, and encouragement; and let me conclude with his words:

> If you find nothing in the corridors open the doors, if you find nothing behind these doors there are more floors, and if you find nothing up there, don't worry, just leap up another flight of stairs. As long as you don't stop climbing, the stairs won't end, under your climbing feet they will go on growing upwards. (from Advocates).

Z

Ukanian Discussions and Homo Britannicus

RICHARD WYN JONES IN CONVERSATION WITH TOM NAIRN

Annwyl Tom,

You've been providing a running commentary on successive UK governments at least since Wilson's first term as Prime Minister. It strikes me that the present administration provide an almost paradigmatic example of that Ukanian governmental trait which you've highlighted with such mordant effect - namely the frantic, rhetorical focus on rebirth, renaissance and renewal in order that, what we might term the 'deep state', can remain essentially unchanged. In fact, the present lot are such perfect exemplars of the Ukanian psychodrama that is almost approaches pastiche. The stress on renewing the financial basis of the state – and the almost sadistic self-righteous pleasure being extracted from the delivery of public spending cuts – while all the while defending the very regulation structures that led the world economy to the brink, is particularly choice. The readiness of the Liberal Democrats to trade their long term commitment to democratic reform for a referendum on just about the only democratic electoral system that might serve to give first past the post a good name, is surely another example of the ability of the deep state to keep on keeping on under the guise of renewal? And of course, the unmistakable, undeniable reek of class privilege that surrounds the UK coalition government is almost beyond parody: satire is dead, and all that...

And yet, some things do seem to have changed. The obvious social liberalism of the upper echelons of the Conservative Party is, to my mind, noteworthy. Indeed, the transformation in social attitudes on sexuality and race is perhaps the most positive intended outcome of the New Labour years and it seems churlish not to admit that.

In terms of devolution, and as you've argued to great effect, it's the unintended effects that are the most interesting: the ways in which a reform on and at the margin, that was regarded as a means of allowing the core to remain untouched and unchanged, has, nonetheless, developed a momentum and a dynamic of its own that – ultimately – cannot but have an impact on the centre. That dynamic has been par-ticular obvious since May 2010, as the political sub-systems revolving around Cardiff and Edinburgh have become very rapidly detached from – and, on my reading, rather contemptuous of – London. It's here, surely, that we find the most striking change from the narrative of Ukanian statecraft that has become familiar through your work?

But before we move to the periphery, how would you characterise the present UK administration and the condition of the deep state of which it adorns?

Richard

Dear Richard,

Thank you very much for your thoughts about post-devolution politics! The 'condition of the deep state' of Great Britain (as you put it) goes right back to the beginning of nation-statehood. Both Ernest Gellner and Liah Greenfeld placed that beginning in England: the original motor of industrialisation and its political manifestation: the 'nationalism' informing and shaping the world process over (approximately) 1789–1989. This development has provisionally concluded with 'globalisation'. Not because the whole globe is industrialised naturally: but the overall shape and meaning has been settled by the defeat of 'Leninism', or Socialism as a comprehensive alternative mode of socio-economic modernity. The reality-mode that started with England has concluded with China: state sponsorship of capitalism in the world's greatest *ethnie* — from England to the 'Middle Kingdom' of the species.

Yet, this concluding stage reveals an oddity, of which the British-Irish archipelago periphery remains a part. Simply because it was 'first' in this grand process, the English nation would never become a typical part: the prime mover could never turn into a nationality like the hundreds of others generated by commercial-industrial development. I have argued in Open Democracy that the English equivalent has been a 'bigger-than' ideology, originally vehicled through empire, then willfully perpetuated via the Special Relationship with the USA: anything to avoid 'little England', ordinariness, being *une nation comme les autres.*

The dilemma of the periphery is that Scotland, Wales and Northern (Protestant) Ireland were always too small to affect this larger trend. They are unmentioned in Greenfeld's definitive account, and found themselves carried forward (and outwards) on the back of England's 85 per cent majority expansion: adjuncts of empire, Anglo-British Commonwealth, half-hearted EU Membership, and American lackeydom. Now they have to find themselves as left-overs, 'also-rans', attempting to realise political identities long after de-colonisation and 'national liberation' in the mainstream sense. The process started in 1915, but is still unfinished. But they now have to do so in the uncomfortable shadow of an England itself troubled by inevitable decline, and the breakdown of 'Britishness' — the ideological vestment of prolonged 'bigger-than' beliefs and claims. As long as they have this contraption, the English feel little need for a democracy 'of their own': such a 'little' nationality continues to signify loss, resignation from a habitual world presence and importance.

Naturally, they are in these conditions vexed by peripheral self-assertion: undermining from within, as if external forces and changes were not enough. Their circumstances aren't unique: Iberia, France, Italy and Germany also had 'peripheries' and sometimes reluctant minorities, and sought to appease them with imperial opportunities — shares in the spoils. However, the comparison at once shows up a longer-term difference. The English were by far the most successful, remaining undefeated in the global conflicts provoked by North-Atlantic expansion. Hence (as you say) the 'deep state' has been able to continue *relatively* unaffected, and capable of stratagems like 'devolution' to render decline and retreat more palatable.

Has this therapy really 'developed a momentum and a dynamic of its own', with 'an impact on the centre' as you suggest? Certainly, no Westminster government would risk undoing devolution. But then, what the Great-Brit political elite wanted was simply life as near normal as possible: keeping the marginals busy with harmless local business, mutual 'respect' allowing non-local affairs to continue unaffected — matters for The Crown, the National Interest with capitals. The historical sublimation of English nationality into British Patriotism had as one implication a weirdly disproportionate emphasis on social class: the absence of identikit national egalitarianism favoured a pathology of stratification — acceptance of a 'Them and Us' society and institutions, including a 'ruling class' identified with the neo-Gothic piles on the London Thames: 'Parliamentary Socialism' (in the words of the father of the Labour Party's new Leader), and as you put it, the 'reek of class privilege' still present in Cameron's coalition regime.

To have an impact on *this* centre may require more than any part of the old periphery can mobilise on its own. Wales, Scotland and Northern Ireland are too different, and too variously compromised in the former manoeuvrings of Britishness to do it on their own. On the other hand, might they not do so *together*? The formula presents no problem: the Great-Brit unitary state should be replaced by some kind of federation. And the sole possible form for that seems to be a confederation where sovereignty is transferred from the neo-Gothic ruins to actual, democratic nations with their own representative assemblies or parliaments...including of course that of England. Such a British-Irish arrangement could take the Helvetic Confederation as its model: chosen union, at the basis of which is the right *not* to belong or continue. 'Independence' is the only way forward allowed by prevailing norms: whether membership of European Union, or of an eventual British-Irish Confederation, or (preferably) of both.

It may be objected that Switzerland has in practice turned into a 'nation-state' of the international arena, its various *ethnies*, languages and faiths agreeing to act largely as one through the convulsions of last century. However, it must be remembered the Swiss had no choice, since they had to modernise in a world of nationalisms. Today, the ex-British confront altered circumstances, an age of 'post-nationalisms', or 'globalisation'. The periphery is ahead of the old game, while the centre insists on sensible archaism: the former is (again in your words) 'rather contemptuous of London', a 21st century Vienna summed up by the feebly re-jigged House of Lords. Unfortunately its version of 'Austria' is demographically and culturally dominant, and quite good at rhetorical up-dating charades with liberal ('Lib-Dem') assistance. Cameron's coalition is the most accomplished yet: 'New, new!'

squiggled over the ancient tripe, and shortly to be buttressed by some actual changes to the historic entrails, through the least harmful-looking of possibilities, 'Alternative Vote' which will (as in Australia) conserve a two-party, 'Ins-and-Outs' structure amidst louder noise from the public, and the 'airing' of alternatives rather than their tiresome embodiment via proportional representation. The Second Chamber may become a system ventilation shaft, if a plausible formula can be dreamt up for farther re-jigging, beyond blood-lines and tradition.

The periphery should surely refuse such pathos: 'confederation' or nothing — i.e. straightforward secession, that's that. The Scottish Government is in the strongest position here, thanks to the early-modern Treaty of Union (1707), an international agreement that could be renounced with enough popular support. However, such self-determination would of course profoundly affect periphery politics as a whole, including (very importantly) Northern Ireland, the territory of 'Ulster Scots' as more than just a dialect. A combination of allied agitation within the 'UK', and appeals to the European Union and other transnational bodies, leading to the equivalent political theatre, Alfred Hitchcock's famed moment in Psycho when 'Mother' is unveiled in her wing armchair as a decayed cult-cadaver?

Regard, Tom

Annwyl Tom,

Having being so heavily influenced by your work it's perhaps not surprising that I find the diagnosis you offer very persuasive indeed! I do, however, have some doubts about the treatment you suggest. In particular, how plausible is it to suggest that federalism or even con-federalism is even a remotely viable outcome? I ask this not from the perspective of the 'periphery', where the appeal is all too obvious. You'll recall that someone like Gwynfor Evans spent decades arguing for a 'Brythonic Confederation'! More recently, the leading intellectual figure associated with the Conservative party in Wales, David Melding, has made a strong case for a federal Britain (*Will Britain survive beyond 2020?* (Institute of Welsh Affairs, 2009); case which has clearly resonated across the devolved section of our political class.

My doubts rather arise from the nature of the institutions at the core. As you have pointed out more forcibly than anyone else, these institutions are buttressed by deeply sedimented assumptions of 'Greatness', 'global leadership', and all that. It's their very *raison d'être* and obviously visible even through such apparently realistic attenuations as 'punching above our weight' and the even more risible 'being Greece to Washington's Rome'. In light of this, isn't the idea that those core institutions would be willing to accept the fundamental constraints that would be imposed upon them by a federal, or even confederal, constitution simply implausible? It seems to me that to believe that is to set aside the very insights of your work tracing the development of the English (then Ukanian) state from the early modern period to the present. One might even want that this is made even more implausible by the availability of an alternative that would allow the core – 85 per cent of the whole, as you say – to remain pretty much unchanged at only a marginal (sic) cost to itself: that alternative, of course, being independence. While I certainly understand the rhetorical and even emotional appeal of federalism or confederalism for the periphery, what's in it for the core?

Richard

Dear Richard,

Many thanks for your comments, and for the important and pointed question posed by all aspirations towards federal or confederal solutions to the post-UK Dilemma: 'What could be in it for them?' meaning at once the English, and the Anglo-British governing stratum? After all, as you suggest, the near-absence of political 'little England' does imply a large, possibly uncomfortable shift for an 85 per cent majority confident of deciding the direction and sense of 'Britishness'.

But look at it from another angle, one surprisingly absent from almost all recent debates about the United Kingdom's: *the monarchy.* My earlier remarks about the non-history of English nationalism, and their relative indifference to England-only identity, made the mistake of neglecting this factor. In fact, such neglect is invariably a kind of muted triumph for the All-Brits. Over-amplification of Windsordom has a half-hidden other side, in an 'exceptionality' that justifies the indifference, and the accompanying feeling of not being 'like that' (i.e. 'ethnic'). 'Multi-cultural' in the Britannic sense is very close to the same thing. All 'races' and nationalities are not only drawn together by 'civic' statehood, equal rights, and so on, but also by a kind of worship: loyalty to 'the Crown', an idealised institution with a personalised embodiment that channels a good deal of the emotion now usually devoted to national identity. In addition, this transcendence is fortified by a semi-sacred elderly lady who has followed Queen Victoria into an untouchable limbo: thus 'Britishness' has acquired a halo that compensates for absent 'ethnicity', making the homeland into a sort of holy land. Anglicanism alone could never have achieved this by itself: the point is that other Protestants *and* non-Christian faiths can join in, or at least feel happy going along with it. Canalisation of identity-sentiment is very important in modernising societies — and one can reasonably doubt that globalisation will divert or diminish that significance. The salience of monarchy is part of the explanation of the absent English-national voice, and also of its surprising bondage to the ultra-right-wing 'British' National Party: ordinary civic-secular nationalism has been usurped in advance, by the glamour of backwardness. The glamour is real enough, and currently being polished up by Prince William and Kate Middleton. Elizabeth II won't last forever, and it's doubtful if King Charles III will live up to her standards of backwardness. This is why the official non-Republicanism of both Welsh and Scottish nationalism is so dubious. There may be few votes right now in 'strident' anti-monarchism; but there could soon be fewer still in supporting Carolingian restoration. A staunchly non-committal position would at least offer fewer hostages to fortune.

As for the English nation itself, it has thus benefited not only from historical priority — the 'launching' of the standard-issue nation-state and nationalism — but from an ongoing identification-machinery that justifies and sustains that unique path. And the aim of the forthcoming referendum in May 2011 is additional blessings for the Anglo-Brit way. An alternative vote system has been accepted by Cameron and his party for that reason. It's the 'Australian' system, and it's worth observing some recent criticism of this. The most incisive is Peter Botsman's *The Great Constitutional Swindle: a Citizen's View of the*

Australian Constitution (Pluto Press Australia, 2000). 'A great swindle or sting is one in which the victim walks away feeling a winner...' The Constitution in question 'was never approved by a majority of Australians (he continues)...and was in large part written by a man whose ideas and principles were never acknowledged or articulated'. Not only were its imperfections glossed over, 'worst of all, it could only be changed with the greatest of difficulty' via farther and more complex referenda (p.50).

If it takes place at all, many will support next May's referendum as a 'first step' towards more serious reform, hoping that a *process* will emerge in its wake. Many Liberal Democrats naturally support it for this reason; but Conservatives and Labourites are mainly assuming the contrary — that such an historic shift will itself *be* the 'process', and endure thereafter with only minor adjustments. They are counting on the inherited inertia of an old and self-satisfied order, plus a degree of popular indifference (or even hostility) to politics as such. The aim of the approaching AV referendum is to provide a zimmer-frame for the old order, enabling it to stagger forward more convincingly in the new century. 'Voices' are fine, providing democratic look-alike features — notably in devolved regions where anti-stagger politics have been gaining ground.

This is why I feel some doubt about your characterisation of Cameron and 'the upper echelons of the Conservative Party' as 'social liberalism'. It is surely more like the psychology of victors, reassured by the evident defeat of Socialism and the absence of any plausible successor. Boosted farther by the coalition with the Liberal Democrats, they can afford to relax a little ideologically. In the same period we have also witnessed (notably in Scotland) the rise of what I'm tempted to call 'Right-wing Trotskyism', a loud journalistic clamour for return to the sacred truths of Neo-liberalism and free enterprise undefiled by what they call 'the public sector'. Commentators like Michael Fry and Tom Miers maintain that Scottish autonomy should be consecrated by return to these truths, rather than advance to independent statehood. Miers's *The Devolution Distraction* (2010) is an outstanding recent example. Just as many right-thinking socialists and communists never forgave later leaders for their betrayal of Leninism, these apostles of capitalist righteousness denounce the abandonment of Friedrich Von

Hayek and Thatcherism. Perhaps no single figure sums up the true road quite in the way Leon Trotsky was made to by disappointed Leftists from the '30s up to 1989: however, the traitors have become so numerous, scattered and powerful that angry Rightists never lack suitable targets.

The tone and emphasis of their arguments strike a familiar chord to many older Leftists. For many missionaries, for about half a century the truth lay in a *return* to gospels unheeded, or at least misunderstood. Stalin in the East and 'social-democrats' elsewhere had either forgotten or travestied the real message of history, and the way forward demanded rediscovery and 'radical' implementation of this primal plan. Hence, abortions like the USSR and the UK Labour Party had to be denounced, so that a new start could be made. It doesn't occur to the new apostles of capital that another abortion has taken place: even as they were composing their sermons, the global economy foundered into a crisis as yet unresolved, and was only partially saved by the assorted 'public sectors' of various states. 'Social Democracy' has been at least partially vindicated by these moves and acquired a new status and new possibilities. On the other hand, Leninism and counter-Leninism alike had been exposed by the course of events. A new start is indeed being imposed, but not one delivered by 'history' or disregarded Messiahs.

Nationalism is part of that new start, and so (therefore) is what has been launched in both Wales and Scotland since 1997. We have the great good fortune to participate not in 'belated' national-liberation movements, but in ones linked to the awakening process of 'globalisation': therefore early days, therefore, not just left-over problems and the hang-over from empire and first-round industrialisation. The Welsh input is probably vitally important here. Wales is closer to England, not separated from it by a broad marchland like the Scots, and also, as Neal Ascherson has pointed out, 'English attitudes to Welshness... are often genuinely hostile' (see 'Future of an Unloved Union', in Tom Devine's collection *Scotland and the Union 1707–2007*). We jointly confront *Homo Britannicus*, as he says, like the people of Northern Ireland. While most voters in the periphery would probably still prefer a confederation as the successor to 'Britannicus', this answer presupposes the sovereignty of its parts, including England. I hope the March 3rd referendum of this new year gives the Welsh Assembly more of the 'law-making powers' it needs — a more confident step in the direction of sovereign independence. Acquiring new powers is no longer just 'devolution': in the context of a declining British realm, that process itself gets new meaning every day. The vital thing here is that 'the notion of 'Britain' is weakening as identity politics — already embedded in Scotland and Wales — take root in England... The gentleman class has left the public stage, and the repackaging of Victorian bourgeois ethics as 'British values' is too vapid to be a substitute'.

Let's help them along! In time, I hope this dialogue will in time swell into a joint approach from Edinburgh, Cardiff and Belfast — into a demand for England too to rid itself of *Homo Britannicus,* and establish a different style of association over these islands. There will be nothing 'little' about such a result: rather, something worthy of the global times — a house of many colours that will bring new life to the opening, broader scene, a 'universal' that does not suppress but demands contrast and variety.

Regard, Tom

Annwyl Tom,

That's such a fascinating and wide-ranging response that I'm tempted to respond by digressing wildly! In particular, I was very interested in what you had to say about the position of the Ukanian monarchy, even at the end of the first decade of the twenty first century. I've often wondered how much of the argument of the genuinely brilliant *Enchanted Glass* you believe has survived the post-Pont de l'Alma process of public disenchantment with the Windsors? More than one might imagine, seems to be the answer – at least for the time being. But I'm not so sure.

I still recall with some embarrassment the response in my home village to the Silver Jubilee in 1977. With the sole, dubious distinction of being the original home of the *Tuduriaid* – better known to most of our readers by their sanitised (i.e. Anglicised) moniker of the Tudors – the tiny rural community of Penmynydd on Ynys Môn (Anglesey) has few claims to fame. But for a student of Welsh nationalism like myself, one interesting thing about the place is that in the late 1930s quite a substantial group of the community's young farmers joined *Plaid Genedlaethol Cymru* (Welsh Nationalist Party – after 1945, Plaid Cymru). Given how marginalised and even despised the party was in that period, this was far from an obvious – or cost-free – choice. By my time, this same group of men had transposed into the community's organic (all-male) leadership – forming the deaconate in the chapels, the parish council, and so on. I'm pretty sure that their voting behaviour never wavered in the interim yet, in 1977, there they were visiting every home in the village asking for financial contributions in order to hold a village sports day (all to be held through the medium of Welsh, of course) in honour of the Queen's Jubilee.

For them and that generation it was simply *unthinkable* not to do this. By contrast, I think that it's equally unthinkable that the same thing could happen today; the contemporary equivalents of those good, honourable men simply wouldn't feel obliged to behave in the same way. Perhaps the 'Wills and Kate' show can get the show back on the road. It certainly won't be through lack of trying, that's for sure. The BBC – with Huw Edwards, son of one of the 20th century's most prominent and passionate Welsh nationalists, to the fore – will doubtless try their best to enthuse us all about the 'great historic significance' of it all. But the sense of social conformity – let alone the monarchical magic – that led the village elders of Penmynydd to traipse from house to house 35 years ago has surely dissipated for good? And, dispiriting though it is to admit it, it's not republican sentiment or the force of some better argument that has done for them (principled opposition to the anti-democratic effects of the royal prerogative, or some such), but rather the logic of (late) print capitalism. The Windsors are now an inextricable part of the celebrity industry in which all those interested enough – sedated enough, may be better – are invited to speculate with increasingly wild and prurient abandon about their clothes, their diets, their sexual proclivities or their views of some prominent contestant on the reality show *de jour*. The dignified part of the constitution is doomed once it's fighting for attention with ballroom dancing rugby players.

But let me try to stick to the point and return to the nature of post-devolution Ukania. In particular, I'd like us to focus on questions of motive and agency. I must confess that I still remain deeply sceptical of the notion that the UK's ruling stratum may yet be persuaded to undergo the huge traumas that would be necessitated by a move to a federal or confederal system. My own view of this has been cemented by contrasting experiences when talking to central state bureaucrats in Madrid and London. In the Spanish capital, mention of Catalan or Basque national aspirations – and in particular the former – leads almost instantly to nigh-on incoherent rage. The unity of the Spanish national territory is a deeply felt article of faith. Any deviation is treated as a personal affront; any genuine threat (even if wholly democratic in nature) is regarded, by more than one might imagine, as a legitimate *casus belli*. In our imperial capital, by contrast, a very different attitude seems to prevail; this notwithstanding Neal Ascherson's observation about the particular complexity of attitudes towards Wales (and at this point I can't help but recall an encounter with one very animated member of the current UK cabinet who was explaining to me, finger pointed, that 'Wales simply isn't a nation!') My impression is that most officials in London seem to be very relaxed about the implications of devolution. Rather, the prevailing attitude seems to be one of more or less benign indifference. So long, that is, that it doesn't affect them. Indeed, I strongly suspect that if forced to choose between undergoing a radical change in order to create a sustainable post-devolution system or simply letting the 15 per cent go, few would hesitate long before plumping for the latter. Likewise, what remains of the monarchy would adjust easily enough to a situation of several post-Kingdom Kingdoms. The one genuinely significant group within the UK's ruling stratum and political class that does seem to share a Madrid-style commitment to the territorial integrity of the British part of the UK state is the Labour Party. In this case, of course, it's very easy to see 'what it's it for them'!

All of which brings me to your sense of where the Labour Party is likely to go now; both the British party and its Scottish incarnation? The party's situation here in Wales is very interesting. They are just about to complete four years of sharing power with Plaid Cymru and even many of those who initially resisted governing with the 'Nats' seem desperate to repeat the experience. Even if the election result in May leaves them technically able to govern alone, you strongly suspect that they won't. They would prefer to renew the coalition. Meanwhile the new UK government's decision to reduce the number of Welsh MPs from the current 40 to around 30 means that Welsh Labour MPs, until now a key block on further reform, are set to lose even more of their power – yet another of those unintended consequences! Indeed it seems to me that the Welsh Labour Party is now more united in its support for home rule than at any time in its history. With so much of the traditional Labourism you first started to analyse back in the mid 1960s having been undermined – by social change as well as New Labourism – the Welsh party seems to be feeling its way towards becoming a patriotic, moderately social democratic formation. In other words, something that looks remarkably like latter day Plaid Cymru, albeit without the latter's cultural inheritance. You'll also recall the remarkable Phil Williams, one of the most interesting characters in the recent history of Welsh politics – Cambridge Apostle turned key nationalist activist. Phil used to tell me that he believed that the key role of Plaid was to persuade the Labour Party to give us independ- ence! He would say that with a characteristic twinkle in his eye, yet, equally characteristically, he was making a serious point. It's one of those Adornian formulations, I suppose. One in which the truth resides precisely in the exaggeration. And while we are clearly a very long way off anything like independence, and almost everybody in the Welsh Labour Party would still baulk at the suggestion that we could or should ever get there, you nonetheless get the feeling that they are now increasingly aware of the fact that they are embarked on a journey that will lead inexorably to what we might term 'ever looser union'. They are increasingly relaxed about that too.

From this distance, however, it looks very different in Scotland. Yet you would suspect that if Labour do get to form a government in Edinburgh, they will rapidly find themselves pushed by the same logic into a position roughly analogous to that of their Welsh colleagues; particularly so now that the 'big beast' generation of Scottish Labour politicians have lost all power and influence in Westminster. If that does turn out to be case then even the most current fervent supporters of Ukanian territorial integrity and unity will have departed the scene.

Richard

Dear Richard,

I too recall fuses being blown on the sacred subject of Hispanidad, clear indications of an insecure metropolitanism — deprived of an earlier overseas empire, yet unconsoled by subsequent 'little Spanish' nationhood and -ism. Spain has to remain big, or it would be...well, nothing. Wasn't it Harold Wilson who uttered something similar about Anglo-Britain? One tempting position here from the 'peripheral' angle is to reply: '*Damn you*... Get used to it, ceasing to be Bigger Than doesn't entail intolerable smallness, just being like most other peoples and nationalities. Kindly stop being ridiculous, and adjust to the normalcy of globalisation!' Such reproaches don't go down well, in part because grandiosity tends to be sustained by so many intellectuals: big-city mental expansionists (brainy body-builders) who can't help feeling that contraptions like Spain and Great Britain remain closer to The Universal than parish-pumps like Wales, Catalonia and Brittany. They feel like be-medalled veterans of early modernity, being requested to turn in their decorations for scrap.

But globality was supposed to be a sensible Big Lads' arrangement, not an all-round collapse of stout parties! Isn't this why the roads to littler Italy and Germany have been quite easy, while those leading to a similar condition in France, Russia, Spain and Britland are so daunting? Those who made it too big, too early, find themselves today unfairly re-dimensioned, struggling to tread water in shallower seas. And yet, the earth emerging beneath their feet *is* the real thing: humanity's diversity at last establishing itself, after the phoney phase of 'nation-alisms' that were largely driven by the first-round need to industrialise, on a scale that tended to neutralise variety (and sometimes did obliterate it). Now, thank God, the survivors can re-group and begin to put things right via 'globalisation'. The latter is the liberation of human-national nature, not its coalescence into All-the-Sameness. Common ground-rules and recognition of being 'in the same boat' are one thing; homogeneity is quite another. Or to put it another way: equality of tongues and cultures is one thing, together with transla-tion-devices; 'globish' is something else.

The former has another outstanding advantage: it accords easily with the wider and generally accepted perspective of natural selection. In his *Origin of Species* (1859), Darwin concluded by looking forward to a *societal* 'struggle for life' based on 'Divergence of Character': 'There is grandeur in this view of life, with its several powers, having been originally breathed into a few forms or in to one; and that, whilst this planet has gone cycling on according to the fixed law of gravity, from so simple a beginning endless forms most beautiful and most wonderful have been, and are being, evolved' (*On Natural Selection*, Penguin Books 'Great Ideas' selection, 2004, pp.116–7). It took global-what's-it to (at last) put us in our place: out there, and evolving.

Far from apologising for your examples of old and new Royalism, shout them out: that's where it's at, or rather, where we are all at. I can't reply in kind, having just come home from a decade in Australia. However, distance is more than a tyranny: it has some consolations, among them what Levi-Strauss called 'The View From Afar'. There, the Brit-Irish periphery can be viewed as a living fossil, dragged along a prolonged detour of imperialism to globalism, but currently finding its assorted places: that's why even England should find its own eventual place too: the first shall be almost last, and deserves a hand, which is in part be provided by us doing our own things. With any luck, even Northern Ireland will go on and complete its 'own thing' too, as beautiful and surprising as anyone else's, another lucky break in Darwin's grand view of life!

Best wishes, Tom

Contributors

ANTHONY BARNETT is the founder of Open Democracy and Co-editor of its UK section, Our Kingdom. He was the first Director of Charter 88, the constitutional reform campaigning group.

ZYGMUNT BAUMAN is Emeritus Professor of Sociology at the University of Leeds. His numerous books include 44 *Letters from the Liquid Modern World, Liquid Times: Living in an Age of Uncertainty* and *Liquid Modernity.*

KEIR BLOOMER is an independent education consultant, Vice-Convenor of Children in Scotland and Chair-designate of Queen Margaret University. He is a former Executive Director of Education and Community Services and local authority Chief Executive.

DAVID DONALD is Senior Fellow at the Department of Economic Studies and International Business at Glasgow Caledonian University and Senior Research Fellow at the Stirling Centre For Economic Methodology (SCEME) at the University of Stirling.

KATIE GRANT has been a freelance journalist and medieval historian and is a bestselling author of children's fiction. Her books include *Belle's Song* and *The Perfect Fire Trilogy* of *Blue Flame, White Heat* and *Paradise Red.*

PHIL HANLON is Professor of Public Health at the University of Glasgow. His previous roles include Director of Health Promotion for NHS Greater Glasgow and numerous academic, medical and health management posts in the UK and internationally.

ALAN HUTTON is Senior Fellow at the Department of Economic Studies and International Business at Glasgow Caledonian University and Senior Research Fellow at the Stirling Centre For Economic Methodology (SCEME) at the University of Stirling.

WILL HUTTON is Executive Vice-Chair of the Work Foundation and author of *Them and Us: Changing Britain: Why We Need a Fair Society*.

PAT KANE is a writer, musician, consultant, player, theorist and activist, one half of Hue and Cry and the author of *The Play Ethic: A Manifesto for a Different Way of Living*. He can be contacted at: www.theplay ethic.com.

MICHAEL KEATING is Professor of Politics at Aberdeen University and author of *The Independence of Scotland*.

JOAN MCALPINE is a columnist on *The Scotsman* and was Deputy Editor of *The Herald* and Editor of *Sunday Times Scotland*. She is an SNP Parliamentary Candidate for the South of Scotland in the forthcoming elections. Her writing and comment can be found at her website *Go Lassie Go*: http://joanmcalpine.typepad.com.

JIM MCCORMICK is Scottish Advisor to the Joseph Rowntree Foundation (JRF) and was previously Director of the Scottish Council Foundation.

JOHN MCLAREN is Honorary Research Fellow at the Department of Urban Studies, University of Glasgow and Centre for Public Policy for Regions.

FERGUS MCNEILL is Professor of Criminology and Social Work at the University of Glasgow.

JAMES MITCHELL is Professor of Politics at Strathclyde University and his latest books include *Voting for a Scottish Government: The Scottish Parliament Election of 2007* and *Devolution in the UK*.

NEIL MULHOLLAND is Director of the Centre for Visual and Cultural Studies at Edinburgh College of Art. His website can be found at: www. neilmulholland.co.uk.

TOM NAIRN is Professor and Institute of Advanced Study Fellow at Durham University and was previously Research Professor in Globalisation at Royal Melbourne Institute of Technology. His books include *The Break-up of Britain, The Enchanted Glass, Faces of Nationalism* and *After Britain: New Labour and the Return of Scotland*.

SUE PALMER is a freelance writer, consultant and adviser on education and literacy, a former headteacher in Scotland and author of *Toxic Childhood, Detoxing Childhood* and *21st Century Boys*. Her writing and research can be found at: www.suepalmer.co.uk.

DOUGLAS ROBERTSON is Professor of Housing Studies at the Housing Policy and Practice Unit at University of Stirling.

EURIG SCANDRETT is lecturer in Sociology at Queen Margaret University.

DREW SCOTT is Professor of European Union Studies at the School of Law, University of Edinburgh and Co-Director of the Europa Institute.

ALAN SINCLAIR is an independent policy analyst who has written on early years development, author of *0–5: How Small Children Make a Big Difference*, and was previously Director of Skills and Learning at Scottish Enterprise and Chief Executive of the Wise Group.

FREJA ULVESTAD KÄRKI is a clinical psychologist and senior adviser in the Department of Mental Health and Substance Abuse in the Norwegian Directorate of Health. Her international tasks include being the WHO Focal Person for Violence Prevention in Norway, as well as the WHO National Counterpart for Mental Health.

ANDY WIGHTMAN is an independent writer and researcher on land rights, land tenure and land reform. His latest book is *The Poor Had No Lawyers*. His work and activities can be found at: www.andywightman.com.

RICHARD WYN JONES is Director of the Wales Governance Centre at Cardiff University and author of *Rhoi Cymru'n Gyntaf: Syniadaeth Plaid Cymru: Cyfrol One* and is co-editor of *Europe, Regions and European Regionalism*.

A Nation Again: Why Independence will be good for Scotland (and England too)
Edited by Paul Henderson Scott
ISBN 978-1906817-67-1 PBK £7.99

If you believe in the Case for Independence, this book will provide you with a stirring endorsement of your view. If you are sceptical, it might well persuade you to convert to the cause. If you are downright hostile, this book could be dangerous – it could prompt you to rethink.

Suddenly Scottish Independence is within grasp. Is this a frivolous pipedream, a romantic illusion? Or is it, as the writers of this dynamic and positive collection of essays insist, an authentic political option, feasible and beneficial?

As the Scottish people prepare for their biggest ever collective decision, this book forcefully sets out the Case for Independence. The distinguished authors, from a variety of different perspectives, argue the case for the Imperative of Independence.

Agenda for a New Scotland: Visions of Scotland 2020
Kenny MacAskill
ISBN 978-1905222-00-1 PBK £9.99

The campaign for a Scottish Parliament was ongoing for centuries. Lamented in prose and championed in print. Petitioned for, marched in support of and voted upon. Dear to the hearts of many and whose absence broke the hearts of a few. From Kenny MacAskill's Introduction to Agenda for a New Scotland

It has now reconvened after nearly 300 years. A Devolved Legislature but a Parliament all the same. Unable to address all issues but able to make a difference in many areas. It is for the Scottish Parliament to shape and mould the future of Scotland. But, what should that future be?

This is a series of contributed articles from politicians, academics and Civic Scotland. They outline opportunities and future directions for Scotland across a range of areas socially, economically and politically. This is an *Agenda for a New Scotland*. Visions of what Scotland can be by 2020.